THE CONSERVATIVE REVOLUTION IN GERMANY

1918-1932

A Handbook

ARMIN MOHLER
& KARLHEINZ WEISSMANN

Translated by F. ROGER DEVLIN
Edited by NINA KOUPRIANOVA

New Essays by PAUL E. GOTTFRIED
& ALAIN DE BENOIST

RADIX | WASHINGTON SUMMIT PUBLISHERS | 2018

Washington Summit Publishers
Whitefish, Montana
U.S.A.

email : hello@WashSummit.com
web : www.WashSummit.com

Cataloging-in-Publication Data is on file
with the Library of Congress

ISBN: 978-1-59368-059-6
eISBN: 978-1-59368-061-9
Printed in the United States of America
10 9 8 7 6 5 4 3 2 1
First Edition

In memory of Armin Mohler (1920-2003)

*Each on a different path, we—on the most difficult,
the re-overthrow of an overthrow*

—Rudolf Borchardt

❧

This translation of *Die Konservative Revolution in Deutschland 1918–1932* omits the extensive bibliography and related source citations found in its Sixth Edition of 2005. The editor and publisher have elected to include a new, selected bibliography in the English language and citations and notes of use to this book's audience. A new Preface, Foreword, and Afterword have been added, which did not appear in any German edition.

Photographs of Armin Mohler are owned and were provided by the Verein für Staatspolitik. All other images in this book are owned and were provided by ARES Verlag or were taken from the public domain.

CONTENTS

PREFACE TO THE ENGLISH EDITION / **XI**

By Paul E. Gottfried

FOREWORD TO THE ENGLISH EDITION / **XIX**

By Alain de Benoist

FOREWORD TO THE GERMAN EDITION / **3**

By Karlheinz Weißmann

1. THE HISTORY OF THIS BOOK / **7**

2. THE RECOGNITION OF GERMAN UNIQUENESS IN THE 19TH CENTURY / **13**

    2.1 Origins of Recognizing German Uniqueness / 20

    2.2 Political Effects of Romanticism / 22

    2.3 Anti-Romanticism / 26

    2.4 The Ideas of 1871 / 30

    2.5 Heralds of a "Cultural-Revolutionary Age": Lagarde—Wagner—Treitschke / 34

    2.6 New Movements: Völkisch and Nationalist / 44

    2.7 Nietzsche as Educator / 54

    2.8 Lebensreform, Jugendbewegung, Post-Nietzschean Culture / 58

3. THE WORLD WAR AS CULTURE WAR / **67**

    3.1 The Party of Idealism and Its Disintegration / 71

    3.2 Thomas Mann and Oswald Spengler / 74

    3.3 New Camp, New Spirit / 80

    3.4 The Solidarists / 87

4.   THE UNITY OF THE CONSERVATIVE REVOLUTION / 97

5.   THE GROUPS THAT CONSTITUTED THE
     CONSERVATIVE REVOLUTION / **109**

   5.1 First Group: The Völkisch

   5.2 Second Group: The Jungkonservativen / 125

   5.3 Third Group: The National Revolutionaries / 153

   5.4 Fourth Group: The Leagues / 170

   5.5 Fifth Group: the Rural Population / 184

6.   CLIMAX AND DENOUMENT / **193**

   6.1 Carl Schmitt and Ernst Jünger / 194

   6.2 A Struggle Between Worldviews / 203

   6.3 Conservative Revolution in Europe? / 210

   6.4 Hitler as Educator / 213

   6.5 Resistance / 219

   6.6 Ambivalence and Separation / 223

   6.7 Subsequent History / 226

AFTERWORD TO THE ENGLISH EDITION / **231**

   By Alain de Benoist

ENGLISH-LANGUAGE BIBLIOGRAPHY / **239**

   Primary sources / 239

   Secondary Sources / 242

PREFACE

TO THE ENGLISH EDITION

PAUL E. GOTTFRIED

ongratulations are in order to F. Roger Devlin, Richard Spencer, Nina Kouprianova, and everyone else involved in this timely translation of *The Conservative Revolution in Germany, 1918-1932*. The work that is now available offers the contents of the sixth edition of an extraordinary piece of scholarship, one that came entirely in its earlier forms from a famous figure of the German intellectual Right, Armin Mohler (1920-2002). This edition of Mohler's handbook has been enriched with an illuminating commentary by a leading theorist of the current German Right, Karl-Heinz Weissmann. In this case the additions don't complicate but rather enhance the exposition. *The Conservative Revolution* is one of the premier studies of the interwar European Right, and it was constructed by someone who knew his subjects quite well.

And yet, this personal sympathy in no way detracts from Mohler's achievement. It is now entirely commonplace and perhaps *de rigueur* for leftists to write about their political persuasion in works that become widely and favorably reviewed. And though some of these authors may try to deal in a balanced way with their topics, more often than not, they simply grind axes, by telling us about the romance of American Communism, the "Red Scare," or those valiant, outnumbered Trotskyists who fought General Franco and his Nationalist forces. In contrast to such celebrations of the leftist past, or those predictable effusions of regret by former rightists who are announcing to the world that they've "grown," Mohler writes with almost clinical detachment. His ability to distance himself from his material is all the more remarkable given Mohler's longtime relation to two of his subjects. From 1949 until 1953 he served as a private secretary to Ernst Jünger and for decades was a regular correspondent of Carl Schmitt.

Mohler and his commentator, Weissmann, let us know that the figures and groups under consideration were wiped out during the Nazi period or had their hopes and rhetoric distorted in such way as to become no longer recognizable to these advocates of Germany's Conservative Revolution. The years Mohler chose for his study are the appropriate ones. The "Conservative Revolution in Germany" grew out the experience of the First World War and was generally open to the inspiration of another anti-liberal movement, Italian fascism, which surged forth out of the same struggle. This striking openness of German nationalists to movements and ideas springing from their enemies in the Great War should not surprise us. The galvanizing, life-changing experience that, according to the novelist and war hero Ernst Jünger, distinguished his generation of right-wing rebels from those who went before was belonging to a "Front Generation." Going through the war and enduring the "storm of steel (*Stahlgewitter*)" of battle on either side made soldiers part of the same fraternity, no matter on which side they happened to stand in 1914 or 1916.

The cult of manliness and heroism was integral to the world of Germany's Conservative Revolutionaries; and this went together with a repugnance for the bourgeoisie, and its association with wealth accumulation and the avoidance of conflict. There was also a special bitterness among these German nationalists over the way the war had ended, that is, with the humiliation of Germany and its allies, the ensuing loss of land, forced demilitarization, and the imposition of an indeterminate reparations by the victorious side, as forced acknowledgement of Germany's "war guilt." Some of those whom Mohler identifies as "Conservative Revolutionaries" had fought the revolutionary Left in their own country or in the Baltic region after the War as members of Freikorps units. Others had been embroiled in post-War territorial fights with countries adjoining Germany that had been given land that had formerly belonged to the Empire. Put simply, the most dedicated partisans had tasted the "*Stahlgewitter*" or battled against the militant Left in the streets long before they joined an intellectual movement.

In a memorable review of the expanded edition of Mohler's work in 1972 (an earlier version had appeared in Stuttgart in 1950), a conservative publicist G.K. Kaltenbrunner discerns three characteristics of the German Conservative Revolutionaries covered by Mohler's encyclopedic work. Kaltenbrunner discusses these characteristics, after properly reminding us that Mohler invented the term "the Conservative Revolution." This is a designation that has been used ever since by both adversaries and admirers of Mohler's subjects. One of Kaltenbrunner's characteristic is an explicit or implicit rejection of Christianity, who view history, like Nietzsche, Oswald Spengler and the ancients, as a cyclical process. In contrast to the Judeo-Christian view of time, for the Conservative Revolutionaries, there is no final age of peace or divine judgment toward which humanity is moving. History repeats itself, the Conservative Revolutionaries taught, with alternating periods of social cohesion and social disintegration. Not at all surprisingly, the Conservative Revolutionaries saw themselves as standing on the cusp of a new age of unity, which would in some ways resemble the Middle Ages but without necessarily a Christian core.

Equally apparent was their willingness to borrow heavily from the Left while identifying themselves as the true Right. Like elements of today's Alt-Right, the German Conservative Revolutionaries characterized themselves as traditionalists, while consciously breaking from what they dismissed as urban bourgeois fixations. They rejected capitalism for some of the same reasons as Marxists did, because it operated as a system of profit that was both impersonal and tore people out of traditional social relations. The Conservative Revolutionaries also favored national control over the heights of the economy, but here they broke emphatically from the Left. Like the Italian fascists, they were pursuing national solidarity and seeking to return to an organic community, albeit in modern circumstances. The degree to which the Conservative Revolutionaries moved in the direction of socialism differed from case to case.

Presumably those who gathered in the Juni-Klub in June 1919, under the auspices of Arthur Moeller van den Bruck and Heinrich von Gleichen, to work out the ideas of a German Conservative Revolution, held very qualified views about government ownership. Most of the early architects of this concept came out of the traditional German Right and could hardly be described as socialists. But soon a decidedly left wing developed out of their plan or the prevailing mindset of the German interwar Right; and such figures as Otto and Gregor Strasser and Ernst Niekisch preached a form of socialism that borrowed heavily from Soviet Communism. Whereas most of the Conservative Revolutionaries sympathized with Russia, which van den Bruck identified as "a young nation like Germany," the leftists in their group also enthusiastically embraced the Soviets as ideological allies. Russia-turned-Soviet-Union, like the defeated German Empire, been treated as a pariah by the victorious Allies after World War One. (Neither had been given the status of a negotiating nation at the Versailles conference, and land was ripped away from both.) Equally important for the left-wing Conservative Revolutionaries, the Soviet system represented a model for what they were trying to do in their own country—with one critical difference. Unlike the Marxist internationalism that the Soviet government purported to be upholding, all Conservative Revolutionaries were nationalists. Moreover, unlike the Soviets, far from breaking from the past, they were proudly affirming their history as a people.

Another characteristic of those who identified themselves as "Conservative Revolutionaries"—and certainly not everyone in Mohler's extensive "handbook" did—was a view of themselves as completers of a "right-wing project." In this sense, as Kaltenbrunner observes, these iconoclasts were the heirs of an older Right in the same way that Lenin viewed himself as the completer of Marx's revolutionary doctrines. Those who opposed Hitler as national revolutionaries, according to Kaltenbrunner, never perceived a parallel between their position and that of Leon Trotsky, who fought and was destroyed by Stalin. The analogy between German Conservative Revolutionaries and Lenin would have been much more to their liking. Unlike Trotsky, these German nationalists were not advocates of a global revolutionary Left. They were more like Lenin in the sense that they viewed the Russian leader through their own nationalist lenses.

Equally relevant, the political activists in Mohler's study considered themselves in a meaningful way as occupants of the Right. No matter how much they may have inclined toward the Soviet Union, they would have insisted that their motives and thinking were quite different from those of the Communist or socialist Left. They admired the Soviets as representatives of an anti-liberal "young nation," as fellow-outcast from the Western "capitalist democracies," and, finally, as imperfect implementers of an organic economy. But, as Mohler makes clear, much of the inspiration for Conservative Revolutionary politics came from an older German nationalist Right

ARMIN MOHLER

and from such theorists of the authoritarian Right as Carl Schmitt. If Conservative Revolutionaries chose for themselves mentors, they would more typically have come from the Right rather than the Left.

This brings me to a final point, which I made in an essay on the German Conservative Revolutionary Left, more specifically on the Strasser brothers and their socialist Black Front in conflict with Hitler, in *Modern Age* in the spring of 1969.[1] At that point I was a fairly conventional "conservative" Republican and had to wrestle with the question of what exactly made my subjects part of the "Right," as opposed to left-wing enemies of private enterprise and Western constitutional government. Without having ever swallowed the asininities of Jonah Goldberg and others who view any deviation from the present version of American "liberal democracy" as being somehow on the Left, I felt initially uneasy about approaching the Right in the form of the German Conservative Revolution. This discomfort was not in any way induced by a feeling that my subjects were Nazis. I never bought the unproved charge that these activists had somehow produced the Nazi government, a charge that Weissmann and others have had no trouble refuting. (The Nazis killed, intimidated or drove into exile most of the better known Conservative Revolutionaries after they took power.) The problem was that my subjects resembled interwar leftists too much for me to regard their rightist credentials seriously.

But as a practicing historian, I understood that the Conservative Revolutionaries belonged to a different time and a different political culture; and it would have been ridiculous to expect them to have reacted to the collapse of the German Imperial government and to the dismemberment of their country like Robert-Taft Republicans or Jeffersonian Democrats. Nor should one have expected German patriots in 1919 or 1920 to rush to adopt the latest political fashions or value

---

|1| Paul Gottfried, "Otto Strasser and National Socialism," *Modern Age*, Vol. 13, No. 2 (Spring 1969).

rhetoric of their victorious enemies; and to whatever extent they did, they would have done so to undo the effects of the Treaty of Versailles. But even more importantly, with regard to their worldview, there was no way that I could consider my subjects as not belonging to the Right. They challenged all the fundamental assumptions of the Left, about creating a universal society, the interchangeability of peoples, and the identification of human progress with the advancement of equality and (pardon this loaded, banal term!) the promotion of "human rights." One did not have to agree with the principles and purposes of the Conservative Revolutionaries to recognize their rightist origin.

I would finally note (as another heretical notion) that what the Conservative Revolutionaries chose as an alternative to the Left seems less alien to me now than when I first wrote about this group many decades ago. The cult of "liberal democracy" has not saved us from the occupation of our social, cultural, and political institutions by a far more insidious Left than any that interwar Europeans had to face. The attack waged on many fronts against distinct heterosexual identities and against anything resembling the traditional family, not to mention national distinctions, by a vast, well-organized Left, plus the utter vulnerability of the object of these attacks, suggests that self-described "liberal democrats" have not done well in protecting their left flank. Nor have capitalists proved to be a force of resistance. Providing that corporate executives and their stock-holders can profit, our leaders of industry and finance have rushed toward every cause that the cultural Left promotes, including the human right of lecherous old men who have declared themselves to be transgendered to have free access to girls' showers. The idea that big business embraces social traditionalists has become a lie bordering on the obscene. At the very least this idea is a pipedream, and one particularly common to Republicans who receive funding from large corporations.

February 2017
Elizabethtown, Pennsylvania

FOREWORD
TO THE ENGLISH EDITION

ALAIN DE BENOIST

he idea of the "Conservative Revolution" was first established in the field of political science after the publication of the famous handbook by Armin Mohler *Die Konservative Revolution in Deutschland 1918-1932*, which was first published in 1950.[1] Originally it was a doctoral thesis written at Basel under the direction of Karl Jaspers. Revised and expanded editions were published in 1972 and 1989. Finally, in 2005, after the author's death, an entirely recast fourth edition was published on the initiative of Karlheinz Weissman.

In this book, Mohler distinguishes three principle families: First, the Young Conservatives, with men such as Edgar Julius Jung, Oswald Spengler, Arthur Moeller van den Bruck, Hans Grimm, Othmar Spann, Hans Zehrer, Max Hildebert Boehm, Wilhelm Stapel, Hans Freyer, Leopold Ziegler, Ernst Forsthoff, Albrecht Erich Günther

---

|1| This essay is based on a written interview in the Italian magazine *Terra Insubre* (Varese, 2007).

and Heinrich von Gleichen; Second, the National Revolutionaries, represented especially by Ernst and Friedrich Georg Jünger, Friedrich Hielscher, Ernst von Salomon, Ernst Niekisch, Franz Schauwecker, Beppo Römer, Bodo Uhse, Harro Schulze-Boysen, Arnolt Bronnen, Eberhard Koebel, and Karl Otto Paetel; Finally, third, the *Völkische*, a notoriously difficult word to translate, among whom one finds authors such as Friedrich Lange, Ludwig Schermann, Gustav Frenssen, Adolf Bartles, Paul de Lagarde, Ludwig Ferdinand Clauss, Mathilde Ludendorff, Hermann Wirth, Jörg von Liebenfels, Paul Schultze-Naumburg, et al.

To this may be added two currents significantly less important, insofar as they were directly linked to contingent historical events: the Bündische, an associative tendency descended from the Wandervögel and the Youth Movement, and the Landvolkbewegung or Rural Movement, a social protest movement born of the peasant revolt of the 1920s, especially in Schleswig-Holstein. Finally, mention must be made of certain great figures who do not quite fit into this classification, including the jurist Carl Schmitt, the young Thomas Mann, the theoretician of the *Männerbünde*, Hans Blüher, the economist Werner Sombart, the philosophers Max Scheler and Ludwig Klages, the geopolitical expert Karl Haushofer, the art historian Josef Strzygowski, the Medievalist Ernst Kantorowicz, and more. I will stop here with a list that could be considerably extended, since Mohler in his book presents about 500 different authors and nearly as many groups, associations or movements!

Opponents of the Conservative Revolution (CR) have regularly described it as a movement that supposedly "opened the way" for National Socialism or at least contributed to its "ideological acceptability." In German, the terms commonly employed are *Wegbereiter* or *Vorläufer*. Of course, this interpretation has been favored by the reeducation of the German people after 1945, which has often tried to disqualify not only Nazism but any concept or idea that could be attached to it, even in the most artificial manner: national conscience, patriotism, irrationalism, the "Prussian Idea," the notion of authority, etc. The reality is very different, since the great majority of the authors of the CR saw their ideas plainly attacked under the Third Reich, and some of them were imprisoned or even murdered.

As for Armin Mohler, he describes the CR as a current distinct both from the old reactionary conservatism and racialist national socialism. Under this label, he gathers all currents of the German Right, which, in the time of the Weimar Republic, were distinct both from early National Socialism and from the old-style conservatism represented especially by Alfred Hugenberg's Deutschnationale Volkspartei (DNVP). However, Mohler also sometimes presented them as the "Trotskyists of National Socialism," a clumsy and above all inaccurate formulation, insofar as Trotskyism was born from a dissident tendency within the Communist International, while the CR was never a dissident tendency within National Socialism, but a current that arose in an entirely distinct manner.

It is important to make clear that Mohler, for whom the CR represents a real alternative to the progressive or liberal ideas inherited from the enlightenment, did not coin the term "Conservative Revolution" himself. Of course, it was never used as a general self-description by the authors of whom we have spoken, but a number of them used that formulation in their articles, books, or speeches. Its roots go back to the 19th century. In fact, we find "conservative revolution" mentioned in a speech given by Friedrich Engels on February 22, 1848, to mark the second anniversary of the Krakow uprising. The significance he gives to these two words is, however, very different from what they subsequently acquired, for example, in the writings of Dostoevsky, who in 1876 wrote that the historic role played by the Russians in Europe are grounds for considering them "revolutionaries motivated by conservatism" (*par conservatisme*). In France, the expression was also used by Hugues Rebell in 1894, then by Charles Maurras, who, in his *Enquête sur las monarchie* ("Inquiry on the Monarchy"), published beginning in 1900, said that a "conservative revolution" would be in accord with his wishes; but he only meant it as a synonym of "restauration." In Germany after the First World War, the same expression was used in various forms by Hans Blüher and Thomas Mann, then by Hugo von Hofmannsthal, Rudolf Pannwitz, Arthur Moeller van den Bruck, Rudolf Borchardt, Edgar Julius Jung, Hans Ebeling, Ernst von Salomon, and many others.

The CR certainly never presented itself as a unified movement, never had a uniform strategy, and never resulted in a fully elaborated political synthesis. It was merely a constellation of authors, groups, and journals, which adopted different and even opposed positions in a number of domains. Finally, it must not be forgotten that it unfolded only over a period of fifteen years, from 1918 to 1933. The large number of authors studied and the extraordinary diversity in their personal careers seem, at first glance, to forbid us from placing them all under the same label.

Mohler, however, thought he had identified a certain vision (*Leitbild*) common to all the authors of the CR, that of cyclical time as opposed to the linear conception of time one finds in Christianity, as well as modern historicism. This image derived directly from Nietzsche, more exactly from the theme of "eternal return," which Mohler believes exercised decisive influence on the entire movement. He believed that those belonging to the CR all adhered to Nietzsche's theses on European nihilism, the cyclic conception of time, the rejection of egalitarian universalism, and the expectation of the "Great Noon." And it was this worldview that constituted the ideological base of the CR and gave it its coherence. Was it not Thomas Mann himself who said in 1921 that "the thought of Nietzsche was, right from the start . . . nothing less than a conservative revolution?"[2]

|2| See Göran Dahl, *Radical Conservatism and the Future of Politics* (London: Sage Publications, 1999), 45.

That thesis is in fact no more than partially true, if only because of the presence of a significant number of Christian thinkers within the galaxy of the Conservative Revolution, and also from the fact that authors such as Carl Schmitt or Rudolf Borchardt never concealed their distaste for Nietzsche. From the beginning, Armin Mohler visibly projected orientations that were mainly his own (if not Ernst Jünger's, whose secretary he was at that time) upon a movement with which he sympathized; he ended by acknowledging this himself. In 1988, he even went so far as to say that Carl Schmitt did not in the end belong to the CR. We may also note that he devotes no space to Martin Heidegger in his book, although his work has frequently been studied from the standpoint of the relations the philosopher maintained with Ernst Jünger or Carl Schmitt.

Following Klemens von Klemperer, the sociologist and political scientist Stefan Breuer (author of an "anatomy" of the CR in 1995) was among the first to contest whether one could consider the CR a unified movement.[3] While rejecting all theses regarding the "special path" (*Sonderweg*) of German history—which attempted to explain the failure of the Weimar Republic by Germany's never having experienced a "bourgeois revolution"—Breuer particularly questioned whether one could speak of conservatism or neoconservatism when speaking of the CR. He relied on the research of Panayotis Kondylis, who, in a work appearing in 1986, declared that conservatism, having entered into a phase of irreversible decadence in the second half of the 19th century, could not renew itself in Germany because of its historic ties to the *ancien régime*.[4] For Kondylis, the gradual elimination of the nobility, the class vehicle of historical conservatism, was a death sentence on political conservatism, which was only able to survive itself by coming

---

[3] Stefan Breuer, *Anatomie der konservativen Revolution* (Darmstadt: Wissenschaftliche Buchgesellschaft, 1995).

[4] Panagiotis Kondylis, *Konservativismus. Geschichtlicher* (Klett-Cotta: Gehalt und Untergang. Stuttgart, 1986).

to an understanding with liberalism or by "aestheticizing" some of its foundations.

After making a close examination of the writings of the various representatives of the CR, Stefan Breuer wrote that "in relation neither to the economy nor science nor technology, nor as concerns any concrete foreign or domestic political project can the least doctrine be uncovered common to all the authors described as conservative revolutionaries." He concluded from this that the concept "Conservative Revolution" must be eliminated from the scholarly vocabulary:

> We must acknowledge that the concept "Conservative Revolution" is untenable; it misleads more than it enlightens us. For this reason, it should be struck from the list of 20th century political currents.

In its place, Breuer proposed adopting the term "new nationalism," the novelty of this nationalism consisting in a mystic and charismatic dimension of the nation (which finds itself assigned a global "mission" of a quasi-metaphysical nature), in its "holistic" or "inclusive" character, i.e., not excluding the nationalization/mobilization of the masses, and in the emphasis it places on the martial values, although without imperialist intentions.

But Breuer did not stop there. In a number of books published afterwards, he endeavored to propose his own classification by way of a sophisticated analytic apparatus. His typology, strongly influenced by the Weberian notion of an ideal type, distinguishes two great axes, one concerning the attitude ("regression" or "progression") toward the process of rationalization characteristic of modernity, the other concerning the attitude ("exclusion" or "inclusion") respecting the social dimension of this same process. Regarding the first axis, he cites as examples of regression (or "cultural pessimism") most of the *völkisch* groups, but also the Bayreuth circle around Richard Wagner, religious reformers like Paul de Lagarde, and poets like Stefan George; and as examples of "progression," the majority of National Revolutionaries, including their most incandescent branch, the National Bolsheviks.

Different criticisms were formulated in 1996 by the "national liberal" Henning Eichberg. In particular, he asked in what way men such as Carl Schmitt or Martin Heidegger could ever have been "revolutionaries," and was surprised by the absence in Mohler's book of left-wing theoreticians like Theodor Lessing (a friend of Ludwig Klages's youth), Gustav Landauer, Hans Paasche, or even Martin Buber—all authors in whom he sees the thinkers of a "revolt on the part of life" perfectly in accord with the "historical potential of really existing nationalism."

The theses set forth by Stefan Breuer called forth many reactions. In France, the Germanist Gilbert Merlio offered a number of criticisms, even as he recognized the well-foundedness of many of Breuer's observations.[5] Merlio thinks that in spite of its imperfections, what he calls the "paradoxical formulation" deserves to be preserved, for it has the advantage—which the label "new nationalism" does not—of expressing well the tension between opposed impulses inherited by the CR. Rolf Peter Sieferle sided with Merlio: in the end, it is better to preserve the concept "Conservative Revolution," even if it must be fitted out with quotation marks.[6]

The label "new nationalism" proposed by Breuer is in fact somewhat equivocal. It is true that practically all authors of the CR were unanimous in considering their country humiliated and demeaned by the Treaty of Versailles and in considering liberalism a foreign element—an "England within"—from which Germany must

---

|5| Gilbert Merlio, "Y a-t-il eu une «Révolution conservatrice» sous la République de Weimar? *Revue Française d'Histoire des Idées Politiques*, 2003/1, 17).

|6| Rolf Peter Sieferle, *Die Konservative Revolution: Fünf biographische Skizzen* (Berlin: Fischer Taschenbuch, 1995).

free itself; and for all, the idea of "nation" was invested with a certain importance. But their conception of the nation is not always the same depending upon whether they let subjective and even voluntarist elements predominate or objective criteria of national belonging. More generally, the idea of "nation" is only really fundamental among the National Revolutionaries (who are, besides, the only ones who called for a "new nationalism"). The Young Conservatives often prefer the notion of *Reich*, and the *Völkische*, that of a "people" or "blood." As for the National Bolsheviks, they try to replace class with nation, while remaining within a revolutionary, if not Marxist, framework. Finally, among certain authors, and those not the least important, we find the idea that modernity calls for a planetary order clearly going beyond the nation: great space (*Großraum*) and a new "Nomos of the Earth" in Carl Schmitt, *Reich* in Leopold Ziegler or Max Hildebert Boehm, the reign of technology in the young Ernst Jünger, "Faustian Imperialism" in Oswald Spengler.

For my own part, while conscious of the extreme diversity of inspiration among the authors of the CR, I think that beyond everything separating and sometimes opposing them, these authors still share much common ground. Beyond the generational unity (most representatives of the CR fought at the front between 1914 and 1918, and the experience of the trenches was decisive for them), the principle point in common is in my view their unanimous condemnation of political liberalism, and with it individualism, materialism, and the primacy of economics, along with a rejection of the purely reactionary spirit, as well as a refusal to interpret history as a simple reflection of the struggle between races. No author of the Conservative Revolution, particularly in its two main families of Young Conservatives and National Revolutionaries, puts economics in the forefront of his vision of the world. None defines himself principally as a reactionary or racialist. With these three refusals, we are at the heart of the Conservative Revolutionary galaxy. It is in this respect that the use of the formula "Conservative Revolution" remains in my view fully justified.

The CR has complex relationship to, on the one hand, technology and modernism and, on the other, 19th century reactionary Romanticism. I have already mentioned the two interpretive axes proposed by Stefan Breuer. Each of them is in a different way related to the attitude adopted by the representatives of the CR toward modernity. In this domain, obvious differences can be observed. Certain currents of the CR resolutely accept industrial and technological modernity, whether in the name of a certain "Prussian socialism" or that of mere will to power, while others reject it totally in the name of what Breuer justifiably calls an aesthetic or religious "fundamentalism" derived from pietism or romanticism. A number of the *Völkische* also take this second position, the first being more common among the National Revolutionaries, as witness the famous book by Ernst Jünger *The Worker* (1932)[7].

Others, such as Jeffrey Herf, have especially insisted on the "reactionary modernism" of the CR, that is, the re-appropriation by various right-wing currents of certain aspects of technological modernity.[8] However, the term "modernity" remains ambiguous as long as one has not specified what is to be understood by it. Gilbert Merlio, whom I have already mentioned, has clearly shown how the supporters of the CR, even when they adhered entirely to "instrumental modernity"—what Jaspers calls the "mass technological order"—reject "reflexive modernity," that is, the "great foundational stories" of modernity: the ideology of progress, the disenchantment of the world, the rationalization of all domains of life (the "dream of reason" Max Weber spoke of). To define the CR's attitude toward modernity, we would have to speak of "anti-modern modernism," this new oxymoron defining a certain way of challenging the achievements or ideas of

---

|7| Ernst Jünger, *Der Arbeiter. Herrschaft und Gestalt* (Stuttgart: Klett-Cotta, 2007 [1932]).

|8| Jeffrey Herf, *Reactionary Modernism: Technology, Culture, and Politics in Weimar and the Third Reich* (Cambrdige: Cambridge University Press, 1984).

modernity with modernity's own tools, of turning those tools against the normative project of modernity.

The "modernism" of the CR is in any case intrinsically linked to its "revolutionary" character. Mohler speaks of a "Conservative Revolution"—what, exactly, is to be understood by the first of these two words? I think two answers are possible. The revolutionary inspiration of certain members of the CR cannot be doubted: they themselves called openly for a social and political overturning. This is obviously the case above all with the National Revolutionaries, whose radicalism is evocative at once of the Jacobin nationalism of 1793, the revolutionary syndicalism of Georges Sorel, and Italian Futurism. The Young Conservatives, to say nothing of the *Völkische*, do not go so far. But the conviction that animates them is that the state in which their country finds itself is such that even a return to eternal values implies a total upheaval. In both cases, the word revolution is opposed to reformism and especially to restoration

So Julius Evola was quite mistaken in calling the CR a *rivoluzione mancata* ("failed revolution") and trying to identify it with a "counterrevolution" in the French sense of the term. To paraphrase Joseph de Maistre, the champions of the CR did not want "the contrary of revolution," but *did* want a "revolution in the contrary sense"—even if, in Carl Schmitt, the influence of counter-revolutionaries such as Donoso Cortes or Joseph de Maistre is obvious. The CR is basically a conservatism turned toward the future, and not a restoration. Its representatives are not reactionaries, whose goal was to restore a past social and political order. They did not dream of the Hohenzollerns nor wish a return of Wilhelmianism. Nor did they defend the interests of a particular class, but aspired to a "great turning" involving the whole of society. The war of 1914-18 marked an irreversible caesura for them. They could also be considered conservators (of the past) in respect to values, and revolutionaries (of the future) in respect to ideas.

The other term of this book's title worthy of scrutiny is *Germany*. Specifically, was the CR an intrinsically German manifestation or was it part of a broader phenomenon? In other words, was it a German Conservative Revolution or the Conservative Revolution in Germany?

Armin Mohler was very impressed, perhaps overly so, with the work of Zeev Sternhell, who studied the French revolutionary Right.[9] This led him to push back the axial period (*Achsenzeit*) of conservative thought. So he did admit that the "prehistory" of revolutionary conservatism can be traced back to late 19th century France. Stefan Breuer, for his part, thought he could discern in the German "new nationalism" of the 1920s certain French, but also Italian, influences. One reason why he thought the expression "new nationalism" preferable to CR is that his concept better permits useful comparisons with other European forms of nationalism.

Personally, I have some reservations. Sternhell's books are extremely interesting, but they are not free of facile anachronistic or teleological interpretations (the very concept of "pre-fascism" is, in my opinion, extremely ambiguous). A comparison between the CR and the "French Revolutionary Right" is not without its pertinence, but it involves simplifications that risk masking what is irreducibly German in the CR (which is considerable). Moreover, there have been attempts to use Mohler's typology by applying it to authors from other countries. The results, it must be said, have been rather disappointing. For various reasons, the *Völkische* and *Bündische* scarcely have equivalents outside Germany. This leaves the Young Conservatives and the National Revolutionaries. But outside Germany, the classification of right-wing authors under either of these labels often amounts to no more than applying a simple gradient of radicalism to them, without really clarifying the identity of any of the families studied.

|9| Zeev Sternhell, *La droite révolutionnaire: 1885-1914: les origines françaises du fascisme* (Paris: Éditions du Seuil, 1978).

On the other hand, it remains true that the German Conservative Revolution was not the only movement that tried to have recourse at once to ideas of the Right and Left, to look for a synthesis and overcoming, in the sense of a Hegelian *Aufhebung*, between revolutionary aspirations and conservative attitudes.

In 1977, for example, the philosopher Günther Anders, husband of Hannah Arendt, wrote:

> *Today it is no longer enough to transform the world; above all, it must be preserved. Afterwards we can transform it greatly, even in a revolutionary fashion. But above all, we must be conservatives in the authentic sense, conservatives in a sense which no man who proclaims himself a conservative would accept.*

Quite recently, Jean-Claude Michéa, in his little book *Impasse Adam Smith* (2002) wrote:

> *Not only is a certain conservative sensibility not incompatible with the revolutionary spirit, but history shows that it is generally a condition for it, and that originally it is often the desire to protect ancient things which leads to the most radical transformations.*[10]

That is my conviction as well.

---

[10] Jan-Claude Michéa, *Impasse Adam Smith* (Paris: Climats, 2002).

THE
CONSERVATIVE
REVOLUTION
IN GERMANY

1918-1932

FOREWORD
TO THE GERMAN EDITION

KARLHEINZ WEISSMANN

After publishing the third edition of *The Conservative Revolution*, Armin Mohler gave up his plan for a complete reworking of the bibliography and turned the project over to a younger person. Together, we decided—due to the changed state of scholarship—to conceive the text itself anew as well. This entailed changes not only to the content but, by necessity, to the method as well. The bibliography[1] has, for the most part, retained its original structure, but it has also been corrected where necessary and supplemented with the most important recent works, as well as the data and corrections included in the appendix to the third edition. Considerations of space required limiting the addition of new authors and themes; some entries have been updated.

---

[1] As mentioned above, the English-language edition of *The Conservative Revolution* omits the extensive bibliography and related source citation found in the German edition used for this translation. Instead, the editors chose to include a selected bibliography in the English language relevant to this subject. (*Ed.*)

3

Like Armin Mohler, the present author views the Conservative Revolution, above all, as a continued search for a German "world alternative." Today, perhaps even more strongly than in the immediate postwar period, we can recognize the inner unity of conservative-revolutionary efforts to keep Germans true to themselves, lead them back to themselves, or realize their own potential. This unity has often been observed from the outside by the Left, with its attack on German ideology, and from abroad especially by the French as the guardians of the counter-revolutiony heritage of 1789. However, the central figures of the Conservative Revolution themselves were also aware of it, as shall be explained below. The impact of the Conservative Revolution was not limited to worldviews in the narrower sense; it was, in many respects, the spiritual expression of a "nation that still believed in itself."

Work on the new edition of this "handbook" required an investment of time. I must thank not only the late Armin Mohler, for the trust reposed in me, but also the Leopold Stocker publishing house, and especially its director Wolfgang Dvorak-Stocker, for having the patience necessary to complete this project. I would also like to thank those who assisted me with references and recommendations and who read the manuscript in whole or in part, above all, Dr. Ulrich Hintze. Finally, mention must be made of the support I received through the Institut für Staatspolitik and its director, Götz Kubitschek, without which continued work on this complex project would have hardly been possible.

Summer 2004
Göttingen, Germany

1

THE HISTORY OF THIS BOOK

hen one of Armin Mohler's sharpest critics declared that the expression "Conservative Revolution," which Mohler introduced, is "one of the most successful coinages in the recent historiography of ideas," this feat can hardly be explained as the result of fortunate circumstances. The objectivity, with which the first edition of *The Conservative Revolution* was greeted, when many of its protagonists from the 1920s and 1930s were still alive, and their literature was accessible, seems surprising from today's standpoint. Yet the change in the intellectual atmosphere since 1945 had already strengthened the positions of those who considered the Conservative Revolution "fascist," as well as over and done with, or "fascist" and dangerous as ever.

If Mohler occupied himself intensively with the Conservative Revolution in spite of all this, and if it, in some respects, became the theme of his entire life, then there are biographical and philosophical reasons for this. Among the former was Mohler's process of intellectual self-discovery starting from the late 1930s, the writing of *The Conservative Revolution*, and its cathartic effect. Among the philosophical reasons was that the book—although submitted to the Faculty of Philosophy at the University of Basel as a doctoral thesis— was never intended to serve purely scholarly ends, but was meant as an "aid to the right-wing intelligentsia in Germany."

When *The Conservative Revolution* appeared in 1950, Mohler had just turned 30 and begun his work as secretary to Ernst Jünger in Ravensburg. Born on April 12, 1920, in Basel in modest circumstances, he completed school and took up the study of philosophy and art history in his native town. He was moving in left-wing circles at the time, especially among the Jewish intelligentsia that had emigrated from Germany. Mohler himself could hardly explain afterwards what led him to break with his previous ideas. Reading, particularly the works of Nietzsche and Jünger, must have prepared him for this conversion. In his view, however, the decisive event was the beginning of the Russian campaign, June 6, 1941.

Six months later, Mohler illegally crossed the border, but distanced himself from his initial wish to volunteer for the Waffen-SS. Confronting certain realities of the NS regime—"the beginnings of a commissar-state on German soil"—led him to see that the Third Reich was obviously not the realization of the Conservative-Revolutionary program. In any case, Mohler registered at the University of Berlin and spent much of his time in the city's libraries, making excerpts or complete copies of the books and essays written by the leading thinkers of Revolutionary Conservatism. In December of 1942, he returned home and was officially charged with "forbidden border crossing, failure to complete military service, and attempted weakening of the army," and was sentenced to six months in prison. In the period after his release and the resuming of his studies, he met Hans Fleig, the man of whom he said—in the dedication to the first version of *The Conservative Revolution*—that, without him, "this book could not have been written."

Flieg was four years older than Mohler and had a doctorate in history, following a second course of study in law, and was then working as a journalist. Toward the end of the war, he undertook his own German adventure, getting himself sent to the collapsing Reich as a correspondent. Fleig used his time not only to gather information on the effects of modern aerial bombardment warfare but also to visit all the available leading figures of the Conservative Revolution, above all, the religious scholar and protagonist of *völkisch* religion, Jakob Wilhelm Hauer. Only in November of 1945 did Fleig return to Switzerland. Now began an intensive exchange of ideas between him and Mohler over all aspects of the Conservative Revolution, lasting until his departure for London in 1948 as a correspondent of the Zurich newspaper *Tat*.

It is remarkable how intensely both men focused on the National Revolutionaries. Mohler's emphasis that his "spiritual  family" consisted of Nietzsche, Spengler, Jünger, and Niekisch also reveals the predominance of this group. Fleig, perhaps, put greater accent on the possibilities for concrete political action—for instance, in the form of the reunification of Germany with Russian help—while Mohler was mainly fascinated by the project for a gigantic "organic construction" like the one that Jünger outlined in *The Worker*.

JAKOB WILHELM HAUER

What united Mohler and Fleig was their awareness of a common destiny with Germany. In a letter dated October 1, 1949, Fleig wrote to a friend: "'The not-given that represents a value' seems to me a fitting way of characterizing what the Germans are pursuing." Undoubtedly, the existential literature of that day—especially Benn and Camus—influenced both men, but nowhere did what they were seeking seem more fully embodied than in the ideas of the Conservative Revolution.

Fleig accompanied Mohler's further work on the dissertation and supported his friend, above all, in two ideas: the incompatibility of the Conservative Revolution and Christianity and the key importance of the notion of "eternal recurrence." And it was precisely to these two points that the sharpest criticism was directed following the publication of *The Conservative Revolution* in book form. This was not only the result of identifying conservatism with Christianity, which was still common in the 1950s, but also the protests of the Conservative-Revolutionary survivors such as Hans Zehrer and Wilhelm Stapel. The objections to the cyclical image of time were reflected on a different level. As important as it was for Mohler to make eternal recurrence the focal point of his reflection, he was unsuccessful in demonstrating its influence on the individual protagonists of the Conservative-Revolutionary camp.

WILHELM STAPEL

Although Mohler declined to change the text for the 1971 edition, with its greatly expanded bibliography, he did—in the course of his further engagement with this subject—make three decisive corrections to his original interpretation. These included the reference to the "axial age," the significance of "heroic realism," and the relationship with European fascism.

In an essay on the history of German conservatism in the post-war period, which first appeared in 1974, Mohler developed the thesis that conservatism had undergone an axial age since the end of the 19th century, with widely varied effects in different European countries, abrupt or drawn out. The concept of an axial age, which went back to Karl Jaspers, referred to a reorientation of conservative thought in Mohler's usage:

> [B]efore the passing of the axial age, conservatism
> was turned toward the past, afterward, it oriented

itself toward the future. Before the axial age, conservative efforts focused on preserving what had been handed down or even on recreating a lost scenario. The axial age, thus, became the time of disillusionment. In it, the conservative recognizes that other groups have established a status quo that is unacceptable to him, and that earlier conditions can no longer be restored. From now on, his gaze is directed ahead. [2]

Although Mohler had already indicated that there was a continuity between the Deutsche Bewegung and the Conservative Revolution, now, for the first time, he outlined more clearly that neither the First World War nor the Bolshevik Revolution nor German collapse of 1918 provided the decisive influence; it was rather a change in the climate of the time at the fin de siècle. With certain justification, one might speak of a changed mentality. Already in the first edition of The Conservative Revolution, Mohler had made clear that despite all differences between the groups that composed the Conservative Revolution, "heroic realism" can be considered a foundation, a set of attitudes that united the entire camp—the *völkische* (*völkische* Bewegung [Movement]), Jungkonservativen (Young Conservatives), Bündische (Youth League Movement), Nationalrevolutionäre (National Revolutionaries), and Landvolkbewegung (Rural Movement)—even if their thoughts varied. Later, Mohler investigated this phenomenon from two directions: concerning himself with the basis of "right-wing worldviews" in general (he believed that they were essentially determined by "myths of embeddedness") and through discussion of the "fascist style."

What Mohler tried to make clear in his extensive, widely reproduced essay of 1973 on this subject was the connection between a certain

---

[2] Armin Mohler, "Deutscher Konservatismus seit 1945" in *Die Herausforderung der Konservativen: Absage an Illusionen,* ed. Gerd-Klaus Kaltenbrunner (München: Herder, 1974), 35.

social and cultural atmosphere (which arose before the First World War and underwent its greatest expion before the end of the Second World War) and the appearance of a certain, specifically "fascist" type , which brought forth the "nominalistic turn of the modern age." Under the influence of the Israeli historian Zeev Sternhell, Mohler clarified the concept further and reached the conclusion that the Conservative Revolution should be employed as an umbrella concept for a great variety of worldviews. These worldviews originated in the 1890s and responded to the collapse of the classic Left-Center-Right paradigm by creating new ideological concepts characterized by the acceptance of ideas—that had traditionally been ascribed only to the Left *or* Right—through the abandonment of the backward-looking attitude of the old conservatism and the affirmation of modernity (even if not in all its expressions). Their goal was to establish conditions, the preservation of which would be worthwhile.

In the third and final version of *The Conservative Revolution,* which appeared in 1989, Mohler allowed these new insights to creep into an appendix, if not the text, where, along with extensive digressions, he engaged in a confrontation with then-current research. This presentation was a compromise that Mohler was prepared to make after it became apparent that his plan for producing a "complete bibliography" of the Conservative Revolution was impossible to fulfill due to the scope of material; on the other hand, he still desired to note his changed position.

The present author played a certain, although quite limited, role in the preparatory work for the third edition, and this probably made Mohler's decision easier to hand the work over to him. Such a transfer is always problematic, especially since the book *The Conservative Revolution in Germany* has long since become a part of history. But becoming a part of history makes the use of a work explicitly intended as a handbook more difficult, and Mohler was more concerned with its practicality than anything else.

2

THE RECOGNITION OF GERMAN UNIQUENESS IN THE 19TH CENTURY

ORIGINS AND DEVELOPMENT

he development of political philosophies in the 19th century is usually understood as a process that necessarily led to the foaqrmation of conservative, liberal, democratic, and socialist parties. Yet this development was no seamless continuum. Considering the period from the French Revolution to the outbreak of the First World War, we see that the ideas of conservatism, liberalism, democracy, and socialism were changed by eliminating or effectively questioning Absolutism, constructing constitutional monarchies (or republics in exceptional cases), industrialization, the transition from a society of estates to one of classes — and later masses—the triumphant progress of the natural sciences and the spread of Europe overseas, to name only the most important factors. Moreover, around the middle of the century, the old doctrines saw themselves questioned by new political movements that did not entirely fit, or no longer fit, into the existing system.

All political philosophies have a pre-history. In the case of liberalism, democracy, and socialism, this pre-history was characterized by the assumptions of 18th-century Enlightenment thought, altered by them for their own purposes. Conservatism, on the other hand, had two roots: one grew from the defense of the *societas christiana*, not only against innovators but also against the tendency of Absolutism to make everything uniform; the second originated from the Enlightenment itself and brought forth the *anti-philosophes*, who carried out the counter-revolution by using the same means as the Enlightenment in order to reveal the dangers of this intellectual movement and contain it. The significance of the French Revolution, therefore, lay not in creating political doctrines but in its cataclysmic effect: it forced a clearer decision in favor of specific positions and party formation, insofar as it forced followers of a political philosophy to band together in order to be effective.

The new party system was hastily arranged with the help of the labels "Left" and "Right." Yet only for a short time had the defenders of the existing system been placed to the Right and its detractors to the Left of the presidium of the National Assembly. The public absorbed this terminology so quickly that a change in the order of seating could no longer alter it. The Left of 1789 consisted essentially of a moderate liberal current that sought to reform the *ancien régime*. The limitation of royal power, the elimination of privileges, parliamentary participation, equality before the law, and freedom of commerce are among the demands of classical liberalism that determined French constitutional development in the years following. The Left represented, above all, the middle classes, but the urban and rural lower classes also joined their movement.

In comparison with the social and philosophical homogeneity of the Left, the Right was characterized by "extreme complexity" from the beginning. Above all, this assessment concerns their political philosophy. Among the conservatives were partisans of theocracy, while others favored the re-establishment of Absolutism; a third party wanted a monarchy limited by estates like those in France before the 17th century, and one minority wanted to take over the English constitutional model. Heterogeneity also characterized the social composition of the conservatives. Along with the clergy and aristocracy, peasants and, later on, a part of the urban middle class followed them.

The real "founding of the Right" took place in the debates of the National Assembly on the future position of the Church and the struggle against the "despotism" of the Constituent Assembly, which destroyed French tradition with its projects for a constitution. The failure of the conservatives in this struggle and their ousting from parliament led, at the beginning of the 1790s, to the development of a broad counter-revolutionary movement, which unleashed a long-lasting civil war in the west and south of the country.

The barely victorious liberals saw their position threatened not only by the Right but also by a second front. A democratic movement arose against them, unsatisfied with what had been achieved. This new Left forced the old one to defend the barely maintained *status quo*, so that they, in turn, appeared as "right-wing." The spearhead of democracy was formed by the Jacobin party, which repudiated the liberal middle class altogether in favor of representing "the nation." As democrats, the Jacobins distrusted all forms of representation and demanded—taking up Rousseau's idea of the *volonté générale*—direct exercise of power by the "people." The *sans-culottes* nation ended up finding its will better expressed in a dictator than in a parliamentary committee and brought about—under the rule of the Jacobins—the paradox of a "totalitarian democracy." It was an experiment laden with consequences, but under the circumstances, it could only last a short time.

In relation to conservatives and liberals, democracy remained in a weak position for the entire first half of the 19th century. This applies *a fortiori* to aminority in democratic ranks that demanded not merely a thorough equalization of society and the immediate participation of the people in political power, but wanted, over and above this, the elimination of the existing property order. Socialists or communists, in the precise sense, did not yet exist, in any case, at the beginning of the 19th century.

From 1789 to 1848, the political development of Europe was determined by the struggle between the *parti de la résistance* and the *parti du mouvement*, the partisans of the "status quo" and the partisans of "progress," the conservatives and the liberals. This constellation first changed under the influence of industrialization, in which the proletariat emerged, which could be assimilated neither into the new bourgeois society nor into the existing parties. That the so-called dangerous classes had become a political factor was first perceived in the Revolution of 1848. This Revolution started out everywhere in Europe as a bourgeois revolution and seemed to complete the process of emancipation interrupted by the fall of Napoleon. The principal demands were suitably liberal, and the liberals assumed the loyalty of the lower classes as self-evident.

The course of the Revolution in Paris, where the fall of the monarchy and establishment of a republic were followed by massive unrest on the part of the proletariat, taught the liberals of a new "red danger." Unlike the 1790s, now this was not merely a matter of constitutional conflict; the whole system of property was being challenged. Fearing a socialist overthrow, the French middle class allied itself with a ruler as popular as he was authoritarian. The coup of Louis-Napoléon Bonaparte reminded his contemporaries of his great uncle's 18th Brumaire. Yet whereas the rule of Napoleon I bore many of the traits of a classic military dictatorship or of a belated case of enlightened Absolutism, "Caesarism," "Napoleonism," and this later "Bonapartism" was something new.

Napoleon III erected a political system at the center of which stood the personal exercise of power by the Emperor, who appealed to the agreement of the people by the means of a plebiscite and allowed a parliament to exist, but largely trimmed its powers. Bonapartism was difficult to fit into the political currents of the time. One the one hand, a democratic cast was hard to deny: many former Jacobins supported the rule of Napoleon and his descendants; on the other, the Bonapartists could appear as the party of order, and thus as a modernized form of conservatism. This assessment was emphatically contradicted by the representatives of the authentic Right, who clearly recognized the instability of a Constitution that entirely depended upon popularity and the latent readiness for the use of force; but logical consistency had its price. When conservatives rejected the Bonapartist solution, they found themselves thrust back upon the vanishing basis of their own political position in all of Central and Western Europe.

Conservatives—who had, once again, risen to be a dominant political factor in the states of continental Europe in the era between the Congress of Vienna and 1848—lost importance. This was closely bound up with the great economic and social changes that gradually undermined the basis for a conceptual realm referring to a social order that consisted of estates. Because of their strong social views, conservatives succeeded in preserving a large segment of their positions until the end of the First World War, but the conservative philosophy became, in part, obsolete, and, in part, adapted to other doctrines.

This adaptation had already occurred in Great Britain. Protected from an encroachment of "Gallic principles" by its position as an island, the old Toryism was only reorganized as a conservative party at the end of the 18th century. A liberal crossover—Edmund Burke came from the ranks of the Whigs—played an important role in this process. Thus, the conservatives saw themselves forced, following bitter political defeats, to make essential liberal demands, such as freedom of commerce, extension of suffrage, and religious tolerance, into their own causes in order to recapture political influence.

On the continent, conservatives and liberals were moving towards each other, as liberals after 1848 sought a way of adapting to the old institutions and were more interested in preventing a proletarian revolution than in eliminating monarchical power or the vestiges of feudal privileges. This realistic turn, above all, caused liberalism to grant a much more important status to the "power" factor than in the past. It led to a certain observable convergence between the liberal and conservative program until the end of the 19th century, although differences of principle did not entirely disappear. For the sake of this mutual understanding, liberals abandoned their utopia of the "classless civil society" and accepted a great deal of inequality in the distribution of wealth; yet they insisted upon equality before the law and parliamentary consultation. The conservatives abandoned all dreams of recreating a corporative order and accepted the curtailment of their privileges, but defended the prerogative of the crown and a strong position for the army and Church.

In view of this development, it is hardly surprising that socialists commonly viewed conservatives and liberals as a *single* enemy. Under difficult conditions, socialist organizational efforts were first successful in the 1880s, incorporating the smaller democratic movements and undisputedly forming the left-wing in parliament, while the liberals moved to the center and the conservatives continued to form the Right. Many socialists promoted the violent overthrow of existing political and social order and the erection of a society without private property; but, in fact, the party leaders gradually adopted a strategy meant to allow them to reach their goals through the continually growing number of their followers. Even if the Left was not the first mass movement of the 19th century—political Catholicism had already begun to form mass parties much earlier in response to the policies directed against it— never before had the organization of the masses been so unmistakably tied to the threat of overwhelming the existing order.

In the last two decades of the 19th century, there began a discussion of alternative forms of mass politics in reaction to endangerement of the middle class. The central question was as follows. Growing population and the decomposition of the social order unleashed new and unpredictable social masses; could a new method be found to discipline them? Old ideologies seemed to offer an unsuitable solution, and even Bonapartism, being bound up with a specific time and persons, was unable to provide a satisfying answer to the question. Only a few of its efforts appeared promising. Ideologies that were now emerging, such as "integral nationalism" or the doctrines that appeared in order to justify imperialism, were appropriated by the Bonapartist model, insofar as they were compatible with the militarizing and ideological education of the people, and they were oriented towards national prestige and charismatic leadership. Yet none of the new philosophies had proven capable of becoming the focus of a new political force. The old "global movement" unleashed by the French Revolution had still not run its course.

At the turn of the 20th century, one perceives less a political change than a change in atmosphere, determined, above all, by the "disappointment of expectations" that affected the European intelligentsia. In view of successful economic and technical developments and of the enormous increase in power experienced by many "Old World" countries, it may seem paradoxical that a feeling of decline was spreading among the educated, but the fact itself is incontestable. The then-influential and widely read Max Nordau observed in his 1892 diagnosis of decadence, "The *fin de siècle*' state of mind is met with everywhere today...."[3]

It is true that there had been concern about "decadence" all through the 19th century, despite the strong belief in "progress," but this fear was never displayed with such intensity as during the *fin de siècle*. The perception that one's own age is "decadent" was in no way restricted to one political camp. Conservative thinkers such as Carl Volgraff and Ernst von Lasaulx were among the most consistent analysts of collapse, but liberals like Alexis de Tocqueville and Jacob Burckhardt had agreed with their pessimistic judgment to a great extent. In the

---

|3| Max Nordau, *Entartung* (Berlin: Duncker, 1892), 3.

ranks of the socialists, the idea that bourgeois-feudal society was in the grip of unstoppable decline continued to operate, despite the fact that Karl Marx's doctrine was entirely based on historical development.

2.1 ORIGINS OF RECOGNIZING GERMAN UNIQUENESS

Because of its intellectual tradition, Germany was a fruitful ground for the perception of decadence, for that "cultural criticism" which understood the problematic aspects of modernity in a particular way. On the eve of the First World War, Ernst Troeltsch wrote,

> *Just as Rousseau, neo-humanism, Romanticism, and the nation-state were the reaction against the spirit and culture of the Enlightenment and its corresponding utilitarian absolutism, so cultural criticism followed the development of the democratic capitalist imperialist technical century.*

Troeltsch linked the situation at the beginning of the 20th century with that at the beginning of the 19th, because it was at that time that the unique spiritual position of Germany first became clear. Simply put, this was the contrast between Germany's "idealistic" disposition and the "positivistic" position that dominated France and England. In spite of its industrial and political developments, which were by then comparable to those of Western Europe, Germany continually demonstrated this disposition and its own extraordinary intellectual significance anew.

Unlike France and England, Germany at the beginning of the 19th century was not a state. Even after the decline of the Holy Roman Empire and the downfall of Napoleon, national unification of Germany failed. Instead, the dualism of Austria and Prussia characterized the following age: this was not merely a political but religious dualism, since Austria was considered the dominant German Catholic power and Prussia, the dominant German Protestant power. Yet the confessional divide was not simply a burden: the Reformation had contributed decisively to the growth of the idealistic disposition and the development of a peculiar "psychology of the German conception of the state." It differed from that of France and England in two respects: by fundamentally supposing an ethical nature of the state, which could never be conceived as entirely separate from society, and by a certain skepticism regarding the "Western" concept of freedom.

The particular German state forms of the 17th and 18th century—the "Christian police state" and enlightened Absolutism—can only be understood in this context. Their success had considerable influence on the political mentality in Germany, even outside the Protestant parts of the Reich, which brought about both a justified confidence in the effectiveness of administrative measures and a notable depoliticizing of the citizenry, especially of the middle class. The Enlightenment was supported by the middle classes in Germany as in the other European countries, but the spread of political doctrines was restricted to very narrow circles before the outbreak of the French Revolution. There were sympathizers of the Revolution in the Reich, but they were hardly "German Jacobins"—rather, supporters of a careful reform of enlightened despotism.

Next to this early liberalism, the predecessors of German conservatism were in the process of development, receiving a certain theoretical foundation in the writings of Justus Möser and a few spokesmen of the counter-Enlightenment. Influenced by radicalizing the revolutionary process, this camp took up an ever more rigid defensive position that could be sure of support from the governments of the individual states. National ideas were widespread among the early conservatives as they were among the champions of the Enlightenment, but without achieving any particular effect.

That changed with the advent of Romanticism. In its origins, Romanticism was not limited to Germany, but there it attained a certain influence on thought, including political thought and the nascent consciousness of German uniqueness. The latter was influential even with respect to the spiritual and political counter-movements that were constantly forced to debate the subjects of Romantic thought.

2.2 POLITICAL EFFECTS OF ROMANTICISM

At first, many Romantics showed sympathy for the French Revolution. Yet this propensity faded and gave way to a conceptual world that rejected not only the Revolution itself but also the Enlightenment that produced this great change. The rejection of rationalism moved to the center of Romantic thought, as well as the emphasis on history and the relationship between things and the "whole," which was to be given priority over the particular.

The so-called irrationalism of Romanticism was directed, above all, against the tendency of the Enlightenment to be suspicious of all feeling, using reason as a weapon intended to destroy existing conditions and even threatening to annihilate life itself—an "unbroken stream," according to Novalis. Yet Romanticism did not merely counter Enlightenment with emotion and intuition but also the idea of a great relationship into which smaller relationships were "organized."

Romanticism connected its critique of the faith in reason to the rehabilitation of religion. The latter was considered not only the most beautiful expression of man's emotional life, but also the bond that connected the individual to an ethical community and made it possible to access a higher truth than that of reason. This conception became so influential that it explains not only the continued religious orientation of German thought in the 19th century but also its defensive position against the Western European version of natural right. After all, the wish to penetrate existence religiously and comprehend the world as a divine and natural order was accompanied by skepticism toward the idea that there could have been prehistoric conditions from which the inalienable rights of man might be derived "mechanically." The view that man had never been a natural being in the sense intended by the Enlightenment, but rather was metaphysically and historically determined, is linked to the Romantics' interest in the past and historical thought, which turns away from the idea of linear progress. Latent fear of decline played a role here, but the notion of an alternating process of *corso* and *ricorso* was more important.

The vitality of the 19th-century German "conservative attitude toward life" (*Lebensgefühl*) is rightly traced to Romanticism. By recognizing longevity as the variable that determines history, the life of an individual as well as that of society overcame the sterility of all purely backward-looking ideas and opened up space for an "organic" understanding of the present and future. In noticeable contrast to this thesis stands the observed lack of practical influence of all properly conservative romanticism after the restoration of 1813-1815. It is true that Schlegel, Görres, and Adam Müller acceded to a pact with absolutism against revolutionary tendencies, but they did so unwillingly and at the price of submitting to the logic of Metternich's system. As a reaction to this, the Romantics' tendency toward theological speculation became stronger—along with the inclination of Protestant Romantics to "return home" to the Catholic Church—as well as their tendency to withdraw from politics altogether.

Romanticism did not only influence conservatism, however, but also defined a very influential group within German liberalism, which has been labeled "historical liberal" or "corporatist liberal." Among its most important representatives, besides Jacob and Wilhelm Grimm, was Friedrich Christoph Dahlmann. That these men all belonged to the Göttingen Seven who protested against the unconstitutional behavior of the Hannoverian king was no more an accident than that Dahlmann's *Politics* (1835)—which in a peculiar way mixed constitutional demands with an organic image of the state—can be considered the programmatic statement of this tendency.

The borderline between the historical liberals and what has been called the "Deutsche Bewegung" (German Movement) was blurred. The "Deutsche Bewegung" was not what this group called itself, but it was a concept introduced by Wilhelm Dilthey and clarified by Herman Nohl in order to mark off a tendency otherwise difficult to delineate. It fused influences from Sturm und Drang, Classicism and Idealism with those of Romanticism. Their leading ideas were marked by the notion of a culture-creating hero, "subjective religion," and the directing of all politics toward the "*Volk*."

Although Herder still thought in 1765 that *Volk* commonly signified the same thing as "rabble and canaille," an enduring change came about through his influence and that of Romanticism. Because of the central position that the *Volk* assumed in the thinking of the Deutsche Bewegung, the latter was difficult to classify in terms of the Left-Right schema. "*Volk*" signified not only the ethnic and cultural community, and not only the political community in the sense of the French Revolution. As before, "*Volk*" served to signify the "crowd," the "poor folks," which imbued every appeal to the *Volk* with a certain "democratic sentiment." This necessarily awakened the displeasure of aristocratic or monarchical authorities at the beginning of the 19th century. In the work of Ernst Moritz Arndt—the most important representative of the new *Volk* idea—there are many references to the decadence of the princes and lords, and to the natural goodness, or at least the impressive regenerative power of simple people.

Arndt connected the positive conception of the *Volk* with other ideas. These ideas have, since the age of humanism, left a lasting impression on the German notion of nationhood: above all, that the unity of the Germans is not based on the link between the state and territory but on the shared qualities of language, culture, and descent. The idea of *Volk* in this sense was perfectly suited to Romantic guidelines, since it formed an organic unity that had arisen historically, guaranteeing continuance and assigning a place to the individual.

It was the excesses of the French Revolution and the experience of Republican and Napoleonic rule that first effectively politicized the development of the *Volk* idea in the direction of German nationalism. In spite of this, the idea that politics was not everything for the nation survived in the Deutsche Bewegung. This aspect that surpasses politics explains the enthusiastic movement for a "*Volksstaat*" ("*Volks* state") "*Volksreligion*." (*Volk* religion"), and "*Volksbildung*" ("*Volk* education") as the basis of a new order for common life.

The *Volksstaat* was oriented toward the idea of the Greek *polis*, and thus combined civic rights with the duty of military service. But there was seldom any precise idea of the individual's involvement in the state. The reason for this was repugnance for both mechanical equality and the preservation of traditional privileges. Especially under the influence of Baron von Stein, the idea of an order based on professions, out of which an organic constitutional structure was to grow, took center stage.

"*Volksbildung*" was meant to raise men up to support the new state. The Deutsche Bewegung played a large role in the educational enthusiasm that characterized the transition from the 19th to the 20th century, including not only the ideas of Pestalozzi and Fröbel, but also Wilhelm von Humboldt's plans for school and college reform and Jahn's practical measures for the physical fitness of young men.

According to the Deutsche Bewegung, the ideal man could only be thought of as a religious man. Their projections of a *Volk* religion were different from that of a patriotic civil worship such as the French Revolution promoted, especially in its serious effort toward a new inwardness of faith. This also explains the gulf that separates the Deutsche Bewegung in this respect from the conservative protagonists of Romanticism. The Deutsche Bewegung was entirely rooted in Protestant soil. Arndt criticized the converts by saying that there was no "way back," that Christendom—in fact, religion itself—would have to be completely renewed.

The Deutsche Bewegung had direct political impact only in the Prussian Age of Reform (1807-1819), including such leading minds as Stein, Gneisenau, Scharnhorst, Clausewitz, Schleiermacher, Fichte, and Arndt. But until 1830, it continued to maintain its rank as the spiritual and intellectual "leading power of the age." Yet it remained without any organizational context, even though the student fraternities, gymnasts, and singers were strongly influenced by them. They were unable to achieve their political goals—above all, German unity, even accepting the Prussian-Austrian dual headship. Under existing circumstances, they appeared as a segment of the liberal or even "Jacobin" camp and, as the fate of Arndt and Jahn proves, were thus viewed by those in authority.

2.3 ANTI-ROMANTICISM

The special inhibition experienced by German liberalism in the first half of the 19th century was, above all, connected with the lack of national unity. None of the guarantor powers of the Vienna Congress settlement, not even Prussia and Austria, were interested in allowing a nation-state to arise at the center of Europe, and the "German Bund" founded in 1815, formed only a loose confederation of sovereign princes and free cities, which had no shared constitution. For this reason, liberals were forced to adapt themselves to the conditions in each member state, without thereby giving up their long-term goals: unity and a constitution.

The collapse of the Revolution of 1848 dealt a decisive blow to the plan for national unification and the idea of an all-German state, including the Hapsburgs. Afterward, the further course of development was largely determined by Prussian policy, which, following a short period of hesitation, gave up its openly proclaimed wait-and-see attitude. Prussia (in contrast to Austria) came to an arrangement with the liberals not merely by including a part of their demands in the constitution granted by the King; under Bismarck's leadership, the old military monarchy seemed to even put itself at the head of the liberal "Lesser German" national movement.[4]

This current was prepared to accept an arrangement with Prussia that did not arise only at the moment of Bismarck's great political success, but had been planned long before. Up until the 1850s, there had been no "national party" in Germany capable of action. This changed under the leadership of a younger generation prepared to draw radical conclusions from the failure of the Revolution. The new National Liberalism included the traditions of the Deutsche Bewegung in its worldview, along with a power politics strongly influenced by Hegel.

In contrast to the Romantics, Hegel did not want to refute the Enlightenment with his conception of idealism, but to outdo it. With regard to political positions in the narrow sense, there were points of agreement between Hegel and those of the Romantics, such as the rejection of natural right and admiration for the hero, but also considerable differences. Thus, Hegel certainly did believe in historic progress insofar as world history itself was "progress in the consciousness of freedom."[5] His efforts were directed to tracing the plans of the "World Spirit." Each "folk (Volk) spirit" served only as a "step" in its development. Like Romanticism, Hegel saw in the folk spirits of the Greeks and Germanics and in Christianity the most important historical factors, but he considered the pre-political Volk, which the Romantics had adopted with such empathy, as "dull" and incapable of historical action. The Volk was not a unified entity at all. This made state formation a serious business that had nothing to do

---

|4| "The Lesser German solution" (die kleindeutsche Lösung) was the contemporary term for a plan to unify German lands and exclude those in the Austrian Empire. In contrast, the "Greater German solution" would have included those lands. The Lesser German solution was realized by Prussia under Bismarck's leadership in the period 1864-71. (Ed.)

|5| Georg Wilhelm Friedrich Hegel, Vorlesungen für die Philosophie der Geschichte, vol. 12 (Frankfurt am Main: Suhrkamp, 1986), 32.

with self-development, but was thought instead as an agonal process, like everything else in history.

Hegel's admiration for Napoleon, and then the Prussian monarchy, can be explained by his anti-Romantic position. His rejection of democracy and advocacy of a "second royalty"—i.e., the recreation of the original constitution of the human race on a higher ethical level—corresponded to the subsiding of "the National" as an intrinsic value. The decisive point was not the nation-state, but the state power that would be in the position to fulfill the law of history.

Hegel, too, saw in the ancient *polis* the ideal fusion of citizenry and state, and believed in the superiority of Protestantism as the basis of a civil religion. Yet his affirmation of political order went considerably further than that of the Deutsche Bewegung. The admiration of Machiavelli that was also familiar in the Deutsche Bewegung—even if in a rather naïve form—became of decisive importance for Hegel early on. In him, wrote Friedrich Meinecke, Machiavelli's basic attitude came to life once again: the sense of the "truth that lies in power."[6]

The Deutsche Bewegung always remained relatively distant from this truth. Any of them who moved closer to it—the Historical School of Law or scientific history that followed upon Leopold von Ranke—fell under the influence of Hegel and the so-called right-wing Hegelians. This is especially true of the "National Party" that wanted to draw conclusions from experiencing the failure of all politics that ignored the "laws of power." This *Realpolitik* then projected by Hegel's disciples was not merely a reaction to the changed intellectual atmosphere of the 1850s, characterized, above all, by the growing influence of Schopenhauer's philosophy; quite consistently, they turned away from the illusion of the brotherhood encompassing all European peoples. "Against the *pensée immuable* of the West and East," said Theodor

---

|6| Friedrich Meinecke, *Die Idee der Staatsräson in der neueren Geschichte*, vol. 1 (München: Oldenbourg, 1957), 418.

Mommsen, we should raise up "the unshakeable protest of Germanic nationality."[7] Hegel's disciples turned towards Prussia as the kernel around which a future German nation-state could crystallize. Even at the high tide of the Prussian armed conflict, this camp was prepared, in principle, to acknowledge the necessity of enhanced means of war and, in connection with this, to provide the military aristocracy with a place in the future Germany as well. The hope that the Prussian *Junker* class would eventually evolve into a gentry based on the British model corresponded to the assumption that a unified German state created by authoritarian means would follow the liberal model in the long run.

With the will toward *Realpolitik*—a term coined by the liberal Ludwig von Rochau under the influence of the failed Revolution—a step was taken, bringing the German liberals much closer to their goal, without the price appearing too high. By contrast, the rejection of Bismarck by the conservatives destroyed their chance of further development. The forcible ousting of Austria from Germany, eliminating the historical rights of the small- and medium-sized states that had sided with the Hapsburgs in 1866, and Bismarck's wish to round out his conquests were useful, but morally and politically unacceptable to the conservatives. It was this principled stand that sealed their fate. In the "new Reich," they fell victim to the realignment of the parties. The conservative formation established in 1871 not only approved national union, but also accepted other liberal positions.

So there were good reasons to think that Germany had become a normal European nation-state, like the other developed countries of the continent, as well as to expect that the development of political-philosophical "camps" would follow the same pattern that had gradually prevailed over the course of the century: a socialist Left, a liberal Center, and a conservative Right. The deviations from this pattern in

---

|7| Otto Westphal, *Welt- und Staatsauffassung des deutschen Liberalismus Eine Untersuchung über die Preussischen Jahrbücher und den konstitutionellen Liberalismus in Deutschland von 1858 bis 1863* (München - Berlin, Oldenbourg 1919), 300.

Germany hardly seemed to matter: the rapid rise of social democracy as a consequence of universal suffrage, the continued division of liberals into an independent and a national-liberal wing, and the appearance of the Catholic party, which had not been destroyed by the *Kulturkampf* but rather strengthened for the long run.[8]

2.4 THE IDEAS OF 1871

Bismarck used neither the term *Realpolitik* nor the term *Machtstaat*. He was certainly no Hegelian, even if he often "did what Hegel and his disciples had earlier expressed."[9] He was satisfied to speak simply of politics and the state, because they seemed unequivocal to him and he suspected all prefixes of being ideological. Even though there were representatives of the Hegelian tradition about him in the persons of Constantin Rössler and Johann Eduard Erdmann, he himself cannot be counted a member of this school. On the other hand, Bismarck's ideas were not purely opportunistic, as has sometimes been suggested. That he did, indeed, possess a philosophy is clear especially in the interweaving of conservative and revolutionary ideas in his thought.

Although Bismarck did not shy away from using revolutionary methods, or at least from threatening to do so; although many older conservatives considered him a "revolutionary"; and although the founding of the German Reich seemed like a revolutionary achievement to many others—as the "German Revolution," in fact—Bismarck

---

|8| *Kulturkampf*, or "cultural struggle," was an anti-Catholic (and, to a lesser extent, anti-Polish) legislative campaign unleashed by Bismarck in Prussia in the 1870s. It backfired, resulting in the creation of the Catholic Deutsche Zentrumspartei (German Center Party), which became the second largest party in Germany and played an important role in German politics for 60 years. (*Ed.*)

|9| Herman Heller, *Hegel und der nationale Machtstaatsgedanke in Deutschland: Ein Beitrag zur politischen Geistesgeschichte* (Berlin: Teubner, 1921), 185,

himself insisted that German unification was a "conservative act."[10] His conservatism, after an early advocacy of reaction, approached the concept developed within Romanticism and then within the Deutsche Bewegung. In his view, conservatism did not preserve obsolete forms, but maintained those vital powers that might sometimes only be possible through the destruction of old forms and the creation of something quite new. The latter, however, must be made out of the dynamic, germinating elements of existence and not against them.

Bismarck had little interest in the theoretical side of the connection. He made use of the current ideas about what was conservative as well as the Hegelian doctrine of the state—i.e., he saw in the state a "living corporation," a "personality," an "organism"—but mistrusted every doctrinaire position. It was precisely the recognition of the givens of power politics that lastingly informed his "realistic conservatism." He himself would have never used this expression either, and, if only for this reason, one can hardly speak of an independent school of thought or "Bismarckism." Yet Bismarck was not alone in his beliefs either. The proximity of his reflection to that of Helmuth von Moltke is as striking as its distance from that of the third *Reichsgründer*, Albrecht von Roon, to whom Bismarck was much closer in terms of origin and biography, but who must be considered with the older corporative conservatism. The halo that surrounded Bismarck and Moltke, and even more the fact that both came forward as authors, ensured that their ideas would spread far beyond the realm that statesmen and military men usually reach. The reading of the writings or the popularizing of their central concerns undoubtedly had considerable political consequences.

Bismarck's conservatism was not only "realistic" in regard to external politics, whose primacy he always stood for, but also in regard to internal societal development. Bismarck had certainly recognized that

---

|10| Gustav Adolf Rein, *Die Revolution in der Politik Bismarcks* (Berlin: Musterschmidt, 1957), 176.

the old order had become fragile and that the anchorage of Prussian conservatism in the agrarian structure of the east was antiquated. His readiness to rule by circumventing his own social peers and thus deny the central element in the conservative credo—the legitimate leadership position of the nobility—did not stop him from being conservative according to his own understanding and actions.

The means available for applying such a variant of conservatism was the "revolution from above," a concept which had been highly influential in Prussia since the time of enlightened despotism and the Age of Reform. This connection was probably never so clear as in Bismarck's social legislation. Its particular character can be satisfactorily explained neither by Bismarck's personal piety not by the wish to bribe the proletariat through benefaction. In Bismarck's mind, it was rather "social conservatism" that played an important role.

Already in the first half of the century, conservatives, especially in Prussia, had discovered the "social question" and the new reality of the class society and attempted to find answers other than those offered by traditional paternalism. Among these attempts were Laurenz von Stein's idea of "social royalty" as well as Victor Aimé Huber's practical recommendation for the overcoming of the housing shortage and the poverty of workers, or Carl Rodbertus's demand for a non-violent but realistic "transition" to the new industrial form of society. Ideas from this milieu strongly influenced Bismarck during the last phase of his chancellorship and contributed to the practical shaping of social legislation.

The Chancellor never went as far as the "state socialists" or "armchair socialists,"[11] whose goals also included a reformation of property relations. Yet their ideas made a strong impression on a younger generation of educated persons. In his memoirs, sociologist

---

|11| *Kathedersozialisten*, literally "lectern socialists;" a pejorative term for the historical school of economics, which consisted largely of academics.

Johann Plenge describes the atmosphere in the seminar of the "armchair socialist" Adolph Wagner:

> *We discovered there that we all stood for socialism, some of us—for the conservative and loyalist socialism of Rodbertus, others—for the democratic socialism...of Bebel and Liebknecht, for the Bismarckian variety...or for the armchair socialism of our respected teacher, or even occasionally for all of these socialisms put together; but everyone was passionately opposed to every sort of liberalism and individualism, which we believed to be a superstition of our fathers, a ghost of 1848, by now obsolete and long since done with.* [12]

This was not a phenomenon restricted to Germany: toward the end of the 19th century, the term "socialism" became increasingly unmoored from its background in party politics and became a cipher for a comprehensive reordering of society. In both France and Great Britain, one found proposals for a new religious, ethical, civil, or even a national socialism. This "boom" was connected not only with the understanding of the need for economic reforms but also with the general crisis of the liberal ideas which had predominated since the great Revolution. But in Germany, its influence only slowly came into its own and was always called into question because of the strong Prussian tradition. It was typical to understand it as a mortgage. Yet one could also see—in the backwardness of Bismarck's Reich—the precondition for the emergence of that "German model of the future," which recognizably differed from the previously dominant prototypes taken from Western Europe and which, for this very reason, would shape the "Social Age."

---

[12]   Johann Plenge, *Zur Vertiefung des Sozialismus* (Leipzig: Der neue Geist, 1919), 45.

2.5 HERALDS OF A "CULTURAL-REVOLUTIONARY AGE": LAGARDE—WAGNER—TREITSCHKE

The certainty "that the days of liberalism were coming to an end" was announced with special emphasis by the religious scholar and orientalist Paul de Lagarde. Born Bötticher in 1827 to a strict conservative and pietistic family, he succeeded only with great effort in achieving the academic career he sought due to his modest social background. He spent years in the school system until his 1869 appointment as professor of the Faculty of Philosophy at the University of Göttingen.

PAUL DE LAGARDE

Lagarde's meticulous research of ancient Oriental[13] texts and those of the Church Fathers are of incontestable scholarly importance, and he exercised considerable influence into the 20th century. In his view, theology was a purely historical discipline; he rejected the obligatory character of the Biblical canon and the dogma of the exclusive revelation of God in Jesus Christ. His emphasis on the historical character of Christianity, derived from historicism, did not prevent his high appraisal of religion—which he considered a necessary element of the personality—nor his avowal of the original teaching of Jesus. By this he meant a view (*Anschauung*) purified of all Pauline elements and focused on ethics and one's relationship with God.

Lagarde's criticism of the Church's preaching always had a certain unmistakable political thrust and implications for popular education.

|13| Here, Middle Eastern. (*Ed.*)

In his view, the throne and altar should be strictly separated, and the denominations forced to set aside their disputes and be assumed in a single "national Church," whose teaching must be a "national religion." This future faith community, as envisaged by Lagarde, had clearly Catholic (but by no means "Roman") features. This was related to his sharp criticism of Protestantism—which he accused of being "ignoble"—and of Luther. He accused the reformer of overestimating the importance of historically conditioned abuses and of causing Jewish ideas to predominate in Christendom by taking up the Pauline doctrine of salvation.

Lagarde's sharp position regarding the Jews, which also found expression in this context, rested upon his assertion that they were not simply a religious community but a "nation within the nation." This made them a continual challenge to the Germans among whom they lived, because a nation could have only one soul. Lagarde demanded variously the complete incorporation of the Jews and the resettlement of the part that was not assimilable. He, however, rejected racial ideas in the strict sense: "Germanness does not lie in the blood, but in the heart," therefore a Jew could perfectly well become a German.

Much of Lagarde's thought was a response to the immediate influence of the Deutsche Bewegung. He had known Arndt, Heinrich Leo, and Jacob Grimm personally and, according to his own testimony, felt himself especially indebted to Romanticism. This tradition explains not only his distaste for Hegel, but also his emphatic conception of Germanness. For him, Germany was not a political-geographic quantity but "the totality of Germans with a German sensibility, German thought, German will." For this reason, Lagarde criticized the *kleindeutsch* unification, which excluded Austria and promoted the formation of a great power in Central Europe under the leadership of the houses of Hohenzollern and Hapsburg. He considered a war against Russia an unavoidable part of this, while he simultaneously hoped for an alliance with Germany's cousin nation of Great Britain.

Lagarde's enthusiasm for Germany's future stood in remarkable contrast to his fear that the nation was as threatened by materialism and atomization as by the effects of modern technology and industry. "Inner unity" was more important for him than all external-political or imperial considerations. He believed that the nation needed a "new ideal" to liberate itself from decadence and bring it outside itself again.

Lagarde's cultural criticism led him to side with the conservatives even more than did his earliest influences.[14] Yet his conception of conservatism clearly differed from the political programs of contemporary conservative parties. Already in a text from 1853, he declared that under existing circumstances, only "reform is conservative, and is radically conservative." The Program for the Konservative Partei Preußens (Conservative Party of Prussia), which he produced in 1884, read, "There is no question for the conservatives of preserving everything that exists: they direct their concern not to the work results of any and all powers, but only to such powers as maintain themselves when the conditions for their survival are not removed."

Lagarde's "radical conservatism" displayed a whole series of traits that made it difficult to reconcile with the orientation of the conservative party. For instance, he never doubted the justification of revolutions, such as the French Revolution of 1789, based on principle. Lagarde also rejected the restoration of the old corporative order, along with Absolutism. His aversion to all forms of despotism—he even considered Bismarck's chancellorship as such—and his trust in individualism are reminiscent of old liberal ideas. This context even applies to Lagarde's sympathy for the English constitution, making his outbursts against liberalism as the dregs of Jewish Celtic theorizing hardly seem consistent. This contradiction can be resolved, however, if one assumes that the impulse of the Deutsche Bewegung with its attempt at a new synthesis continued to linger in Lagarde's philosophy. This also explains why the "actual *Volk*" always remained the focus of his efforts.

|14| *Seine Herkunftswelt*, lit. "his world of origin." (*Ed.*)

Lagarde's influence was rather limited during his lifetime. Yet already at the time of his death in 1891, people spoke of its "prophetic nature." And, in fact, he was among the key inspirations for the next generation. Up until his death, only other outsiders, such as Constantin Franz, Nietzsche, and his friend Franz Overbeck, referenced Lagarde. Yet before the First World War, Christian Morgenstern called him the most influential German thinker next to Nietzsche, and Thomas Mann called him *"praeceptor Germaniae."*

The reasons for the extraordinary increase in his influence lay, in part, in the popularizing of Lagarde's ideas through a very successful book, *Rembrandt als Erzieher* (*Rembrandt as Educator*). Its author, Julius Langbehn, explicitly considered himself the custodian of Lagarde's legacy. Also, this influence was the result of the significance that Lagarde's thought gained for Jugendbewegung (Youth Movement). Although his *Deutsche Schriften* (*German Writings*) sold poorly at first, a compendium that the Diederichs publishing house brought out in 1913, under the title *Deutscher Glaube* (*German Faith*), achieved massive dissemination. Among the prominent minds that noticed Lagarde early on—but did

not only absorb him very selectively in the manner of Nietzsche and Overbeck—was Richard Wagner. In 1878, Wagner invited Lagarde to complete a treatise he had begun on the subject, *What Is German?* Lagarde did not comply with this request and kept his distance from Wagner. However, there were many Lagarde sympathizers in the Bayreuther Kreis (Circle). They saw a plan related to the Master's intentions in his project for a German religion, in particular.

RICHARD WAGNER

Wagner (1813-1883) had at this time, in the first decade following the establishment of the Reich, arrived at an endpoint of his rather mutable ideological development. Like Lagarde, Wagner was strongly influenced by Romanticism, although, in contrast to him, in the 1840s, he attached himself politically to the ideas of Young Germany and democratic radicalism. His active engagement in the Revolution of 1848 followed years of instability and exile, which only seemed to lead to a triumphant homecoming following his meeting with the Bavarian King Ludwig II.

Yet Wagner was faced not only with ever-new obstacles (not merely financial). In his attempt to realize his ambitious festival plans, he was forced to realize that the national unity he had longed for had not led to the apotheosis of the German spirit and German art for which he had hoped. Although Wagner succeeded in becoming the most influential German composer after 1871 and in making Bayreuther Kreis the center of a new opera concept, this did not satisfy his grander ambitions. The sharp aesthetic opposition between the ruling political and social conditions moved to the forefront of his thought, along with the idea that he, Wagner, was the appointed trailblazer for an "attempt to regenerate the human race."

For this project, Wagner wished to unite a renewal of Christianity with a return to certain elements of Germanic myth. The basis for these conceptions was also prepared by Romanticism. However, the notion of the Germanic origins of the Germans received a new and incredibly effective expression through the world of Wagnerian opera. Furthermore, Wagner developed a heroic and, in part, bleak self-image for the German nation, which exerted influence far beyond the musical and artistic realm. If one considers the reworking of his motifs by painters such as Hans Makart, Hans Thoma, Franz Stuck, or Franz Stassen, and sculptors such as Rudolf Maison, one gets a vague idea of the influence these motifs received, popularized through cheap prints, which were widely disseminated and even found expression in schoolbooks and were taken up by popular literature.

Wagner's notion of a broad renewal of national culture and a new form of idealism, as well as that of Germanizing Christianity and his corresponding rejection of Jewishness, showed a strong affinity for the ideas of Lagarde. But the effect they had was much more immediate. This was because of the success that Wagner enjoyed within his own lifetime. In addition, a smaller discipleship, the Bayreuther Kreis, was available to spread his ideas and combine them with other philosophies.

One of the most effective combinations may have been "Gobinism." Arthur de Gobineau's *Essay on the Inequality of the Human Races* had

not achieved much dissemination since the appearance of the first volume in 1853. One reason was that as time passed, this racial theory fit ever less well with scientific knowledge. Yet an even larger role may have been played by the fatalistic philosophy of history that formed the basis of Gobineau's *Essay*, and which considered the decline of the white race unstoppable.

ARTHUR DE GOBINEAU

Wagner, who met with Gobineau several times in the 1870s and again once more just before his death, could not, from the beginning, reconcile himself with Gobineau's pessimism. He broke lances with him over Wagner's hypothesis that Christianity was suited to become the basis for a renewal of the "blood." But it was the extraordinarily influential work of his son-in-law, Houston Stewart Chamberlain— *The Foundations of the Nineteenth Century*, which appeared in two volumes in 1899—that first changed the foundations effectively created by Gobineau. This occurred through the identification of the historical Germanic peoples with the contemporary Germans, through adopting the dualism "Aryan/Semite" (which Gobineau was not interested in), and through the presumption that there was no necessary downward development but rather that a new choice in favor of breeding was possible, and thus a regeneration of the race could be envisioned.

Heinrich von Treitschke (1834-1896) was nearly a generation younger than Lagarde and Wagner, and his thought belonged more unmistakably and more fully to the "New Reich." Yet he also displayed an oppositional temperament from early on. He broke with his father

and joined the "lesser German" national movement early on. As one of the most prominent champions of the "realistic" conception of politics—he was lastingly influenced by Hegel and considered Rochau's book *Realpolitik* one of the most important political philosophical treatises ever. He also came into conflict with the segment of liberal opinion that still believed—after the failure of the Revolution—that national unity could be achieved by one's own effort and "from below."

HEINRICH VON TREITSCHKE

Treitschke, along with a group of historians that had, since the 1860s, centered around the *Preußische Jahrbücher* (*Prussian Yearbooks*), pursued the goal of uniting the liberal center (along with the more reform-ready conservatives and moderate democrats) and simultaneously bringing the Hohenzollern monarchy to join its forces with those of the national cause. With this view in mind, he went quite far in his readiness to recognize the autonomy of the Prussian military monarchy, stipulating that a compromise was necessary to prevent a repetition of the mistakes of 1848, as well as the danger of intervention by outside powers in the event of German unification.

Treitschke's path after 1871 was not only determined by his being the "Herald" of the Reich or that he enjoyed prestige as an influential mind of the so-called Borussian school of German historians. More important, perhaps, was that after a short period of complete agreement, he turned away both from Bismarck and from Nationalliberale Partei (National Liberal Party)—for which he occupied a Reichstag seat until 1878— and without thereby being left isolated. Instead, his independence was strengthened, and his undeniable rhetorical and pedagogic abilities—he had been credited with possessing something "magical"—earned him the reputation as one of the most influential academics anywhere.

He used this position, above all, in the seminar on politics he regularly held after 1874 in order to propagate a philosophy that made possible a ruthless look at history and the present. Already in his earlier writing, Treitschke had turned sharply against certain liberal views, contradicting the idea of a freedom based on natural rights in favor or political freedom in a "free state," and rejecting the notion of an independent society in favor of the necessary incorporation of all society within the state. Like Hegel, Treitschke negated all organic conceptions of the state and valued the political *verismo* of Machiavelli. Yet he did not go as far in his admiration as Hegel, who shared Machiavelli's conception of the moral autonomy of politics, but instead demanded that politics be bound by ethics (albeit one suitable to his own political demands).

Treitschke advocated a clearly authoritarian monarchical state model, which limited the power of the legislature, and he considered a conflict with the other great European powers—especially England and France—unavoidable. On the other hand, he rejected all Absolutism as inconsistent with German tradition; was at least suspicious of the imperial endeavors of his time; and was inclined to defend classical liberalism as it concerned domestic and economic issues.

In spite of his growing sympathy for the conservatives, Treitschke never abandoned the key elements of his original philosophy. Hans Herzfeld has somewhat rightly spoken of Treitschke changing only into a "liberal Tory." This verdict applies in principle to his later years as well, despite his participation in the "Berlin anti-Semitism Dispute" of 1878-79, in which he sharply criticized Jewish influence, especially on the press, which had grown too large in his view. Treitschke not only expressly rejected all properly "racial" arguments, as well as an "unclean anti-Semitism," but he also insisted that, above all, every Jew who wished to assimilate could become a German.

Yet one must differentiate between these nuances, as well as his reservations about unleashing a life-and-death struggle among the nations, from the effect Treitschke had. And this impact, in fact, lay in the strengthening of the new anti-Semitism, on the one hand, and a more clearly emerging nationalist current, on the other. It is only viewed from a distance, however, that this seems decisive. Important contemporaries of Treitschke were, at his death on 1896, above all, certain that Germany had suffered "a great national loss."

The connection between Treitschke, Lagarde, and Wagner is not obvious. They belonged to different generations. The Revolution of 1848 was an important break for each of them. Treitschke experienced it in a passive manner, having just reached adulthood, Lagarde—as a spectator, Wagner—as a leading actor. Their initial political orientations also offered little indication of similarity: Wagner came from the far left, Lagarde—from the traditional Right, while Treitschke's sympathies lay with the liberal Center, Wagner as well as Lagarde belonged to Romanticism in terms of many of their ideas, while Treitschke stood for the Protestant intensification of politics in the Hegelian sense.

The decisive point, however, was that all three adhered to a pronounced nationalism, were hopeful about the coalition of the patriotic movement within Prussia, and were curiously disappointed by the results of the great exertion and great success. Finally, this disappointment was detectable in Treitschke, whose career, growing public renown, and great political influence belonged to the decades after the establishment of the Reich. Lagarde and Wagner experienced "*Reichsverdrossenheit*"[15] much earlier. Their plans were more ambitious, their hopes—greater than those of Treitschke.

|15| Dissatisfaction with the state (Reich). (*Ed.*)

What did Treitschke accomplish for the later development of political consciousness in Germany? Above all, this was the sharpening of the political will to knowledge. That he was denounced abroad as the representative of a typically German, i.e., barbaric, conception of international politics must not deceive us as to how minor the legitimacy of such attacks seems compared to the "specifically German need" not to disguise questions of political power with moral pretexts.

One may describe Treitschke's influence as direct, but that of Lagarde and Wagner must, for the same reason, be assessed differently. After all, their idea of a "total" reformation of the German people always targeted achieving an inner form of change. Both shared the pedagogical impulse with Treitschke. However, their expectations for a new national form of education were more comprehensive and, for this reason, had a delayed effect—all that much stronger in certain areas. The central place of religious questions in their projects is characteristic of them.

We have not mentioned the agreement between Treitchke, Lagarde, and Wagner as the most obvious thing in the world. The importance that all three attributed to the "Jewish Question" cannot be explained only by referring to the virulence of modern anti-Semitism after the 1870s. It was never merely a matter of the negative experiences the emigrant Wagner had with Offenbach in Paris and his dislike of the Orléanist middle class, which seemed to be vividly represented by certain Jewish bankers. It was also never merely a matter of Lagarde's initially theologically motivated anti-Judaism, which only slowly affected the "racial" argument. And it was also never merely a matter of Treitschke's dislike of the Jews (probably even influenced by that of Lagarde) or the public "calamity" that the wealth of the Rothschilds signified for him.

Fundamentally, the Jews seemed to be a suitable "counter-type," a cipher that stood for a world that one rejected and believed to be especially well-embodied in the Jews—one around which everything connected with "materialism" coalesced. For Treitschke, Lagarde, and Wagner, "Jewish" and "materialistic" coincided—an effective abbreviation for nourishing that anti-materialistic sentiment which arose from weariness and revulsion at a world they and many others felt to be getting increasingly flat, monotonous, and ugly.

2.6 NEW MOVEMENTS: VÖLKISCH AND NATIONALIST

The turn against "materialism" and "Jewry" was first broadly influential in Germany during the economic depression that followed the "great crash" of 1873. The fact that a large segment of private banks was under Jewish ownership resulted in blaming "Jewish capital" for the crisis. [16] Isolated demands for an anti-Semitic party that would combine social reform with a struggle against Jewry already surfaced at this time. This plan took shape in 1879 as the Imperial Court Pastor Adolf Stoecker abandoned his original intention of forming a Christian Social Workers' Party. Instead, he began his anti-Semitic agitation among the middle classes of Berlin, which were threatened by the economic crisis and competition from heavy industry as well as department stores. It appears that he had only hesitantly given up his original idea of winning over the proletariat for a conservative form of "state socialism," which had been damaged by the violent polemics of the influential liberalism in the capital. He then used his demagogic talent all the more to make anti-Semitism the starting point of a mass movement against the Fortschrittspartei (German Progress Party) and social democracy.

Yet the determination of the enemy remained unclear: Stoecker insisted that the Jews were to be combatted only as individuals and

---

|16| *Gründerkrise*, lit. "founder's crisis," i.e., the economic crisis that followed the founding of the German Reich. (*Ed.*)

because of their individual characteristics, not as a "race." Despite his charisma and the sense of having a mission, he remained a man of the old days, who wanted to put the Deutschkonservative Partei (Conservative Party) on broader foundations, to make it a *Volkspartei* (populist party) with the help of the social question and anti-Semitism.

The failure of the Berliner Bewegung (Berlin Movement), as the groups and projects that followed Stoecker were called, led to an attempt—at the beginning of the 1880s—to make anti-Semitism something independent. This, however, only succeeded in 1886 with the establishment of the Deutsche Antisemitischen Vereinigung (German Anti-Semitic Union. Here appeared two new leaders of the movement, Theodor Fritsch and Otto Boeckel. They attempted to undertake a reorganization from Saxony and Hesse, respectively.

Boeckel's sharp opposition to the "Cohenservatives"[17]—the Hessian "Farmer-King" voted in the Reichstag with the Deutsche Freisinnige Partei (German Free-Minded Party) and social democracy—was approved only by some anti-Semites. Fritsch rejected it and contributed to establishing the Deutschsoziale Partei (German Social Party) in 1889. This Party—following the Reichstag election of 1890, where it gained a single seat—characteristically declined to form a fraction with Boeckel's Antisemitische Volkspartei (Anti-Semitic Party) with its five seats. After a period of insignificance, anti-Semitism was again considered a political factor. This was obvious, for instance, in the German Conservatives' decision to add a plank to their program rejecting Jewish influence in religion, culture, and the state at their so-called Tivoli Party Convention of 1892.

At the elections of the following year the Anti-Semites were able to increase their representation from five to 16 seats. But this marked

---

[17] Kurt Wawrzinek, *Die Entstehung der deutschen Antisemitenparteien (1873-1890)* (Berlin: Ebering, 1927), 127.

the high point of their movement. The rampant leadership struggles within the Party destroyed all attempts at efficient organization or practical politics. Up until the First World War, the Party tried to keep its adherents together, but without lasting success.

Many people, particularly among the younger activists in the movement, had long since gone over to the great academic Verein deutscher Studenten (Union of German Students) or economic associations like the Bund der Landwirte (Farmers' Federation), which were anti-Semitic without being exclusively so. The most influential segment of the old Right, on the other hand, found its original reserves once again. Along with the lack of qualified personnel, it was the largely negative program that explains the lack of attractive power in anti-Semitism. Indeed, it promoted a certain national and social idealism from the beginning, but failed to place these aspects at the forefront or turn them into a philosophical foundation. This distinguished the older anti-Semitism from the *völkische* Bewegung.

The "*völkisch*"[18] concept first emerged in Austria in the 1880s as an emphatically German replacement word for "*national*." From there, it was quickly adopted by right-wing groups in the German Reich. At the center of this philosophy stood the comprehensive renewal of the *Volk*. A political program in the strict sense was a rarity. The *völkische* Bewegung clung to a kind of "yeast principle," believing that "*Volksbildung*" was the most promising way to spread its own convictions. Together with groups like Verein für das Deutschtum im Ausland (Union for Germanness Abroad), established in 1881, or Allgemeine Deutsche Schriftverein (Universal German Writing Union) along with Deutschnationale Vereinbewegung (German National Club Movement) in the Habsburg Monarchy, it devoted itself to the care and protection of the German minority and especially its culture, and sometimes acquired large memberships. There were also

---

|18| *Völkisch*: a populist, ethno-cultural perception of one's homeland (here, German-speaking lands) emphasizing organic customs and traditions. (*Ed.*)

influential professional organization, such as the Deutschnationale Handlungsgehilfen-Verband (German National Commercial Employees' Association) and countless smaller groupings that devoted themselves either to philosophical projects or to all possible questions of practical existence. A few of these groupings, especially those that pursued religious goals, had sectarian character. Others, such as the Deutschbund (German League), formed in 1894 by Lagarde's disciple Friedrich Lange, operated expressly as political-influence groups.

The growing influence of *völkisch* ideology in the period before the Great War can largely be explained with reference to the Deutsche Bewegung. The *völkische* Bewegung drew its basic impulse to reform national existence from it. There also was a personal continuity for the many former 1848ers among the *völkisch* leaders. Yet the philosophical environment had greatly changed since the first half of the 19th century. This becomes especially clear in the concept of *"Rasse"* that was, next to *"Volk,"* central for the *völkisch* ideology. There had indeed been a bridge between these concepts by the means of identifying *"deutsch"* with *"germanisch"* in the Deutsche Bewegung, including both Fichte and Jacob Grimm. The new race conception, however, was filled with very different content than that intended by the Romantics—for instance, when they discussed the significance of origin and heritage. The reason for this development lay in the new paradigm that was used with extraordinary success in order to interpret all social and political processes: Social Darwinism.

Social Darwinism not only transferred the idea of evolution from nature to history, but also asserted that man was and must remain subject to a "struggle for existence," and that "higher development" was dependent on the advancement of the "fit" and "eradication" of the "unfit." Although neither Darwin nor his followers had a clear idea of the causes of variation and the laws of "natural breeding," many Darwinists believed from the beginning that it was possible to improve the evolution of human society, understood by way of analogy with natural evolution. "Eugenics" became for the Social Darwinists the starting point for the demand that human reproduction must no longer be left to chance, but required scientific control and legal regulation. Concern for the preponderance of asocial tendencies, such as criminality, drunkenness, prostitution, and feeble-mindedness, quickly came to the fore.

In Germany, the idea of eugenics was quickly replaced with that of "racial hygiene." Although it was constantly emphasized that here race referred to the "vital race of mankind," the reorientation in the direction of the *völkisch* ideology was a short step to take. Social Darwinism in Germany could only be enforced with difficulty, because the doctrine of descent was considered materialistic. This changed around the turn of the century. The interest in eugenic problems increased through links with more general problems of public health and demographics that were ever more intensively discussed and met with interest in the *völkische* Bewegung. Their ranks contained many of those who believed that humanity was degenerating both spiritually and bodily as a consequence of urbanization and industrialization, but also of racial mixture, that the "unfit" were increasing disproportionately, while the "fit," especially if they belonged to the higher social classes, were raising too few children. They argued that, in order to improve the situation, positive eugenic measures were to be taken to support an increase in healthy offspring by pro-natalist policies, while negative eugenics would prevent the marriage of those with hereditary defects or the birth of children to them. *Völkisch* breeding concepts such as those of the chemist Willibald Hentschel, who sought to create racially pure colonies in which a new Germanic man would be produced through hybridization, remained without broad influence. Some, however, made no secret of considering the state's reluctance to intervene in the name of racial hygiene regrettable and thought that breeding back a purely Germanic race would likely remain a "lovely dream."

In spite of the close connection between *völkisch* ideology and Social Darwinism, certain reservations against the "sordidness of evolutionary theory" remained among the movement's members.

Also, their central goal of preserving the *Volk* spanned far beyond the mere biological understanding. This was the result of the above-mentioned tradition of *völkisch* thought, lastingly influenced by educational idealism, the possible effectiveness of which would negated by any strict determinism.

This unpolitical aspect played a lasting role in the *völkische* Bewegung, as seen especially in the interest in religious questions and enthusiasm for German prehistory. Archeology in Germany had first begun to interest itself in findings from the Middle and Germanic Ages in the second half of the 19th century, and thereby became an "outstandingly national science." It corrected the image of the past, above all, by showing that the Germans' ancestors were by no means barbarians; the notion of an unbroken cultural identity thus became more convincing.

Around the turn of the century, other clear changes to previous ideas about the ancient Germanics emerged. A more "realistic" image, derived mainly from the Icelandic sagas, was now opposed to the previous notion of "happy natural peoples." Their rediscovery also dealt a blow to the assumption that there was a special affinity between Germanic Man and Christianity. Herder and Arndt already hinted at the fact that Christian missionary work could be seen as an act of foreign infiltration. Jacob Grimm's *German Mythology* revealed how much pagan content lay hidden beneath the veneration of saints and Church customs. But they, along with the majority of the Deutsche Bewegung, clung to a "Christian-German" view. Only a minority desired (already in the years leading up to the Revolution of 1848) a return to the Germanic gods. This idea seems to have already been dismissed in the second half of the 19th century.

That a decisive turning point was reached in regard to this question was not least due to the novels of Felix Dahn. Dahn, who taught law at several universities, had occupied himself not only with Germanic legal history but had also begun publishing numerous books dealing with Germanic past in the 1870s. Dahn's novels differed from other popular works on the subject, such as Gustav Freytag's *Die Ahnen* (*Ancestors*), by their particular way of portraying Germanic—in some ways even Indo-Germanic—men. Dahn was not inclined to any sort of naïve glorification, but he emphasized courage and faithfulness as fundamental values. Through contact with the philosophy of Schopenhauer and with Darwin's teaching, his portrayals took on a dark heroic cast, especially evident in the closing pages of his most famous work, *A Struggle for Rome*.

Dahn considered the Christianizing of the Germanics historically unavoidable, but did not sympathize with it; he was far from any thought of renewing the old faith. The twilight of the gods seemed to him a great act, through which Germanic Man forwent all religion in the traditional sense, in order to found a new autonomous, purely this-worldly and tragic ethic. The process was supposedly interrupted by the Christian missions, but now, once again, became possible under different conditions. This expectation was disturbing insofar as Jahn himself had indicated that man's religious need made entirely abstract ideas unbearable. Perhaps, this explains why his ideas spread widely through the extraordinarily high sales of his books, but found broad acceptance only in the *völkische* Bewegung.

Quite apart from the practical obstacles to any departure from a Christian Church in the German Empire, the hardness of Dahn's teaching may have had an offputting effect. The neopagan grouplets— that began emerging after 1911—sought in any case an entirely concrete form for their religious ideas: whether they organized in the form of a community of sentiment (especially Deutsch-religiöse Gemeinschaft [German Religious Community], then Deutschgläubige Gemeinschaft [German Believing Community] of Otto Siegfried Reuter), an occult lodge (such as Wodangesellschaft [Odin Society] of Josef Weber or Neutemplerorden [New Templar Order] of Jörg Lanz von Liebenfels, both of which characteristically arose in Austria) or a sort of pagan Church, such as Deutsch-religiöse

Gemeinschaft, later, Germanische Glaubensgemeinschaft [Germanic Community of Faith], of Ludwig Fahrenkrog).

While the number of those who joined these groups remained very small—amounting to a few hundred before the First World War—there was a much larger group which believed that the generally perceived religious crisis of the time could be overcome by modernizing Christianity by Germanizing it. These ideas were not merely found by going back to the Deutsche Bewegung. They were also represented in Bayreuther, the members of which believed that Wagner's work signified not only the rediscovery but also the "fulfillment of the Aryan Mystery" in Christianity. Finally, this tendency received a strong impetus from the progressive historicizing of Christianity, whose historical and cultural determinedness was more clearly emerging. The Catholic Church was much less affected by this tendency to question the dogmatic form of the faith than the Protestant Churches. Here again, we see the parallel between the *völkische* Bewegung and liberal Protestantism, pointing to similarities between the *völkisch* and liberals, in general.

Wilhelm Schwaner, for instance, whose periodical, *The Volk Educator*, exercised considerable influence on the movement, not only called for the election of Left liberals (since they preserved the legacy of 1848), but also cultivated an intimate friendship with Walther Rathenau. Many of the *völkisch* sympathized with the Deutsche Freisinnige Partei[19]—the only Party to hold fast to a "greater German" program, and later—with the national-social ideas of Friedrich Naumann. In Austria, the whole German National Movement was considered part of the liberal camp.

|19| Deutsche Freisinnige Partei (German Free-Minded Party) was founded in 1884 from a merger of the Deutsche Fortschrittspartei (German Progress Party) and the Liberale Vereinigung (Liberal Union). In 1893, it split into Freisinnige Volkspartei (Free-Minded People's Party) and Freisinnige Vereinigung (Free-Minded Union); these two merged again to form Fortschrittliche Volkspartei (Progressive People's Party) in 1910. All of these groupings were broadly liberal. (*Ed.*)

Like every other attempt at an unambiguous political orientation, however, this was met with reservations from the *völkisch*. Their affinity with the remnants of anti-Semitic organizations was as obvious as their sympathy with the "Lagardian Right," which came together in new nationalist organizations outside the party system. The influence of Lagarde, as well as that of Treitschke, played an important role for the nationalists. Lagarde was valued by them (unlike *völkische* Bewegung) precisely for his "tough" demands, including widening the area of German settlement; Treitschke's ideas were extended and radicalized until they became useful for the nationalists' own program.

The zeal of the nationalists was essentially comparable to that of "integral nationalism," which experienced increased popularity in all developed European countries after the end of the 19th century. The ideas around the full integration of the individual into the nation varied, but could go as far as demanding a new racial aristocracy and eliminating the hereditary type and its privileges in order to organize the proletariat through a "national socialism."

The selection of a new elite was of decisive importance for the nationalists, but its willingness to compromise with existing social relations was considerable. "External" Social Darwinism was more important to them than its "internal" counterpart, i.e., they concentrated on the struggle for life among the nations. All great powers, they believed, were faced with the alternative of belonging to the "living" or to the "dying" peoples; all great powers, therefore, had to compete continually: economically, militarily, and politically. Where necessary, they must let things come to a fight for "world power or destruction." The acquisition of colonies played a great role in the preparation for this struggle.

The new nationalism substituted Darwinian arguments for the older, mostly religious, ethical, or economic arguments for imperialism. Along with racial and ethnographic considerations, geopolitics and strategy also played an important role. German nationalism mirrored that of Britain, perhaps in spite or perhaps of German nationalism being directed as sharply against England as British nationalism was against the German Reich. The similarity is immediately obvious from the almost identical list of organizations beginning with "Naval-" and "Defense League" passing by the Deutsche Kolonial-Gesellschaft (German Colonial Society) and all the way to the Alldeutscher Verband[20] (Pan-German League), ADV. This league was founded in 1891; its relatively weak membership (18,000 in 1914) must not deceive us as to its significance as an umbrella organization.

Heinrich Class, elected president in 1908, understood the ADV as the kernel of "national opposition." The latter demanded the introduction of dictatorship in order to fight for Germany's position as a world power and to suppress all domestic revolutionary activity with a heavy hand. It also asked for the abolition of Jewish emancipation, since it threatened the German *Volk* with "disintegration through Jewish blood and the Jewish spirit." The Pan-Germans hesitated to incorporate anti-Semitism into their program. That addition signaled that the close connection that bound the Pan-Germans and all other nationalist associations with the traditional right wing, above all, the German Conservatives and National Liberals, had become weaker. Instead, the influence of *völkisch* ideas (and *völkisch* influence groups such as the German League) was growing and the idea of a new "German National" right wing was born.

The term *"deutschnational"* (German National) spread especially in Austria as a parallel to *"völkisch."* After defeat at the hands of Prussia (1866), a whole series of organizations sprung up there. They primarily defended the privileged position of Germans in that multinational state and maintained close relations with the liberals. On the fringes, however, a radical tendency formed under Georg von Schönerer, which did not want to limit itself to defensive positions. Schönerer combined nationalist with socialist and anti-Semitic agitation in order to win the

---

|20| Allgemeiner Deutscher Verband until 1894. (*Ed.*)

support of the masses. He was quite successful at this, but ended up a victim of his political immoderation.

Schönerer considered the Germans of the Habsburg Monarchy as irredentists, and his final goal was the abolition of the dynasty and the annexation of Austria by the German Reich. The future *Alldeutschland* ("Total Germany") would form not merely a political but a religious unity. For this reason, Schönerer openly called for the destruction of the state and for withdrawal from the Catholic Church. But the "Away from Rome Movement" he organized in the 1890s marked the end of his political career.

Many of his followers were already irritated by his admiration for Prussia and Bismarck, but they were most certainly not prepared to definitively break their traditional religious bonds. The deep roots of Catholicism in Austria permitted participation in the great spiritual movement of Romanticism and Idealism, but already presented an obstacle to the influence of Hegel in the first half of the 19th century. The departure of Austria from the German League led, despite the persistence of older ideas of loyalty to the Reich and new "greater German" and German National sentiment, to the rise of a mental disposition that differed from that of Bismarck's state and would later prevent a broader influence of Nietzsche in Austria.

2.7 NIETZSCHE AS EDUCATOR

Even Nietzsche, the godless despiser of Luther, thought that "our good Protestant air" was an advantage, though this does not sufficiently explain his extraordinary intellectual influence on Germany at the turn of the 20th century. This influence is traceable, above all, to his diagnosis of European decline. In his view, its cause was "nihilism," which, he believed, was determined not only by the Enlightenment and positivism but fundamentally by the whole history of the Christian West, if not all developments since the errors of Plato.

Nietzsche saw his contemporary world as in apocalyptic labor pains. He believed it was perishing from that "reflective barbarism," to which Vico first ascribed key importance for decadence. He contrasted it to poetic barbarism of the beginnings—yearning for its return—in his struggle with the Philistines, the Educated, and, finally, the Last Man. But Nietzsche also spoke—as if to defend himself against a hasty interpretation of his talk of the "blond beast"—about "another sort of barbarian who comes from the heights: a sort of conquering and ruling nature in search of a material it can shape." The idea of this "other sort of barbarian" held great fascination for the *fin de siècle*. The individual proclaimed by Nietzsche as an *"Übermensch"* and "Zarathustra"—creative, freed of all ordinary conventionality, thus, amoral and capable of establishing new values and, indeed, for forging a new aristocracy—was appealing to those who hoped for a comprehensive renewal.

FRIEDRICH NIETZSCHE

In view of Nietzsche's origin and the chronological framework of his life, it was hardly to be expected that he, of all people, would be the one to proclaim this great renewal. Born in 1844 in Röcken as the son of a Lutheran pastor, he only gradually overcame the narrowness of his milieu. Only after the collapse of his University career at the end of the 1870s appeared the treatises in which he dealt polemically with the dominant morality and conception of reality. His physical decline, abandonment of his professorship and isolation, his withdrawal to the south, first to Italy and then Switzerland (Sils-Maria) impaired his outward life from then on. In spite of this, he worked tirelessly, gradually reforming the center of his reflection. This became unmistakable with the appearance of *Dawn: Thoughts on Moral Prejudices* and *The Gay Science* in the years 1881-82. After turning away from Schopenhauer, the idea that the "Will to Power" was the real driving force of all life moved to the very center of Nietzsche's thought. This thought became correspondingly important for his principal work, *Thus Spoke Zarathustra: A Book for All and None*, published shortly afterwards (1883-85).

Karl Löwith has spoken about *Zarathustra* being "a unique attempt at 're-engagement' (*Wideranverlobung*) with the world, from which the successful struggle of Christianity against the pagan reverence for the Cosmos has separated us." This "re-engagement" occurred through the decision to see not God's Providence, but fate as an active principle in the life of individuals and nations; and not to merely accept, but to affirm this fate. Nietzsche called for *amor fati*, not fatalism. In the "eternal return,"[21] the great cycle, he thought he saw an adequate expression for recognizing the unsurpassable power of what is destined—but in this vision there was also something comforting for him, a kind of ultimate cosmic harmony.

In the polemical writings that appeared after *Zarathustra* and were directed, above all, against Judeo-Christian values as well as, one last time, against Wagner, signs of his coming mental breakdown could already be seen. It took place in January of 1889, and left Nietzsche in the care of his mother and sister for the last 10 years of his life. But it was only with this collapse—which gave him a halo of martyrdom in the eyes of his disciples—that Nietzsche's impact took on spectacular forms. Indeed, in the last decade of the 19th century, it led to his exercising the greatest imaginable influence on the European intelligentsia. If Lou Andreas-Salomé already then

---

|21| *Die Ewige Wiederkehr (Wiederkunft) des Gleichen. (Ed.)*

suspected in him the founder of a new religion, then this was right on target, as veneration of Nietzsche was preparing a following that could be characterized as the "religiously faithful (*gläubig*)." Shortly after Nietzsche's death in 1900, a circle, centered around the brothers Ernst and August Horneffer, quite seriously developed a plan to transfer the philosopher's remains to Weimar and construct a shrine, with a temple and stadium based on the ancient model, where public readings and games were to be held in honor of his *manes*.[22] The list of supporters reads like an index of the cultural avant-garde in Europe at that time: Gabriele D'Annunzio, Maurice Barrès, Anatole France, André Gide, Gerhardt Hauptmann, Hugo von Hofmannsthal, Harry Graf Kessler, Gustav Mahler, Charles Maurras, Edvard Munch, Walter Rathenau, Richard Strauss, and Herbert George Wells.

What appealed to these men, accompanied by many second- and third-rate minds, about Nietzsche was his "total understanding: the ambiguous character of our modern world—these very symptoms could indicate decline or strength." Nietzsche stood beyond the belief in progress or nostalgia, he had declared the world godless, senseless, planless, and hopeless, and yet still demanded that it be affirmed: his "pessimism of strength" had a bold character, was elitist and without sympathy for liberalism or democracy, but also without regard for the old order; it was intellectual and full of suspicion of life-killing reflection, sharply set against Christianity, but demanding faith, archaic in its imagery, and futuristic in its vision. For all these reasons, Nietzsche's message found an echo all over Europe and determined the *Zeitgeist* of the outgoing 19th century.

This effect was nowhere stronger than in Germany. This was partly because of the language—of which Nietzsche had a masterful command—but also because Nietzsche himself suspected that "we, Germans, are still closer to barbarism than are the rest of the civilized peoples in the West." The existence of certain dispositions

---

|22| Deities that represent souls of the dead in Roman paganism. (*Ed.*)

in Germany, which contributed to the new gospel falling on especially fruitful soil, may be cited in favor of this diagnosis. A unique German consciousness formed the decisive precondition for Nietzsche to be heard late in his own homeland, but then all the more attentively.

It is disputed, however, how far any political conception can be ascribed to the philosophy of Nietzsche: whether his demand for "Great Politics" should be understood as an abstract counterplan to the promises of liberalism and socialism, or whether he seriously thought about forming that Partei des Lebens (Party of Life), of which he occasionally spoke, so as to practically apply his ideas in the titanic struggles for the future. This need not be cleared up for our purposes. After all, it is uncontroversial to think that Nietzsche's thought has political *consequences* and that his admiration for Machiavelli and the Renaissance prince, as well as his statements about Napoleon and his elitism, found followers. These followers made a political program out of it, while others were indebted to him at least for their political foundations. Very early on and very accurately, Nietzschean politics was described as "aristocratic radicalism."

2.8 LEBENSREFORM, JUGENDBEWEGUNG, POST-NIETZSCHEAN CULTURE

If Nietzsche must be assigned to a side in the conflict between Romanticism and anti-Romanticism, then it must certainly be the latter. His interest in Latin culture, his criticism of German formlessness and German nationalism, his distaste for Wagner's turn towards Christianity, and his Catholic tendencies speak in favor of this. Yet one can sense Nietzsche's uncertainty in the forced character of this turn; his remark about "German double nature" applies to himself more so than to almost anyone else. Nietzsche's language had Romantic traits, his yearning was Romantic in many ways, and, for this reason, he had an impact on neo-Romanticism, especially.

Although Nietzsche's high expectations were not fulfilled in his own lifetime, he observed in a 1887 letter that he was gaining "an 'influence'" that was "very subterranean, of course." He continued:

> *Among all the radical Parties (socialists, nihilists, anti-Semites, Orthodox Christians, Wagnerians), I enjoy a surprising and almost mysterious respect.*[23]

In fact, his followers were initially as heterogeneous as he observed: the Frauenbewegung (Women's Movement) and the Jugendbewegung, socialists, anarchists, Zionists, and anti-Semites, even pacifists or occultists wanted to appeal to him. A great part of these groups stood in close association with a partly accepted, partly underground current that has been described as *"Lebensreform"* (Life Reform), meaning—in the German context—everything that tried to achieve a fundamental change in the modern way of life since the first third of the 19th century.

One must not seek any system of ideas equally applicable to all efforts in the Lebensreform Movement: impulses from the Enlightenment, Idealism, and Vitalism were involved along with materialistic, Darwinist, or monarchist tendencies. The kernel of their philosophy was formed of vegetarianism, homoeopathy, nudism, and clothing reform; comparatively marginal were projects for garden cities, land reform and attempts at forming new settlements, along with anti-alcoholism. Common to all these currents was that they sought, as far as possible, a new form of human existence and were convinced that neither technical progress nor political or social reaction was appropriate for reaching this goal.

To some extent, there were counterparts to Lebensreform in England (vegetarianism, abstinence, and garden cities, along with William Morris's Arts and Crafts project), but the real center of the

---

|23| Steven Anschheim, *Nietzsche und die Deutschen: Karriere eines Kults* (Stuttgart: Metzler), 18.

movement always lay primarily in Germany. German Lebensreformers developed alternatives to all predominant models of civilization that they not only saw as responsible for acute crises (such as the "social question") but fundamentally rejected. Enmity for the metropolis, industrialization, and capitalism; the struggle against the enjoyment of alcohol and tobacco, as well as against "movie mischief" and "dirt and rubbish" in popular literature did not play the principal role. More important were the counter-ideas that they offered: the demand for a new naturalness in habitations, clothing, and nourishment, as well as a new honesty in all decisive questions, starting from objects of belief ("religion, not denomination") through to sexuality and pedagogy.

Lebensreform members generally refused to join organizations or parties. Insofar as they were not consistently individualistic, they formed cooperatives or confederations that they oriented in a fundamentally democratic way or as an entourage around a "master." Along with a Romantic understanding of community, Nietzsche's idea of a new elite played a role. They thought that such an elite could be realized in an exemplary fashion through education and autodidactic pursuits.

Although much about the Lebensreform Movement was already considered whimsical by contemporaries, the idea of Lebensreform as a practicable "third way" between bourgeois capitalism and proletarian socialism had an effect far beyond the true kernel of the movement itself. It is easy to understand its influence on bohemian life, for instance, in the artist colonies of Worpswede, Dachau, and Hellerau, which exhibited certain Lebensreform approaches. This connection was even more unambiguous in the Dürer League founded by Ferdinand Avenarius in 1902, which arose from the group of collaborators on the influential cultural journal *Kunstwart*. The Dürer League cooperated on many levels with the

STEFAN GEORGE

Werkbund founded in 1907. Through its criticism of industrial mass production and propaganda about "quality work," the latter had a decisive effect on the renewal and further development of the German tradition of workmanship.

With its international orientation and extraordinary skills of its workers, the Werkbund stood above the intellectual and artistic level usually attained by Lebensreform. But it undoubtedly belonged to that post-Nietzschean culture which appeared across Europe after the turn of the century marked by the poetry of Stefan George, as much as the dramatic work of George Bernard Shaw; the sculpture of Max Klinger and the young Otto Dix as well as the paintings of Edvard Munch and Arnold Böcklin, or the architecture of Henry van de Velde; the influential writings of the Protestant Arthur Bonus, as well as the idea of a Judaic renaissance in Martin Buber and the "God-Building" of the Russian socialists around Maxim Gorky; the philosophy of Max Scheler, as well as Henri Bergson, and, finally, the sociology of Max Weber as well as Georg Simmel.

Obviously, Jugendbewegung that had arisen since the turn of the century was also part of this milieu. Like the Lebensreform Movement, it largely remained limited to the German-speaking world, i.e., the Reich, Austria, Bohemia, the Baltic, Switzerland, and Flanders. Scouting, created at almost the same time in England by Robert S. Baden-Powell, exercised some influence. Yet with its paramilitary conception, it belonged rather to youth *care*, addressed by comparable religious and non-religious organizations in Germany before 1914, for instance, the Jungdeutschland-Bund ("Young Germany League").

The Wandervogel hiking club[24], as the original cell of Jugendbewegung, arose out of a group of Steglitz high-school students founded in 1896 by the university student Herrmann Hoffmann-

---

[24] Literally, "migratory birds"—a play on words, since the verb *"wandern"* also means "to hike, roam." (*Ed.*)

Fölkersamb. The group received a clearer form through the secondary school student Karl Fischer, who replaced Hoffmann following his departure. In 1901, Fischer succeeded in creating a sponsoring organization presided over by the poet Heinrich Sohnrey under the name Wandervogel— Ausschuß für Schülerfahrten (Committee for Student Tours). The movement spread quickly over central and northern Germany, but remained limited to the middle classes; a socialist Jugendbewegung with close ties to Social Democracy arose in the years before the war on its own accord.

The heterogeneity promoted by the spread of Jugendbewegung led to rapid organizational collapse despite Fischer's efforts to preserve unity. Already in 1904, the Wandervogel e. V. (Registered Association) broke off from the old Wandervogel group that remained under Fischer's leadership. In 1907, the Wandervogel: Deutscher Bund für Jugendwandern (German League of Young Hikers) arose in Jena, which was quite important for further development. It permitted girls to join (always a contentious point in Jugendbewegung). Strictly women's leagues sprang up as well. By 1906, there were already 78 local Wandervogel groups, with a total of 1,500 members.

The Wandervogel often proclaimed its ideological neutrality and concerned itself only with the experience of nature, homeland, and youthful camaraderie. However, it was obviously influenced by neo-Romanticism and neo-Idealism, which were closely associated with Lebensreform, and partly by *völkisch* ideology. While Nietzsche's ideas became important for Jugendbewegung only relatively late, those of Lagarde and Langbehn were widespread from the beginning. The Wandervogel, however, adopted almost exclusively the "soft" variants of these philosophies; racial thought and anti-Semitism played almost no role. It is true that the Austrian Wandervogel, founded in 1911, introduced an "Aryan clause" and had a counterpart in a small group formed in the German Reich in 1912, the Wandervogel—Völkischer Bund (League). But the "Jewish Question" was otherwise of little importance to the movement.

First of all, this was the case because the individual groups largely acted autonomously, and could hardly be kept united (especially in an ideological sense). Also, the motives for becoming a member were always personal and seldom or never political. Perhaps, along with the friendship of the members, the provocation of a moderately oppositional lifestyle played a certain role, but without this being of further social significance (apart from the views of a few ambitious leaders).

Immediately before the outbreak of the First World War, serious problems became apparent in Jugendbewegung; they resulted from the emergence of community elders (*Älterenschaft*). For this reason, the plan of the educator Gustav Wyneken was met with approval: to hold a meeting on the Hoher Meissner near Kassel on the occasion of the 100th anniversary of the Battle of Leipzig to promote greater unity within Jugendbewegung. The Erste Freideutsche Jugendtag (First Day Conference) was held on October 11-13, 1913, with 2,000-3,000 participants, but it did not bring the unity that was sought. Only a brief common resolution was passed (the Meissner Formulation), noting the right of youth to shape their own lives autonomously. The Freie Deutsche Jugend (Free German Youth) that was founded in advance, and tasked with forming an umbrella organization, could not fulfill its functions on account of internal disputes; the Wandervogel remained a truly vital element of Jugendbewegung.

GUSTAV WYNEKEN

Even if the notion of a young generation that carried Nietzsche or Faust in their knapsacks in August 1914, and which was more familiar with the *Edda* or Meister Eckhardt than with the Bible, is dismissed as a cliché, one cannot avoid concluding that the cultural atmosphere in Germany on the eve of the war was strongly determined by the impulses that went back to Nietzsche. "Education through Nietzsche" set off the most effective of those spiritual processes that determined the character of Germany in those decades. Nietzsche's books—or, rather, certain individual ideas of his or, rather still, slogans drawn from those ideas—influenced public discussion to a considerable degree. Nietzscheanism had followers in all political camps, but there was a natural affinity for the Right. This was not the Right in the accepted sense, which lived on in the tradition that Nietzsche regarded with hostility, hardly the anti-Semitic or *völkisch* Right, but a "New Right" formed especially from the nationalists and imperialists, with participation from the "National- Social" tendency connected to liberalism, as well as all those, whose worldviews did not immediately relate to any party.

Their ideas were "conservative" in Lagarde's sense, but also Nietzsche's, because the concept of Life was the "most German, Goethean, and, in the highest, religious sense, conservative concept" that "Nietzsche had imbued with new feeling, incased in a new beauty, force and holy innocence, raised to the highest level, led to spiritual lordship." According to Moeller van den Bruck, their ideas were altogether directed against the shackling spirit of pessimism and full of hope for a new synthesis, as well as the establishment of a new style. But many of its protagonists became ever more convinced that a modern philosophy, "which, until now, had only had an evolutionary and revolutionary force, as we needed at the time, must again be rooted in a conservative force."

It is of decisive importance not to relate such worldviews closer than necessary to the notion of a "theory" or a "philosophical system" and then demand too much rigor or completeness from them. Political philosophies are seldom or never the result of pre-thought and separable from the particular situation from which they arise. They must be understood as the "political 'life-feeling' of an age," in which, perhaps, very different impressions and influences were mixed and "brought to consciousness." This limits the refutability of worldviews, whose possibility and unity are often visible much sooner to those on the outside.

There were undoubtedly parallels in the rest of Europe to the development of political philosophies in Germany. The closer the end of the old century—the greater the perception of living in a "time of transition." This increased attention to social and ideological alternatives. British historian Thomas Carlyle was already enthusiastic about Lagarde's ideas; his colleague John R. Seeley advocated ideas very similar to those of Treitschke. Thomas Mann's and Moeller van den Bruck's reception of Dostoyevsky's works not only had literary, but also political motivations. In Italy, there were nationalist intellectuals like Gabriele D'Annunzio and Enrico Corradini who explicitly appealed to Nietzsche. In France, Ernst Renan and Hippolyte Taine formulated a general critique of the path trod since the Revolution, which had led the country into decadence, and recommended a therapy that made use of the "Germanic" spirit. In France, as well, the young generation was affected by Nietzsche; monarchist Charles Maurras formed a new sort of political organization, the Action Française, which combined conservative and revolutionary elements in a peculiar way; and the socialist renegade Georges Sorel developed concepts that made him seem like the "forefather of the Conservative Revolution" in many ways. The Dreyfus Affair led not only to the fall of the classic Right and the formation of a revolutionary counterpart, but also to a split in the Left—into a nationalist wing with an authoritarian tendency and a parliamentary wing with an anti-patriotic tendency. When it comes to these newly arisen camps, there were remarkable alliances and sensational faces. But these were only the outward signs of more essential changes that went beyond both the old and the new ideologies.

Many economic, cultural, and social processes of this age converged to a single point. This was the loss of credibility of the principal hope in the future that had become determinative for the educated class since the Enlightenment, and was particularly strengthened by the 19th-century belief in progress, the idea of which promised to fully humanize man. This realization struck men to different degrees. Bleak prophesies could not surpass many, if not most, people's optimism about the future. This applied to Germany as well, but there was something else at work: a deeper current that came to the surface more strongly than in the rest of Europe, a hostility toward the ruling powers of positivism and "plutocracy."

Immediately before the outbreak of the First World War, British historian John Adam Cramb wrote in an essay about Germany and England that there were decisive, above all, spiritual, differences between them, despite the similarity of the two countries. Germany had, to a large extent, remained untouched by Roman civilization; the Reformation had a different character there; there was nothing in England comparable to the influence of Kant, Hegel, Schopenhauer, and Nietzsche; and the particular character of Germany explained not only the enormous dynamism of that nation but also the rise of a new "faith" in the young generation:

> *While preparing to found a world empire, Germany is also preparing to create a world religion.... This is the faith of young Germany in 1913. The prevalent mindset at universities, in the army, and among the more cultured was towards what may be described as the religion of valor: the glory of action, heroism, undertaking great things. It is in the metaphysics of Zarathustra's amor fati.*[25]

|25| John Adam Cram, *Germany and England* (London: Murray, 1914), 116.

3

THE WORLD WAR AS CULTURE WAR

he First World War was, from the beginning, not merely a military conflict and national war but also a struggle between worldviews—a culture war. The formulation was coined by Troeltsch, a representative of entirely moderate political views similar to those of the historian Otto Hintze. In 1915, Hintze answered the question about the war's significance by calling it a matter of just defense, as well as of breaking England's world domination: not so that it might be replaced by German domination but in order to construct a world politics in accordance with Germany's own national tradition. This tradition was incompatible with imperial models, but rather realized "the principle of freedom and the equal right of all peoples of the earth," so long as "they have reached the necessary degree of civilized behavior."

In Great Britain and France, this war was justified with an expansionist ideology from the arsenal of the Enlightenment, as both claimed to be fighting for "humanity," "civilization," "democracy," the "rights of the individual," and against "barbarism," "reaction," "autocracy," and "militarism." In contrast, the German ideology of identity defined the philosophical (*weltanschaulichen*) war aims defensively as the necessity of refounding its own community, its culture and historical right under changed circumstances, and of defending itself as a world power.

The appeal to the ideas of 1914 was first voiced in autumn of 1915, when the invocation of the August days of the previous year already overtly served the goal of self-assurance and the call to persevere. Plenge[26]—in a lecture at this time—formulated the following thesis. He suggested that 1789 and 1914 must be seen as symbolic years in history, that the outbreak of the World War brought the age of the French Revolution to an end, and that war itself was increasingly proving to be a revolution, in the course of which a new "idea" was being born. He reverted to those ideas that had already been formulated as part of the German war ideology. Above all, this was the notion that the Reich, located in the middle of Europe, was being equally forced and summoned to lead the struggle against the "merchant ideals" of the West and the despotism of the East in order to achieve a balance—a synthesis in the Hegelian sense—that would reconnect freedom and order, the right of the individual and the right of all. The adherents of the "ideas of 1914" disputed exactly what this balance would look like. They fiercely debated the position of the Reich in case of victory, and what political constitution and form of society it would have.

When it comes to Germany's territorial and political considerations after the war, there were two principal views until 1917. The first, represented particularly well in the Pan-German and *völkisch* circles, demanded the expansion of German territory eastward and westward, along with considerable extension of its colonial possessions. The arguments brought forward were either openly imperialistic or cited

---

|26| Johann Plenge (1874-1963) was a German sociologist; he started out as a Marx scholar and Social Democrat and later moved toward nationalism. (*Ed.*)

references to geopolitical and geostrategic necessities that looked ahead to the "militarily untouchable" and "economically unparalleled" Germany. For the *völkisch*, historical and racial reasons also played a role, for instance, particularly over the question of annexing Flanders or the Baltic states. In contrast, the second, comparatively moderate, group posited the establishment of a hegemonic status for the Reich, in which aspects of formal (boundary adjustments) and informal (Central European Customs Union, creating a series of new states, such as the semi-dependent Kingdom of Poland) domination were to be combined.

Another motive for the maximalism of the Pan-Germans was the concern that, without great gains, the existing social and political order of Germany could not be maintained. Their concept of "German freedom" thus clearly differed from that which a weaker, but still influential group among the adherents of the "ideas of 1914" represented. This faction also disputed whether it must take sides against democracy in the name of the Prussian-German tradition, or in favor of an "organic democracy" in the name of the Germanic-Teutonic tradition. However, in principle, they did not doubt the need for a new beginning and the overcoming of older political forms. They went as far as assuming that this war would (like the Napoleonic Wars and the Wars of German Unification) lead to an increase in popular participation: a "*Volksstaat*" and "*Volksmonarchie* (*Volks* monarchy)."

Certain proposals for reordering the social constitution were even more radical than those for the political constitution. The notion of the "*Volk* community," connected, above all, with the notion of harmonizing economic interests guaranteed by the state, was quickly outbid by the idea of a new, not merely warlike, but rather "national" socialism. Plenge himself was among the most eager proponents of this concept. Even before the war, he expressed the idea that the development of industry was itself transforming capitalism into an organic socialism, in which the decisive point would no longer be the entrepreneur's motives for profit but rather objectivity (*Sachlichkeit*) of employed or state-appointed "organizers." The experience of "national comradeship" in the war strengthened Plenge's view that the times were working toward a "national socialism." Werner Sombart, another economist and protagonist of the ideas of 1914, supported Plenge. At the beginning of the war, Sombart asserted the "mediating role of militarism" that was preparing the way for a new heroic order.

These and other similar ideas were not only widespread among the middle class and the intelligentsia; some labor leaders also followed Plenge and Sombart in thinking that the war economy would open an unforeseen path toward the realization of "socialism." Social Democrats, who identified with the ideas of 1914, may have individually had different motives than those of Plenge and Sombart. Yet they were convinced that the liberal age would be surpassed by that of organization, which must necessarily be "socialist." They also thought that Germany, because of its tradition of *étatisme* (until then regarded with hostility by the Left), brought with it the best preconditions for delivering the model of this socialism. According to them, only a German victory could lead toward progress, whereas not only those who opposed the Left's wishes, but the whole *Entente*—tsarist Russia and even the high-capitalist England—embodied "world reaction."

The chief proponents of these views were Paul Lensch, Heinrich Cunow, and Konrad Haenisch. Originally, they all came from the left-wing of the party and had even rejected war credits, but had later taken a different position. This position also differed from that of the party's right-wing, which approved only the defense of the Fatherland. Starting from 1915, these three men published *The Bell*, a journal financed by the Russian socialist and businessman Alexander Helphand (pseudonym "Parvus"). Their influence on the Sozialdemokratische Partei (Social Democratic Party) should not be underestimated, but they were never able to win over the majority. Their opponents described them as "Social Chauvinists," and they produced no convincing leader. Their ideas were too complex and sophisticated to be effective within a mass movement, whose own leaders, eventually dubbed the "red lackeys of the *Entente*" by Lensch, they quickly learned to despise.

3.1 THE PARTY OF IDEALISM AND ITS DISINTEGRATION

The year 1917 marked not only a military and political but also a philosophical turning point (*Ideenwende*). The consensus fell apart under the pressure of war weariness among the people along with the revolutionary events in Russia. Alongside the originally very weak radical Friedenspartei (Peace Party) represented by the Spartacus Group and then the USPD (Independent Social Democrats), and alongside the supporters of an immediate negotiated peace among the Social Democrats and in the moderate parties, there were still proponents of a "German" or "victory peace," who were ever less united as to what these code words meant.

The signal for the breakdown of the social and intellectual civil peace was the resignation of Chancellor Bethmann-Hollweg on July 14, 1917. The government championed the return to the status quo from before the war. It was hemmed in by the military high command that continued to insist on territorial gains and criticized the Chancellor's weakness. This position found support in the latter phase of the war, especially among the Deutsche Vaterlandspartei, DVLP (German Fatherland Party), that stepped forward as the party of national unity. After its founding in September of 1917, it attempted to achieve the total mobilization of the nation for the final struggle and the elimination of all forces prepared to compromise.

As a reaction to the Reichstag's peace resolution of July 19, 1917—that the SPD, Deutsche Zentrumspartei (Center Party), and the left-wing of the Liberals had carried—Vaterlandspartei began to bring together Conservatives, Liberals, and right-wing Catholics. It was led by the architect of the German naval armament,

Alfred von Tirpitz, and the go-getter Director of the East Prussian Agricultural Credit Union, Wolfgang Kapp, who maintained close ties with heavy industry and agriculturalists east of the Elbe. Deutsche Vaterlandspartei engaged in intense propaganda activity. It not only painted in threatening colors the all-devouring tyranny of Anglo-Americanism that would follow German defeat, but also held fast in principle (with certain external moderation) to the goal of substantially expanding the Reich after the war's end through annexations in Belgium and the east.

Although Deutsche Vaterlandspartei initially sought to avoid any debate about domestic politics and decisively favored maintaining the existing constitutional order, its agitation was unambiguously directed against the Left. This was partly out of fear of a revolution based on the Russian model, but also because of the leading role the SPD played in the passing of the peace resolution. There were even expectations that only two parties would survive: Vaterlandspartei and the German Bolsheviks. While Vaterlandsparteilong hoped to win over the nationalists and Left Liberals, resentment toward the "ultramontanists" prevented almost any success among the Catholics. Still more hopeless was the effort to orient the working class toward the ideals of the Vaterlandspartei.

Despite its nominally high membership of 1.2 million and its obviously considerable financial means, Vaterlandspartei was unable to achieve stability. This was bound up not only with the dramatic change in the overall situation over the course of 1918 but also with a series of structural weaknesses. Thus, Vaterlandspartei was never able to attract a large number of individual members and was essentially dependent on group memberships. Alldeutscher Verband (Pan-German League) played an essential role here, for obvious reasons, even though the Vaterlandspartei decided only in the final phase of the war to adopt the Pan-German program regarding a military dictatorship (although not in respect of its anti-Jewish demands).

Decisive for the failure of Deutsche Vaterlandspartei was, ultimately, that it at no time succeeded in embodying the "unity party" (*"Einheitspartei"*) that even moderate forces wished for. It was precisely in those circles of the intelligentsia, which felt especially devoted to the "ideas of 1914," that the aversion to the "war-prolonging party" (*"Kriegsverlängerungspartei"*) was particularly notable. Publisher Eugen Diederichs, who coined this expression, had already repeatedly warned of the "Pan-German danger" and criticized not only the immoderation of the nationalists but even more so their

EUGEN DIEDERICHS

blindness to the need for constitutional reform. At two conferences, he organized at Burg Lauenstein in May and October of 1917, Diederichs gathered important scholars such as Max Weber, Werner Sombart, Friedrich Meinecke, and many others. In his view, they were suitable for demonstrating the spiritual (*geistige*) unity of the nation precisely because they opposed those tendencies that found expression in Vaterlandspartei. In December of 1917, there was an unsuccessful attempt to establish the core around which the support for this group's ideas might crystallize by founding Volksbund für Vaterland und Freiheit (National League for Fatherland and Freedom).

The Volksbund (National League) included such personalities, who—despite their affirmation of German uniqueness—believed in the need for change in the structure of state and society. They thought that this change should be addressed following the (victorious) end of the war at the latest. Yet the utopian counterpart opposed the Machiavellian principle of the nationalists: one that was likewise condemned to failure, if for quite different reasons.

3.2 THOMAS MANN AND OSWALD SPENGLER

The minimal consensus of the "party of idealism" (*"Partei des Idealismus"*) was the concept of a militarism with real popular participation; then this position finds its most splendid defense in Thomas Mann's *Reflections of a Nonpolitical Man*. The book, published in the autumn of 1918, expounded the German position once again in the final hour by the means of opposing culture (*Kultur*) to civilization (*Zivilisation*), Central and Western Europe, music and literature.

Yet *Reflections* had, in comparison with Mann's earlier espousal of the "ideas of 1914," a slightly resigned undertone. He had clearly distanced himself from the expectation of a new synthesis of power and spirit—as invoked in a letter to the editor of *Svenska Dagbladet* dated April of 1915—and from the idea that the World War would be "the bringer of its own third Reich." Mann still maintained that the war had destroyed the materialism of peacetime and created a new awareness of community. He also expressed his satisfaction with the separate peace with Russia and the continuation of the struggle against Western Europe as the principle enemy. Yet even in the case of victory, he considered the preservation of German uniqueness unlikely.

This is especially clear in Mann's discussion of democracy, whose "doctrinaire mendacity" repelled him, but whose success he considered unavoidable, and which he, therefore, did not wish to combat. The most

THOMAS MANN

he hoped for was a specifically German form of the *"Volksstaat,"* but even it would largely comply with the Western European model. As for his own position, which he declared to be conservative, Mann wavered between the concern that he might be pleading on behalf of an obsolete idea and the expectation that conservatism had been strengthened by the war. "This yes-but-no is my own case," he states in one place—an avowal without much practical significance. In all questions that demanded a decisive answer, Mann was either evasive or inclined toward positions that the political Right decisively rejected.

Mann himself noted the ironic fragmentation of his conservatism; he alternated between partisanship and questioning that partisanship, contributing to the "unreadableness" of the book, which he conceded. Nonetheless, *Reflections* was an altogether political declaration, and, in a certain sense, it must be understood as the first programmatic statement of the Conservative Revolution. Mann had used this expression not in the *Reflections*, but in an essay of 1921, parallel to the essay on the "Third Reich":

> *Conservatism must only have spirit (Geist) to be more revolutionary than any positivist-liberal Enlightenment, and Nietzsche himself was from the beginning...nothing other than Conservative Revolution.*[27]

From the onset, *Reflections* provoked a certain irritation on the Right, although the rapidly developing events between the autumn of 1918 and summer of 1919 allowed only a delayed appreciation of it. The lack of practical relevance might also have been felt as a disadvantage. Yet the conservative intelligentsia celebrated Mann as the one who had been correct in his critique of the "bourgeois rhetorician" and assertion of the insincerity of the West, but who had also "represented and defended what was 'conservative' in the deeper sense of the word."

At this time, Mann himself established contact with individual protagonists, groups, and journals that were to play a significant role in the history of the Conservative Revolution. His own political

---

[27]   Thomas Mann, "Zum Geleit" in *Süddeutsche Monatshefte* 18 (February 1921): 293.

thought in the entire transitional period from the autumn of 1918 to autumn of 1922 was marked by ideas that were discussed in these circles. Even the ambivalence—the fluctuations in his judgment about the events that he witnessed—was typical. This wavering occurred between the assumption that the "*coup*"[28] had been necessary and the aversion toward those responsible for it, between mourning for the old German position of power and the idea of a new German mission in the world, between the fear of Soviet power and sympathy for a "National Bolshevism," between the idea that capitalism was obsolete and defending the primacy of education and property, between the hope of preserving tradition in a new form and enthusiasm for a new beginning, between acceptance that Western Europe had won and the faith that Germany was called upon to "invent something new in politics"—and, indeed, something specifically German.

When *Reflections* appeared on October 7, 1918, the first volume of Spengler's *Decline of the West* was already available, albeit in a very

OSWALD SPENGLER

limited edition. In this case, appreciation by the wider public was also delayed until early 1919. Even then the rapid and extraordinary success of this work resulted from a misunderstanding: identifying the book's title with the fate of the nation.

What Spengler meant by the "decline of the West" was the inevitable end and rigidification of a certain culture that had originated in Western and Central Europe since the Middle Ages. This culture, like many others before

---

|28| In reference to the *coup* that created the Weimar Republic. (*Ed.*)

it, had experienced phases of a creative beginning and a blossoming—the time of "culture" (*Kultur*) in the true sense—and since the 19th century was transforming itself into a "civilization" (*Zivilisation*), whose fate would be increasing sterility. Spengler's morphology differed from other philosophies of history in that he had assumed the necessary process of decline in his effort to demonstrate the strictly regular character of this process by referring to parallel developments in other high cultures. What disturbed a large number of his readers was his demand to not merely accept the inevitable but to affirm it in the sense of Nietzsche's "*amor fati.*"

Like Mann, Spengler believed in the German victory right up to the final collapse. In fact, he had written his book with the expectation that it might help orient the military and political elites of the Reich in the reordering of Europe and in preparing for future conflicts, which Spengler believed unavoidable. Defeat surprised him, but it did not lead him to change his predictions for the future. These predictions included the rise of economics to become the decisive factor in domestic politics, and with it, the rise of democracy, their gradual hollowing out of both the decay of the corporative order in society and nations and the building of new empires that would face each other in great wars.

Spengler repeatedly protested against interpreting his view of history as "pessimistic." He wanted his way of looking at things to be understood not as an invitation to resignation, but as an appeal to stoic endurance of the given situation and to the pursuit of "tangible political goals." Spengler discussed this task of his own time in the second volume of *Decline*, which only appeared in March of 1922 and dealt with the development of European history and the foundation of all politics.

The main focus of Spengler's discussion was "Caesarism," which included the looming "advent of formless forces" based neither on tradition nor aristocracy, but only resting on intimidation and personal abilities of the ruler. Spengler compared this "Caesarism" of the European End Times with the early Greek *tyrranis* and Sulla's exercise of power. Yet along with these examples from antiquity, he produced some from Chinese history and asserted that this form of rule belonged to the definitive political constitution of late civilizations. In his assumption that Caesarism rests only upon brutality and the sympathy of the masses, as well as *de facto* leads to a re-primitivizing of political life, Spengler shared the tradition of older conservative interpretations. But for all his ambivalence, an important consideration for him was the perception of the possibilities that would be offered to the "great man of facts," the "great individual" following a phase of equalizing and democratizing. After all, the Caesars were also the last "men of race," who were able to bring their followers (if not the nation) "into form," sweep away parliamentarism and the "dictatorship of money" that goes with it, and replace them with the "will of a master" and a warlike "socialism."

Among those who misunderstood the purpose of Spengler's book was undoubtedly Thomas Mann. He began reading the first volume in June of 1919, and completed it within a few weeks. Mann was lastingly fascinated with Spengler's argument, particularly the analysis of decline. But Mann was far from being convinced of taking Spengler's challenge seriously that "civilization" was inevitable. It clearly irritated him that Spengler—much like he—contrasted culture and civilization, but wanted his diagnosis of the fateful transition from one to the other "to be taken completely seriously and favorably."

Clear as the connection between Mann and Spengler was—both made reference to Goethe, Schopenhauer, and Nietzsche and hoped for renewal from the East—they differed fundamentally on one decisive point. This was the explicit commitment to being "apolitical" (and, therefore, to Romanticism) by Mann and the explicit commitment to politics (and, therefore, to anti-Romanticism) by Spengler. The consequences can be detected in each man's idea of democracy's triumphant progress. Neither evaded this fact, but Mann's affirmation was melancholy, whereas Spengler's—heroic. He was concerned how the Germans' "being in form" [29] might look under changed circumstances. From a letter at the end of December of 1918, we can infer that Spengler—who never made a secret of his admiration for the Kaiser and the old leadership stratum—wished for no restoration in the true sense, but rather for a "Prussian state socialism" to be supported both by the nobility ("once it has been purified of all feudal, agrarian narrowness"[30]) and by the simple people ("after they have separated themselves from the 'masses' out of revulsion and self-respect"[31]).

This already sketches out what Spengler would develop at greater length in his *Prussianism and Socialism*: the idea of the Prussian tradition as the basis for a new *Romanitas* that would have the necessary toughness to create a German Empire in the future. Spengler later asserted that "the national movement took its start from this book." Indeed, *Prussianism and Socialism* enjoyed extraordinary circulation— by 1932, 80,000 copies had been printed—and gained considerable influence on the thought of the younger generation. This was the case, in part, because it did not presuppose the level of argumentation of Spengler's *Decline*. Also, the possibilities for action that Spengler revealed were also noteworthy along with the diminishment of the kind of fatalism that the reading of the *Decline* sparked, even if unintended by the author.

With his political writings, Spengler influenced that specific segment of the intelligentsia that can be considered central to the Conservative Revolution. Here, too, was a similarity with Thomas Mann: both maintained contact with a group of publicists around Heinrich von Gleichen, Eduard Stadtler, and Moeller van den Bruck, in particular. Yet they turned away from them almost simultaneously

---

|29| Oswald Spengler, *Der Untergang des Abendlandes: Umrisse einer Morphologie der Weltgeschichte* (München: Beck, [1918/1922] 1980), 1106.

|30| Oswald Spengler, *Briefe 1913-1936*, (München: Beck, 1963), 115.

|31| *Ibid.*

at the end of 1922. Their motives, however, were quite different: while Mann converted to the Republic, Spengler criticized his disciples' distance from actual politics.

3.3 NEW CAMP, NEW SPIRIT

The German Revolution resulted from the collapse of the old order rather than the determined will to create a new one. Not a hand had been lifted in defense of the Kaiser's Empire, but neither did the Republic meet much enthusiasm. The traumatic experience of commissioned and non-commissioned officers, whose men had torn the shoulder insignia from their uniforms, the resigned silence of the middle class before the sudden outbreak of mob passions, and the hysterical conviction of the radicals that a new age would begin under the Red Flag—all stood abruptly juxtaposed. The overall sentiment in the first half of 1919 was confusion, accompanied by fear of a more radical revolution or a successful counter-revolution. Practical preparations for elections into a national-constituent assembly were combined with utopian considerations about the best form of government, and all of this was supplemented by the population's growing excitement regarding the truce conditions and, afterward, the peace treaty.

The reasons for the decision to sign the treaty were clear and acknowledged in principle by the opposition. The government feared an invasion by the Allies, the disintegration of the unity of the Reich, and, possibly, an attempted Communist revolution in the case of non-compliance. They had neither combat forces to prevent an invasion nor hoped to find the population ready for an emergency *levée en masse* on behalf of the Republic. The leadership circles of the majority Social Democrats did not give into illusions about the effectiveness of surrender propaganda (*Unterzeichnungspropaganda*), which was mainly supported by the independent Social Democrats. Some mentioned that the defense, Minister Gustav Noske—when he heard the conditions of the Versailles Treaty—said, "Our people are so worn out that we must sign."[32]

Thus, he became one of the first Social Democrats to publicly accept the treaty. His motives, however, lay not in the approval of the Allied demands but in his particular experience of the last few months. He found it important that—even before the limitation of German armament to 100,000 men without heavy weapons—with the disintegration of the old army, no troops were available to defend the borders from the greed of the new neighbors, especially Poland, and to maintain order within the country. In addition, the truce conditions allowed German troops to maintain their position in the Baltic countries in the face of the advancing Red Army for as long as the Allies considered necessary.

When Noske had to abandon the early attempts of the Social-Democratic government to win over the proletariat for a militia-like transitional army, he fell back on the men who had shown themselves ready to put on their uniforms again, or who had not taken them off in the first place. *Freikorps* ("Free Corps") arose from the surviving units of the old army; less frequently, they were formed from scratch. The distinction between the *Freikorps* and the "resident defense leagues"— set up especially in Bavaria and East Prussia for the self-defense of villages and regions—was inexact. The estimated 400,000 members of the *Freikorps* were partly professional soldiers, partly men won over by promises made to them—for instance, of land on which to settle.

Concerned citizens gathered in the resident defense leagues. Members of the *Freikorps* in the narrower sense, who were permanently stationed with their units, gradually developed a self-conception as *Praetorians* forced to serve a despised system. They, therefore, made

---

|32| Philipp Scheidemann, *Der Zusammenbruch* (Berlin: Verlag für Sozialpolitik, 1921), 249.

no secret of their dissatisfaction with service. The fundamental ideological attitude was nationalist, but politicization gradually set in. In early 1919, *völkisch* and anti-Semitic organizations began successful attempts to infiltrate the *Freikorps*.

Despite their readiness to fight the radical Left, very early on, there already was a certain sympathy in the *Freikorps* for the concerns of the working class and vague ideas about a "German socialism" that showed affinity with wartime socialism. In most organizations that served until they were dissolved in the autumn of 1920, the outlook of professional soldiers played a more important role than any worldview (*Weltanschauung*). They felt ever less duty toward the government and ever more toward their leaders and units, along with a strong willingness to apply force to achieve political goals reminiscent of contemporary Italian *squadrismo* and *arditismo*. But unlike Italy, there was no large, radical political movement such as fascism that might have availed itself of these men. Until further notice, the old bonds were merely destroyed, and many members of the *Freikorps* had "joined another camp without being aware of it." The question was whether the "new spirit" corresponded with this "new camp."

In the period between the proclamation of the Republic (November 9, 1918) and the day that the Versailles Treaty was signed (June 28, 1919), a feverish atmosphere dominated social life in Germany. Whoever did not join the parties of global Civil War—whether Lenin's or Wilson's—saw himself subjected to the results of a hectic ideological production that constantly tried to blend opposites and offered nothing but the third way between Western liberalism and Eastern collectivism: Christianity and anarchism, asceticism and libertinism, nationalism and socialism, conservatism and revolution.

Most of it was merely despair and a literary exercise, and hardly likely to have any political impact. Many of the ideas can be explained only based on the circumstances of the time, for instance, all those linked with the discussion of the possible continuation of the war. The most radical variant of the demand for a people's squadron was certainly connected to the idea of a German Jacobinism. The moderate variety counted on the repetition of 1813 and accepted a possibly longer time for preparation, as was also necessary in Prussia after the defeats of Jena and Auerstaedt. Max Weber wrote to a friend (November 24, 1918), "We are starting all over from the beginning, as in 1648 and 1807."[33]

The continued attraction of "national socialism" can be explained by the idea that the nation's resurgence would have to be prepared by the concentration of all its powers, especially economic. Even official agencies attempted, immediately following the collapse, to instill a new self-confidence in the population by harmonizing war socialism and the demands of the postwar age, and explicitly combining them with the idea of "Germany's global socialist mission." Prudent voices warned about pretensions that certainly exceeded the capacities of the defeated country, and preferred to understand national socialism merely as a makeshift way of organizing all the powers of the nation in order to avert external and internal threats. The memory of Naumann's national-social policy played a certain role here, but more important were the ideas about "cooperative economy" (*Gemeinwirtschaft*) that were discussed after the end of the war.

The idea of the "cooperative economy" had influenced Walther Rathenau even before the end of the war, and it had a more lasting effect in his conception of an elite-led *"Volksdemocratie"* (*Volks democracy*) on a socialist basis. Rathenau is commonly understood as a representative of political liberalism. Thus, we see here the attraction that the idea of a national socialism held in the early postwar period, and how strongly it worked its way into the very center of political life. National socialism's real power of attraction was exercised where it was understood as a polemical concept opposed to "un-German" parliamentarism and capitalism imposed by the Revolution and the Versailles Treaty. In a certain sense, early "National Bolshevism" also

---

|33| Marianne Weber, *Max Weber: Ein Lebensbild* (Tübingen: Mohr, 1926), 648.

belongs in this context. It had many similarities with national socialism. However, it was distinguished from it thanks to the demands of individuals such as the conservative Paul Elzbacher or the Hamburg national communists around Heinrich Laufenberg and Friedrich Wolffheim. They not only demanded a planned registration of all the productive forces in society in the sense of a "national *Volk* organization," but also called for the support of Soviet Russia in order to prepare for a war of revenge against the Western Powers. This was rejected by many strictly anti-Bolshevik proponents of national socialism, who explicitly considered the "dictatorship of a national socialism" a decisive deterrent against Bolshevism.

In the early days following the Revolution, the fear of a communist coup was not quite as strong as the outrage about the Versailles Treaty.

HEINRICH LAUFENBERG

Yet it was a crucial factor in the development of new ideologies. The decisive point was the concern that the events in Russia of 1917 might serve as precedent for the developments in Germany. Reports of Bolshevik massacres of the old ruling stratum, the arbitrariness and cruelty of their actions during the Revolution and subsequent Civil War related by the returning prisoners of war, as well as the Baltic German refugees and fleeing emigrants essentially contributed to a mood that combined panic and determination to resist.

In this context, anti-Semitism played a special role. It had grown since the last phase of the war, received new nourishment from additional immigration of Jews from East-Central Europe, and was enhanced once more by the recognition that a rather large number of the Bolshevik leaders were of Jewish ancestry. Identifying Bolshevism with Jewry, along with fear of a collective destruction of the middle class, played an essential role in the emotions that defined a segment of the political Right in the immediate postwar period. But since the crucial strength to create something new never lies in negativity, neither anti-Communism nor anti-Semitism was decisive for the formation of a "new camp." The pivotal factor was the expectation of a "new era."

Although one might assume that such aspirations had completely disappeared because of the defeat, they actually received new life under the influence of the great hope for world salvation that aroused both West and East. Between the end of the war and the climactic phase of inflation, Germany experienced a true explosion of religious or quasi-religious quest for meaning. Some of the "inflation saints," who enjoyed a boom between 1919 and 1923, found a huge following with their proclamation of a new age. Most of them were a curious mixture of Nietzschean thought, Lebensreform, sexual permissiveness, and obvious pathology, like the kind that had appeared in Europe during earlier times of crisis.

In addition to these, there were also serious efforts that tried to meet the demand for total political reform. In a letter to the Social Democrat Konrad Haenisch (January of 1919), the conservative Max Hildebert wrote: "The aversion for liberalism among young intellectuals is simply enormous. We do not even take it seriously as an enemy." The conservative youth was beginning, in the context of this enmity and "despite all their serious differences," to feel "a kinship even to socialist circles."

The thought of a conservative-socialist marriage had a few supporters even on the Left, especially in the circles of wartime socialism. *The Bell*, a journal that continued to appear until 1925, was an important forum for this current, seeking to balance nation and socialism. The most important protagonist of this tendency in the postwar period, next to Haenisch and Lensch, may have been August, a sometime representative of the German government in the Baltic states, then the Executive President in East Prussia. Later, he characteristically lost his office because of open sympathy for the Kapp Putsch.

No one from this group of Social Democrats retained any influence on the SPD after the situation stabilized. Young socialists, especially from the Hofgeismar Kreis, approached the national-socialist idea only in the course of the 1920s, and even then it was limited to a minority. Lensch and August Winnig openly joined the Right, but were hardly of interest to the "young conservatives" advocated by Max Hildebert Boehm. This was also the result of the generation gap. The "Generation of 1919," as Moeller van den Bruck was to name them, was more strongly and more immediately marked by the experience of life at the front and the postwar period, by the hopes that arose at the end of the war, and by the feelings of impotence when the peace conditions became known. While many of the older people, who had played a significant role in the Partei des deutschen Idealismus (Party of German Idealism), withdrew from political debate (Otto Hintze, Friedrich Meinecke), the young were powerfully seized by that wave from the Right that had changed the social climate in Germany in the spring of 1919.

AUGUST WINNIG

The collapse of Freie Deutsche Jugend was symptomatic of the generational aspect of this situation. Already before the war, Gustav Wyneken, a reforming educator, exercised lasting influence on the movement. After 1917, he, once again, sought to solidify this loose group and orient it toward his ideas. That the attempt to preserve the independence of the Free Germans had to fail was demonstrated by a conference called in Jena for the Easter holiday of 1919. The organization split along the now-customary philosophical fault lines into the "Resolute Youth," which was taken up in the Kommunistische Jugendinternationale (Communist Youth International) by 1921, and the Jungdeutscher Bund (Young German League).

Above all, Frank Glatzel, Young Germans' leader, brought the group closer to national-social conceptions. Revealing and symptomatic of the whole camp was the comprehensive *völkisch* concept that Glatzel tried to push through. Anti-Semitism "in no way formed the heart and soul of the movement," but was "an expression of the *völkisch* feeling born of the struggle."[34] Glatzel's fundamental idea of a specific "youth movement" contribution to politics, however, remained unrealized both during the war and in the postwar period.

The returnees could not be integrated into the league, although their hopes of coming back to the Wandervogel groups regularly failed. The majority supported an apolitical stance as in the time before the war. New aspects that found expression in the *Bündische* Youth only gained clear contours in the 1920s.

3.4 THE SOLIDARISTS

The policies of the "new camp" included the struggle against the dictated peace conditions and the Communist threat, the creation of a new *Volk* community, and the search for a German way beyond the Eastern and Western constitutional models. Thus, they lead to the question as to whether a greater concentration of the individual philosophical elements on a single point had not occurred even at this early phase.

In fact, one might see this focus in the Solidarist group formed shortly before the end of the war. The organizer of this circle was the former functionary of the Alsatian Center Party (Zentrumpartei), Eduard Stadtler. Stadtler had volunteered at the outbreak of the war, taken part in battles in Northern France, and was transferred to the Eastern Front in the summer of 1916. A short time thereafter, he became a prisoner of war in Russia, and in early 1917, he managed

---

|34| Uwe Puschner, *Die völkische Bewegung im wilhelminischen Kaiserreich* (Darmstadt: Wissenschaftliche Buchgesellschaft, 2001), 15.

to escape. The outbreak of the Russian Revolution strengthened him in two convictions: first, that liberalism was preparing the way for Bolshevism, as the Kerensky government in Russia had paved the way for Lenin; second, that Bolshevism's success was only due to the primitive nature of its conceptions, which corresponded to the primitive nature of the Russian population.

Stadtler believed that the danger of the "Marxist world revolutionary struggle" was culpably underestimated both in Berlin and at the German embassy in Moscow. He also believed that anti-Bolshevism must be made into a rousing political movement that could seize upon the masses. Turned away in official circles—merely charged with delivering anti-Bolshevik educational lectures—Stadtler got in contact with Bund deutscher Gelehrter und Künstler (League of German Scholars and Artists) led by Heinrich von Gleichen after his return to Germany. Formed upon private initiative during the war, the League was meant to defend the cause of the Central Powers to the educated classes in neutral countries. Stadtler said that he met Gleichen for the first time on August 22, 1918—a fateful encounter for both men.

Up to that point, von Gleichen had hardly come forward politically. Even before the war, he had written a work of cultural criticism, but it

HANS GRIMM

was ignored. After taking over leadership of the league when the war broke out (Walther Rathenau also belonged to the board of directors), he succeeded in winning over about a thousand members and engaged in lively activities as a lecturer. He maintained close connections with the Central Office for the Foreign Service, which tried to counter Allied propaganda. Moeller van den Bruck, Hans Grimm, Friedrich Gundolf, and Boehm, all of whom later played an important role in the Conservative Revolution, were active here and in similar organizations.

Even before the collapse, a "Union for National and Social Solidarity" was formed by Stadtler, von Gleichen, Franz Röhr, Karl Helfferich (briefly, Germany's ambassador to Moscow and, later, a Deutschnationale Volkspartei [German National People's Party] politician), Simon Marx, a banker, and the Christian-National labor leader Adam Stegerwald. According to Stadtler, the group never included more than twenty persons. This number seemed insufficient to him for organizing a mass movement not only to blow up the old-new party system but also to sweep away the provisional government. So on December 1, 1918, Stadtler opened the General Secretariat for the Study and Combating of Bolshevism in Berlin, the kernel of Antibolschewistisches Comitee (Anti-Bolshevik Committee), ABC, or Antibolschewistische Liga (Anti-Bolshevik League).

Stadtler claims that a few days later, he noted in a letter that the Solidarists (which continued to exist as an "intellectual and political secret organization") and the Anti-Bolksheviks did not want to limit themselves to purely negative goals, but were working toward "something new, that might be labeled conservative-socialist or national-socialist." In fact, these expressions appear nowhere else in Stadtler's writings. Most plausible is the linkage of the concepts "national" and "social," which had already been made (albeit using different words).

Stadtler referred to contacts with Friedrich Naumann (attested elsewhere as well). Also, he later made a plausible case that his intention had been to present a contemporary and, in every sense, intensified version of the old national-social program. The latter might be characterized as a plan to create a block of states in Central Europe, dominated by Germany, which would form the core of an informal empire encompassing the entire continent. Domestic politics were to be determined by a mixture of social reform, corporativism, and plebiscitary elements.

Like many German intellectuals, Stadtler and von Gleichen believed that one of the mistakes of the German war policy was to ignore propaganda. They were not only convinced of the effectiveness of enemy propaganda—going as far as to think it had caused the revolutionary upheaval—they also believed that any counter-revolutionary movement must be based on modern communications media. At this time, public opinion was "in a state of ferment," which made everything that was possible seem so, if only one could control the instruments for influencing the social mood. Although Stadtler had already shown himself a gifted speaker before public assemblies, and although his brochures had had been printed and disseminated in the thousands, he still lacked the means of exercising lasting influence on public opinion.

In early 1919, Stadtler was able to acquire *Gewissen* (*Conscience*), a

small journal, and make it the central organ of the Solidarists and the ABC. The editorial position of *Conscience* can be sufficiently characterized by citing the third issue (April 26, 1919) with its headline: "Neither Lenin nor Wilson." Like many adherents of the Third Way, Stadtler first came forward with an emphatically left-wing argument. Not only did he champion a "spiritual socialism," but he also openly demanded the socialization of heavy industry. Already in early 1919, he planned a kind of a counter-Soviet, a "general conference of the productive German nationality" that would call into question the legitimacy of the provisional German government and the National Assembly. Still in 1920, when all the dice had fallen in favor of parliamentarianism, Stadtler declared the necessity of the German Council (i.e., a Soviet) Constitution. His ideas probably corresponded with the proposal of an anonymous contributor to *Conscience* to hand executive power over to the Defense Minister Gustav Noske, and to invest him with full dictatorial powers.

It is surprising that the group around *Gewissen* did not view the Revolution unfavorably, or not entirely unfavorably. In one of the first articles that Moeller van den Bruck wrote for the journal (November 11, 1919), he states (underneath the headline "Benefits of the Revolution"):

> *Since the Revolution, a change has come about with us all. It goes about among men as a greater nationalness* (Volklichkeit). [35]

**ARTHUR MOELLER
VAN DEN BRUCK**

There is no prospect of a restoration, and a "young nation" with its history before it will be able to use the Republic as well to fulfill the national mission.

Moeller, born 1876, not only assumed the function of *spiritus rector* (master spirit) for *Gewissen*, but also became, next to Mann and Spengler, the leading figure in the Conservative Revolution in its early phase. Moreover, his life connected the precursors of the movement

---

|35| Arthur Moeller van den Bruck, "Der Revolutionsgewinn" in *Das Gewissen* 31 (November 11, 1919): 1.

in the Wilhemine Age, the "ideas of 1914," and thought about the "new camp," as it arose following the collapse.

Originally Moeller belonged to the Bohemian literary world, a friend of poets Franz Evers, Richard Dehmel, and Theodor Däubler, as well as Ernst Barlach, author, graphic artist, and sculptor. Early on, he made a certain name for himself as a critic and publisher of English and American literature. Initially, he lived in the intellectual atmosphere of literary *décadence*, fled to France to avoid military service, but returned to Germany in the autumn of 1907, after receiving permission to perform his service belatedly. He was able to dispel any suspicions of lacking a national caste of mind by referring to his eight-volume work, *Die Deutschen* (*The Germans*), which had appeared in the meantime.

Returning to civilian life, Moeller spent the coming years in travel, which took him to London, again to Paris, and, most important, to Northern and Eastern Europe. As a result, he became acquainted with Scandinavia, the Baltic states, and Russia. The impressions he gathered there stood in sharp contrast to his experiences in France. Already in his 1905 book, *Das Théâtre Français*, a turn against France and its claims to cultural leadership are noticeable. The latter also had political implications. Moeller criticized the "national character of outwardness" and the lack of authenticity in all the varieties of French civilization.

The idea that the essence of a people is shown in its culture played an important role in his conception of *The Germans*. This work (of very uneven quality) demonstrates, above all, the degree of politicization in Moeller's thought. He relates the "human history" of his own nation—from Germanic prehistory to the end of the 19th century—by attempting to represent the characteristic traits of the "*Volksgeist*" *à propos* of the key figures from the German past. There was a remarkable tension in the work between the optimistic assumption that the German Age still lay ahead and the pessimistic assumption of the necessary decline of all cultures, states, and nations,

Like every race, every nation finally goes under, according to its own destiny; we, too, shall go under in our own way. But we will not do so until we have fulfilled this destiny.

During this time, Moeller was intensively studying organological and Darwinian theories that interpreted the laws of social life according to the model of natural processes. His entire conception of "youth" and the "old age" of nations was determined by these theories. But by "youth" and "old age," he did not merely mean biological facts; they were synonymous with the presence or absence of a life force. France was, in Moeller's view, old, used up, mechanical, and uncreative. Italy, too, was old, but had always experienced rebirths. Moeller considered North Americans different from both—their pioneer spirit nourished the idea that they could start all over again—along with the "race" of Slavs.

The word "race" was no more naturalistically intended here than his statements about the "youth" and "age" of nations. By "race" Moeller meant the unity of a great life form, not a genetically determinable collective. It was in the mixture of races that he saw an important precondition for the power to give life new expression. He believed that this force remained strong in the Slavs, and especially in the Russians. Unlike the urban, civilized, skeptical, and liberal West, the rustic, primitive, faith-oriented, and conservative East possessed the reserves necessary for a new renaissance.

Moeller revived many of the ideas of Romanticism and the Deutsche Bewegung, but also clearly perceived the tension, in the way that they compared to political reality. Therefore, his search was directed toward a philosophical synthesis, toward an answer to the question "how opposites can be overcome." In his book that appeared during the war, *Der Preußische Stil* (*The Prussian Style*), he sketched out a possible answer. The sharpness of his anti-Romantic position is striking, as is his rejection of any "de-Prussification" in the name of what is German:

Style is law; Romanticism is lawlessness. Romantic lawlessness, too, has its rightful place in the life of nations, when it comes from an exuberance on the part of its people, when it is a venture, a challenge to fate, a departure for undiscovered shores. But if a nation does not want to perish from this Romanticism, then there must also be bonds that preserve the life of the people, that hold it together internally—strong bonds of community and fixed forms of tradition.[36]

For Moeller, Prussia was a symbol of the anti-Romantic position, which was characteristic of his political attitude, like the reception of the radical conservative ideas of Lagarde, the cultural criticism of Nietzsche, and a nationalism reminiscent of Barrès. All this put together makes the sharpness of his criticism targeting Wilhelm II understandable. Already in the third volume (1909) of *Die Deutschen*, he had assigned much blame to the Kaiser for Germans' failures, although the accusation was formulated in an opaque manner. In the second edition of *Der Preußische Stil*, which appeared after the war, he attributed Wilhelm's inclination to Romanticism as the real reason for his failure. This inclination did not give way even before the entirely un-Romantic tradition in Prussia: "There is nothing that could have been less Prussian—but it was very German."

This remark is important, because Moeller's rejection of the Republic must not be misunderstood as an expression of political nostalgia. Moeller was no "reactionary." Several times he made known his readiness for peace with the revolutionaries, if they fulfilled their main task: the "nationalizing of democracy." Failure at this task brought much contempt upon the Weimar government and lent political legitimacy to the "new camp." Among the young, specifically, it

---

|36| Arthur Moeller van den Bruck, *Der Preußische Stil* (München: Piper, 1916), 180.

nourished the idea that one must seek the way to raise Germany to its feet again upon other paths.

What arose between the autumn of 1918 and summer 1919 as the preliminary or early form of the Conservative Revolution still had something unfinished about it. This can be seen, above all, in their wavering self-designation. In order to express their position beyond Right and Left, they considered calling themselves the "new Center." The latter was meant to symbolically represent the need to create a comprehensive political and social movement that would overcome the oppositions of the past. This was the goal agreed upon in the group around Moeller, Stadtler, and von Gleichen, along with other individuals and groups that stood outside the "semi-circle" of the usual party spectrum.

4

THE UNITY OF THE CONSERVATIVE REVOLUTION

espite their attempt to position themselves beyond Left and Right, the main protagonists of the Conservative Revolution were regularly classified as the latter category. Their shared opponents—Versailles, Liberalism, and Bolshevism— led to this assessment. Ideological similarities were also present. The Conservative Revolutionaries, however, did not share the restorationist longings of the old Right, which intrinsically felt the loss of their most important point of reference, the monarchy, as a great burden. The royalism of conservatives, national liberals, and the *völkisch* was not only at a loss for a presentable representative; it also had to struggle with the belief of many of its followers that any restoration was hopeless. The crown found no saints and martyrs. The refusal of the "royal sacrifice" by Wilhelm II may have been responsible for the insight into the senselessness of the final attack under his leadership;

but it also appeared to be an expression of resignation and weakened any attempt to build upon the old order.

This shortcoming was intensified by another, namely, that the old names for political tendencies became unusable and had to be replaced by new, popular labels. This applied especially to the concept of a "conservative"; Kuno Graf von Westarp, the leading member of the German Conservatives, said as early as November of 1918 that this label had, in broad strata of the population, fallen too greatly into disapproval for there to be any hope of significantly influencing the politics of the near future under that name.

After the dissolution of Deutsche Vaterlandspartei and the failure of all attempts to create a great civic (*bürgerlichen*) coalition movement, Deutschnationale Volkspartei (DNVP) built upon the organizational foundation of Deutschkonservative Partei (German Conservative Party), but also took in Independent Conservatives, members of Christlich-Soziale Partei (Christian-Social Party) and National Liberals, along with a fraction of the Pan-Germans and the *völkisch*. Its core support included the Protestant middle class, parts of the landowning class and industry; they maintained close contacts with Christian-national labor unions, combatant organization such as the Stahlhelm, agrarian interest groups and the leadership of the Protestant churches. In their program, the German Nationalists demanded the restoration of the Hohenzollern monarchy, but also provisionally recognized existing constitutional realities, and thus the Republican order.

Unlike Deutsche Vaterlandspartei, the National Liberals in Deutsche Volkspartei (German People's Party), DVP, only belatedly succeeded in obtaining an organizational basis, so that they hardly took part in the constituent assembly. The leader of Deutsche Volkspartei, Gustav Stresemann, rejected any union with the German Nationalists, since he was more interested in a pan-liberal party to include the progressives, now known as Deutsche Demokratische Partei (German

Democratic Party), DDP. Only after the failure of this attempt to overcome the old division that dated to the time of German unification did the right-wing liberals decide, in December of 1918, to found the DVP. Their program was similar to that of the German Nationalists in respect of advocating restoration and a strong nation-state. Yet they placed greater emphasis on their willingness to collaborate constructively in the Republic. Like the earlier National Liberals, the new People's Party was especially anchored in the Western part of the Reich, found support in the influential circles of industry, and adopted strongly anti-socialist positions.

One of the causes of Stresemann's refusal to join forces with the German nationalists was his rejection of any cooperation with the *völkisch* and anti-Semites. In March of 1914 just before the outbreak of the war, these groups attempted to bring together the remains of Deutschsoziale Partei and Deutsche Reformpartei (German Reform Party) in a new organization, the Deutschvölkische Partei (German Völkisch Party), DvP. The DvP even gained five seats in the Reichstag from those previous parties, but was hardly able to carry out any political activities during the war. This was the case partly because of heavy military censorship that, along with left-wing papers, struck conservatives and anti-Semites. But this was also the case because other nationalist-influence organizations, such as the Pan-Germans, were essentially better able to respond to the changed situation.

In early 1917, the contest between the German social and reform wings broke out again, and could only be defused by the decision of the Party leadership to integrate the DvP into Deutsche Vaterlandspartei. The goal of undermining the DvP in a *völkisch* sense was presumptuous and condemned to failure from the start; instead, the *völkisch* were sucked into the downfall of the DVLP and practically ceased to exist by the end of the war. In January of 1919, its leadership committee, however, was able to establish Deutscher Schutz—und Trutzbund (German Protection and Defiance Organization), shortly thereafter renamed Deutschvölkischer

Schutz- und Trutzbund (German *Völkisch* Protection and Defiance Organization), DVSTB. The initiative came from the leadership of the Allgemeiner Deutscher Verband. The Pan-Germans were the only large nationalist organization to survive the war, and the goal of this grouping—now established and led by them—was the nationalist and anti-Semitic mobilization of the masses under their secret leadership.

The real power of the DVSTB, therefore, lay with the executive leader of the Pan-Germans, Alfred Roth, who focused its activities on agitating against the immigration of eastern Jews and the struggle against the new order. In 1920 alone, the league distributed 7.5 million leaflets, 4.8 million handbills, and 7.9 million stickers. At that time it had 110,000 registered members, a figure that was to rise to 150,000 by 1922. In those years, the league was banned (outside Bavaria) because of its constant anti-Semitic agitation that the government, in part, blamed for the murder of Walther Rathenau.

The *völkisch* did not have any party organization of their own at this time. The decisive reason for this was the negative experience of all attempts to establish anti-Semitic parties before the war and the hope of being able to reform DNVP in a *völkisch* direction. Indeed, there was a certain willingness to make concessions in this direction among the German Nationalists, but the leadership committee refused any further reception of the anti-Semitic elements of the *völkisch* program. As a result, the main spokesman for the *völkisch* in DNVP, Albrecht von Graefe, began gathering his followers into a German *Völkisch* working group, which was intended to represent *völkisch* interests. The leaders of the German Nationalists reacted sharply against this attempt to organize and forced Graefe and his supporters out of the Party.

ERNST GRAF ZU REVENTLOW

Consequently, in December of 1922, Deutschvölkische Freiheitspartei (German *Völkisch* Freedom Party), DVFP, was founded under the leadership of Graefe, Reinhold Wulle, and Ernst Graf zu Reventlow. The DVFP was able to achieve certain successes through an alliance with other regional *völkisch* lists and parties. After the failure of the Hitler-Ludendorff Putsch on November 8-9, 1923, it even seemed in a position to inherit the banned and leaderless Nazi Party. But it soon became apparent that the Achilles' heel of the *völkisch*—namely, constant leadership conflict, the organizational framework of DVFP, which never rose above the function of an umbrella organization, along with Hitler's tactical superiority—made any lasting establishment impossible. Deutschvölkische Freiheitspartei lived on until 1933, but characteristically was never able to fill its leadership positions after the end of the 1920s.

What united all right-wing groupings especially in the early years of the Weimar Republic was the view that the "Constitution remains wholly unintelligible, if the conditions of this murderous peace are not read as a commentary upon it."[37] German nationalists, right-wing Liberals, and the *völkisch* saw themselves as the defeated party in a constitutional war that Germany had waged between 1914 and 1918 in order to further develop its own version based on Bismarck's Reich. After the defeat, the *Entente* imposed the Western model onto the Reich. At the same time, this weakeness caused by war, revolution, and the fundamental defects of parliamentarism might have led in the end to the system's replacement by the East's counterpart—Bolshevism.

There certainly was overlap between this assessment of the situation and ideas shared by parties that cannot be classified as "right wing" in any narrow sense. To start with, this pertained to parts of Deutsche Demokratische Partei, all the way to the National Catholics of the Center. Deutschnationale Volkspartei, Deutsche Volkspartei,

---

|37| Christian F. Trippe, *Konservative Verfassungspolitik 1918-1923* (Düsseldorf: Droste, 1995), 163..

and the *völkisch*, however, remained the core of the "national opposition," quickly and expressly designated as "the enemy" by the new rulers. Already between the elections to the National Constituent Assembly and the first Reichstag elections of April of 1920, the Right succeeded in nearly doubling its share of the vote (from 16.7 percent to 31.6 percent). Under the impact of the great political crises— domestic (inflation, mass strikes, Putsch attempts, political murders) and foreign (demands for reparations, occupation of the Ruhr, border conflicts in the East)—their share of voters grew to 42.6 percent in the Reichstag elections of December of 1924. But this success could not be made to last. The *völkisch* rapidly lost importance, and up to the end of the 1920s, only a third of the voters regularly voted for the DNVP and DVP, whereby the clear rapprochement between the National Liberals and the Republic produced a gain and the greater distance of the German Nationalists from the Republic produced a loss.

The rise of the National Socialist German Workers' Party (NSDAP) in September of 1930 fundamentally changed the entire syste of political arithmetic that had been valid up until that point. The National Socialists were not only able to mobilize the mass of non-voters in their favor—with the exceptxion of the Catholic population segment—they also showed gains among all social groups. They were able to "inherit" those right-wing parties that had existed until then, and which had lost some two thirds of their seats in the Reichstag.

If one could establish that the right-wing parties in the Weimar period only ever represented a minority in the parliament, even if a relatively strong and stable one, how can it be explained that the "*de facto* dominant ideology in the Germany of the Weimar period"[38] was formed from the political philosophies of the right? The most important reason for this was the influence of the right-wing intelligentsia and their distance from the Republic. This distance was not identical to enmity

---

[38]   Louis Dupeux, "Présentation générale," in La « révolution conservatrice » allemande sous la République de Weimar (Paris: Kime, 1992), 7.

from the beginning, but arose with the perception of considerable functional shortcomings in the Constitution. The more the chain of events confirmed this skepticism, the greater grew rejection and aggressiveness. Right-wing intellectuals did not regard the new order as theirs. But the reasons for this rejection varied. While the older generation rejected it because it did not measure up to the Wilhelmine model, the younger generation was inclined to make the accusation that it failed to give the wartime *Volk* community a new fitting form. Many of the younger generation hesitated to take a political stand at all. They seldom came from the ranks of the prewar Right, even when they were influenced by the radical-conservative approaches or their developments, or certain ideas associated with the national-social, *völkisch*, life-reform or youth-movement currents.

From the beginning of the 1920s, it became clearer that besides the parties of the Right, there appeared newspapers, journals, leagues, and groups, whose goals were not of tactical, but of fundamental nature. Even if they shared similarities, contacts, and personal bonds with the larger organizations, these groups' philosophical convictions and *metapolitical* goals stood apart from the considerations of daily politics. Forms of cooperation varied from formal mergers to establishing loose circles and friendships, from allowing the members of neighboring schools of thought to publish in their

own organs and releasing anthologies containing divergent viewpoints, to lengthy debates.

The movement's consolidation (despite inner pluralism) was first expressed symbolically. All groups considered part of the Conservative Revolution used a black flag as a symbol, not only in opposition to the black-red-golden flag of the Republic or the red flag of the Left, but also against the black-red-white colors of the German Nationalists and the Popular Party and the swastika flag of the National Socialists. Black was an expression of mourning and outrage over the Versailles Treaty and a sign of determination to overcome the existing conditions and replace them with something better.

The old Right understood the collapse of the old order and grieved for it, above all, as an undeserved and incomprehensible misfortune—as the end of the Reich. The "new front" or "youth front," on the other hand—which really did not want to follow the traditional scheme of Right and Left at all—recognized a certain historical justification for the Revolution. The revolutionaries, however, did not live up to their task, because they had not created that Greater German Social *Volksstaat*, the establishment of which they promised, and were thus truly unworthy of the great name "Republicans." For this reason, they desired no counter-revolution, but rather, to triumph in the Revolution by entrusting the revolutionary process to the "Conservative Revolutionaries," similar to Luther, the men of the Deutsche Bewegung, or Bismarck.

KARL ANTON PRINZ ROHAN

Combining "conservative" and "revolutionary" in this sense can be traced back to the time of the collapse. Despite this, the Conservative Revolution as the label for a more clearly construed political and intellectual movement prevailed only gradually and never entirely. At first, older concepts like "Fatherlandish" or "National Movement" were used. Using a part to represent the whole was also common. The whole movement was called "*völkisch*" or "nationalist" or (later) "young conservative." Even Thomas Mann's use of "Conservative Revolution" in the sense of an umbrella term changed little. Only in the second half of the 1920s did particular names prevail for the individual schools of thought. It was at that time that the Conservative Revolution become a key concept, above all, thanks to Moeller van der Bruck's 1923 book *Das Dritte Reich*[39] (*The Third Reich*), through a corresponding statement by Prince Karl Anton von Rohan, and through a lecture given in 1927 by Hugo von Hofmannsthal on *The Written Word as the Spiritual Space of the Nation* (*Das Schrifttum als geistiger Raum der Nation*).

As already mentioned, Moeller called for a balance between the tendencies of conservation and renewal even before the war. Under changed circumstances, he continued his efforts in this direction. Beginning in the autumn of 1921, he published contributions to the journal *Gewissen*, which served as preliminary work for his book *Das Dritte Reich*. There, he placed his own thought explicitly in the tradition of the Deutsche Bewegung, Lagarde, and Nietzsche. Thus, he emphasized the interconnectedness of preservation and change, of conservatism and revolution:

> *What is revolutionary today will be conservative tomorrow. Preservation eternally succeeds in overthrowing and making up for what it neglected, sets right what it got wrong. We do not want to carry the revolution further, but, rather, the ideas of the revolution that lay in it and that it did not understand. We want to combine these revolutionary ideas with conservative ideas that always assert themselves, and we want to drive them in a conservative-revolutionary way to where we reach conditions, in which we can live again.*[40]

|39| The newest English edition is called *Germany's Third Empire* (London: Arktos, 2012). (*Ed.*).

|40| Arthur Moeller van den Bruck, *Das dritte Reich* (Berlin: Ring, 1923), 22.

For Moeller, conservatism no longer had anything to do with preservation in the strict sense, and most certainly not with reaction; it was rather a matter of the ever-new task of uncovering the vital drives. If anything was to be preserved at all, then it was the stream of life that could as easily be choked by dead forms like silt through being falsely diverted. A conservatism thus understood would finish off liberalism and subsume Left and Right in itself. For this reason, Moeller originally wanted to call his book *Der dritte Standpunkt* (*The Third Position*). Perhaps, under the influence of his young friend Boehm, he decided upon the title *Das Dritte Reich*. But this title is curiously disconnected from the book's content, even though in the final chapter, he does speak of the need for Germany to fight for its "Final Reich."

Das Dritte Reich became, following Moeller's early death, the "Bible of all who worked from the Right for a renewal of political life and of the nation." In regard to this renewal, Moeller had preferred to speak of revolutionary conservatism, while Hofmannsthal expressly made use of the concept "Conservative Revolution," thus displacing the emphasis from the dynamic to the static aspect. But the poet also placed the search for a new synthesis in the tradition of that German cast of mind, the origin of which lay in Romanticism and which has been making the ever-renewed attempts to realize a "Conservative Revolution" since the 19th century.

The conception formulated here, that "life is only worth living because of valid bonds,"[41] might be characterized as the conservative credo, and the self-perception of the Conservative Revolutionaries could go so far as to assert a history of conservative decline lasting throughout the entire 19th century and ending only with themselves. The war and collapse of the old order allowed nihilism—that had been present since the Enlightenment, but remained hidden behind the conservative backdrop—to step forward. Only a man with true

---

|41| Hofmannsthal. Hugo von, *Das Schrifttum als geistiger Ratum der Nation* (München: Bremer Presse, 1927), 30.

conservative convictions, who saw through both the illusions of progress and the frailties of the old system, could counter this form of nihilism. What characterized this type was a special mentality that could only be expressed in paradoxes. Early on, Thomas Mann spoke of the "will to fitness for the world" (*Welttauglichkeit*); less happy was the formula "skeptical enthusiasm"; "political realism" was unclear; convincing, finally, was "heroic realism."

The adherents of the Conservative Revolution differed from the older conservatism on the assumption that the bonds, in which the conservative man wanted to live, were yet to be created. In their readiness to found anew "the existing order from the *nomos*"—i.e., to refound the nation's law of life, but to preserve "awe before the inviolable"—they distinguished themselves from the goals of every form of totalitarianism. These distances they preserved did not stop the Conservative Revolutionaries from also seeing themselves as the *avant-guard* of a "new, greater Right" that would integrate the remains of Wilhelmianism and radical mass movements.

5

THE GROUPS THAT CONSTITUTED THE CONSERVATIVE REVOLUTION

5.1 FIRST GROUP: THE VÖLKISCH

In the early postwar period, the *völkische* Bewegung was one of the most commonly used collective terms for various groups within the Conservative Revolution. Yet, the *völkisch* themselves gradually grew distant from the philosophical core of revolutionary conservatism, and, by the end of the decade, hardly anyone would have considered these to be equivalent terms. The causes of this rift lay in the continual infighting in this camp, in the age of its protagonists, in the peculiar rigidity of their ideologists, and in the loss of that "elementary character" that benevolent observers had long granted them.

These factors also help explain why *völkisch* organizations, after the great boom they experienced in the immediate postwar period, sank back into insignificance. Many groups that achieved considerable influence in the revolutionary period were unable to thrive without that soil to nourish them, and carried on a meager existence. Allgemeiner Deutscher Verband still existed, but never recovered the prominence it enjoyed in the prewar years. The Deutschvölkischer Schutz- und Trutzbund (German Nationalist Protection and Defiance Federation) ubiquitous during 1919-1920, fell apart under state pressure. Smaller organizations like the Reichshammerbund (Reich Hammer League)— that had merged into it—reorganized itself after it was banned, but remained insignificant.

All of this was caused by losing all hope for a second, "true" revolution and the predominance of their "negative program." As in the Wilhelmine period, the *völkisch* failed to make their positive goals sufficiently clear. The struggle against Catholicism and Freemasonry—but, above all, their collection of anti-Semitic demands—became less attractive, as the Republic stabilized and the demand for scapegoats diminished. The idea that "all great political events of the last decades are the work of the Jews"[42] had a recognizably delusional character. That said, the assumption of a Jewish-Communist conspiracy—or the "stab in the back" that caused the German defeat—had an increasingly large constituency. It was of central importance for the organs of the *völkische* Bewegung, such as the *Deutsche Zeitung (German Times)* or *Der Reichswart (The Reich Guardian)*, which were widely circulated.

If rigidity can explain the limited effect of the *völkisch* philosophy, it also served as a very strong factor favoring internal integration. This applies especially to the *völkisch*-religious faction, which experienced a lasting shift of its philosophical foundations after the war through the rollback of the German Christian element by the neo-pagan element. Whereas a Germanized Christianity was considered the only tolerable version of *völkisch* religiosity before the First World War—there were scarcely more than 200 consistent pagans at that time—the separation

---

|42| Fritsch, Theodor, "Nachwort" in *Die Zionistischen Protokolle* (Leiptzig: Hammer, 1933), 78.

of Church and state after the collapse made an open break with Christianity simpler.

This new development was all the more surprising for the German-Christian groups in that the war meant an extraordinary boom for their position. From "war theology," with its invocation of the Lord of Hosts, who had little to do with Yahweh Zebaoth and much with the Nordic Thor, to the ideal (widespread in the Jugendbewegung) of the "young soldier," whose Christ bore a bright sword, one could certainly get the impression that the "Germanizing of Christianity" was making progress. Yet the Protestant pastor Arthur Bonus, who coined this expression, already explained in an 1895 essay:

> It is immaterial whether our formula says "modernizing" of Christianity or "Germanizing." For us, a more modern form of Christianity can only be a more German from, a more German form of Christianity will itself be more modern.[43]

And:

> I shall expressly leave undiscussed whether that, which issues from the process of recreation, will still be Christianity, because this is wholly indifferent.[44]

Affected by the war, Bonus definitively broke away from the Church's teachings and declared the idea of the unique revelation of God in Christ no longer acceptable. Bonus thus took a step that a whole series of Protestant pastors followed. Under the influence of liberal Protestantism, these pastors carried out a relativizing and historicizing of the Christian doctrine that in the end left nothing

---

|43| Bonus, Arthur, *Zur Germanisierung des Christentums*, v. 1 (Jena: Diederichs, 1911), 2..

|44| *Ibid.*

behind. In this context, let us name Wilhelm Teudt, who, like Bonus, came from the circle formed around Friedrich Naumann. With his 1929 book, *Germanische Heiligtümer* (*Germanic Shrines*), he won great influence over the *völkisch*-religious movement. There was also Gustav Frenssen, whose popular novels constantly dealt with questions of faith, whereby the author gradually shifted from being an admirer of a "heroic Jesus" to a believer in Nordic paganism. Professors of Theology Jakob Wilhelm Hauer and Hermann Mandel also belonged to this circle. They, coming from the standpoint of history of religion and systematic theology, respectively, finally broke with Christian teaching. The writings of Hauer and Mandel were published from the beginning of the 1930s and experienced rather widespread dissemination. In them, they explained and justified their change of opinion.

Those who were not prepared to make a complete break from Christianity organized themselves at the end of the war in independent German-Christian groups, such as the League for the German Church founded in 1921, or the League of German Christians, founded in 1925. None of these organizations understood itself as a new Church; instead, they sought a "Christianity in a German mould" and wanted to act as a party within the Church, whose final goal was an ecumenical Reichs-Church.

Fundamentally, this initiative was about eliminating the Old Testament from the canon, segregating Jewish Christians, and demonstrating that the religion of Jesus and the Germanic-Nordic worldview were one and the same, according to the line already laid down by Houston Stewart Chamberlain and continued especially by the Protestant Minister Friedrich Andersen. Andersen was Senior Pastor in Kiel and simultaneously Bundeswart (National Guardian) in the German Church. Already in 1917 he—together with other prominent *völkisch* leaders like Adolf Bartels and Hans von Wolzogen from the Bayreuther Kreis—established "95 Theses for the Reformation Festival." It advocated for a "German Christianity on a purely evangelical basis" as the fulfillment of Luther's work. Although the league succeeded in winning over other prominent members of the German Christian tendency, such as Pastor Max Maurenbrecher and philosopher Max Wundt, its effectiveness remained very limited.

Artur Dinter's sectarian organization, "Spiritually Christian Religious Community," was considerably further removed from the historical form of Protestantism than the League for the German Church or the Christian League. Dinter explicitly considered himself the "perfecter" of the Reformation and offered a curious mixture of Lebensreform, esotericism, and *völkisch* ideology, combined with an obvious polemic against Jews and Catholics. His attempt to create a German National Church on the basis of the gospel as restored by him clearly failed. Thus, Dinter followed the path of establishing an entirely independent organization; and his religious community even appointed its own "National Pastor."

Through his brisk and successful activity as author, which early on included scurrilous anti-Semitic novels, Dinter achieved a measure of recognition. His hybrid self-image, however, led not only to lasting conflicts with Hitler—Dinter was a Nazi Gauleiter in Thuringia 1925-8, until his removal and expulsion from the party—but also hindered the spread of his ideas even within the confines of the *völkische* Bewegung. This was so even though many may have shared Dinter's ideas. But the always-potent chaotic element within this current meant that objective thought proximity was perceived as a threat and competition, and, in any case, was all the more combatted. This explains the extraordinary vehemence of Dinter's polemic against Dietrich Klagges, National Socialist Gauleiter of Braunschweig, who, like himself, had attempted to distill an "original gospel" and who, like himself, propagated a German Christianity (but who trod a beaten path because of his submission to Party doctrine).

Although the Federal Church Council as the leadership committee of the Evangelical Church considered it necessary to hold a debate on the German-Christian tendency in 1931, this should not deceive us as to its practical lack of influence. The umbrella organization, the German Christian Association of Greater Germany, founded in 1926, remained without any function, and the German Christians found real support in only a few congregations. This was also due to the strength of forces favorable to the general *völkisch* tendency within traditional Protestantism. On theological grounds, these traditionalists stood against any form of syncretism that blended faith and race, and just as strongly opposed any acceptance of historical criticism concerning the revealed content of the Bible. On the other hand, they were prepared to go rather far in calling for a new unity of Christianity and nationality (*Volkstum*).

An additional reason for the diminished significance of the German Christians over the course of the 1920s was undoubtedly its defensive position against the *völkisch*-religious. Since God had not revealed himself in a victory of German arms, as had been expected during the war, they were forced to go back to cultural Protestant arguments, defending the usefulness of Christianity as a part of German tradition and an indispensable element in the economy of the German soul. As a result, active young members inevitably got the impression of half-measures and wholeheartedly turned to paganism.

Their entry into the already existing *völkisch*-religious groups led variously to marked conflict between generations, new dissention and splintering. Only the Ariosophische Gesellschaft (Society) were relatively unaffected by this. These circles either survived the war (Guido von List Gesellschaft, Ordo Novi Templi, Germanen Orden [Germanic Order]) or were newly founded (Edda Gesellschaft [Society], Ariosophische Gesellschaft, later merged in the Neue Kalandgesellschaft [New Kaland Society]). Along with historical speculation and racial metaphysics, rune magic and *völkisch* astrology (Tyr-Kreis [Tyr Circle]) grew in importance.

Ariosophist books and journals retained a certain influence in the postwar period. New authors, who must be considered part of this trend, such as Josef Strzygowski or Rudolf John Gorsleben, strengthened the camp. Some of their ideas found supporters not only among the *völkisch* but also in the youth leagues, which had fascination primarily with the idea of a mysterious Germanic past. On the whole, however, the Ariosophists, especially the older generation, were disappointed about the neighboring groups' lack of readiness to acknowledge their own preeminence and privileged insight into all of Aryan religion.

Compared with the Ariosophists, the other *völkisch*-religious groups were subject to much stronger change in the 1920s. The oldest organizations of all, the Deutschgläubige Gemeinschaft and the Germanische Glaubens-Gemeinschaft (Germanic Faith Community), lost importance. Their leaders had no shortage of high-flying plans— for instance, Fahrenkrog's proposal for a German Cathedral, for which the small North Hessian municipality of Witzenhausen had already contributed a plot of land—but were short of the support and enthusiasm necessary to realize their project.

The change in generations led not only to new forms of expression in worship and customs (folk songs, folk dances), new formations also arose that made a real impression on the entire movement. In 1924, the Orden der Nordungen (Order of Nordungs) split off from Deutschgläubige Gemeinschaft. In 1927 they lost most of their members to the Nordische Glaubensgemeinschaft (Nordic Faith Community) founded by Norbert Seibertz and Wilhelm Kusserow, which, however, soon fell victim to splintering and refoundings. Although organizational and personal disputes were the most important factor in these events, the labeling of both groups as "Nordic" also reveals a shift in emphasis. Once again, the significance of the "racial" aspect and common Germanic orientation had grown.

On the whole, the spiritual impulse found in the Orden der Nordungen and the Nordische Glaubensbewegung (Nordic Faith Movement) hardly offered anything new. Here as well appeared the old division into occultists (especially among the Nordungen, who also took the organization into lodges) and the strongly rationalist Naturgläubige, Nature Worshipers (mainly in the Nordische Glaubensgemeinschaft). An essential difference from the teachings of the Deutschgläubige Gemeinschaft and the Germanische Glaubens-Gemeinschaft lay, however, in the emphasis placed on the equal rights of women (their oppression being considered the result of Jewish-Christian alienation) and in their belief in polytheism.

Up to this time, the *völkisch*-religious had displayed much ingenuity trying to demonstrate the original monotheism of the Germanics. They remained so strongly bound to the world of the 19th century, with its ideas of "progress" and "development," that it seemed unthinkable to expose their adherence to Christianity by "reverting" to polytheistic "barbarism." The prospect now changed entirely. Belief in a plurality of gods was now emphasized as an expression of pagan tolerance. A text from this time states:

> *Germanic paganism was not founded on a father religion in the sense of the Semitic, Christian, and Mohammedan teachings, and the Father of All is a later, futile attempt at alignment with Christian teaching. In the North, we constantly encounter generative god-couples. Confusion and decline first came to our people with the penetration and autocracy (under the threat of death) of the Semitic Sky God.[45]*

The Nordische Glaubensgemeinschaft was originally planned as a merging of all the *völkisch*-religious. In 1931, along with the NG, the Germanische Glaubens-Gemeinschaft and the Nordungs united to establish the Nordisch-Religiöse Arbeitsgemeinschaft (Nordic Religious Consortium). But all groups retained their organizational independence; the membership was extremely small and cannot have

---

|45| Hildulf R. Flurschütz, *Neugeburt nordischen Naturglaubens* (Berlin: Selbstverl, 1928), 15.

surpassed a few hundred. Because of later political developments, the Nordisch-Religiöse Arbeitsgemeinschaft never even achieved the status of a functioning umbrella organization.

The only formation in this camp that managed to achieve a certain numerical significance was seldom recognized by the other *völkisch-religious* as a peer. Erich Ludendorff's

Tannenbergbund (League), TB, which went public on September 7, 1925 ("Sedan Day"), originally championed no religious goals. Ludendorff organized this grouping as a kind of spiteful response to his defeat in the Presidential election that year and to his falling out with Hitler shortly afterward. Still convinced he was called upon to be Germany's savior, he won over a number of former high-ranking officers attracted to the

ERICH LUDENDORFF

idea of creating a core for the coming German national movement with himself as the leader. His considerable personal prestige led to the TB having 40,000 members by 1927. Ludendorff was unable, however, to integrate these heterogeneous elements. By the end of 1927, the process of members leaving the TB for the National Socialists was under way. Ludendorff lost his most talented colleague, Konstantin Hierl, as a result. In September of 1930, against his stated will, the TB's Frontkriegerbund (Frontline Fighters League) called for supporting Hitler at the polls.

Along with his obvious lack of political leadership abilities, it was, above all, dogmatic narrowness that lead to Ludendorff's growing isolation. After his 1926 marriage to Mathilde von Kemnitz, who exerted an intellectual influence on him, Ludendorff increasingly concentrated on conspiracy theories and the battle against "supra-governmental forces," whose perfidious

MATHILDE LUDENDORFF

plans sought the destruction of the German nation through "world revolutionary finance-Bolsheviks."

Ludendorff expressly included churches, and particularly the Catholic Church, among these supranational forces. This emphasis was unusual, even for the *völkisch* camp, when he stated in an essay entitled *Rom-Priester als Bolschwisten* (*Roman Priests as Bolsheviks*): "Not the 'Marxists', but Rome and Judah are the ones principally responsible." The view that there was essentially no difference between Catholicism and Jewry ran through Ludendorff's entire, increasingly manic-sounding, polemics. He offended a considerable part of his followers, but also brought a small number to draw the same conclusions as the General himself and leave the Church. For these people, the "German *Volk*" was founded in 1928 to be their own organization within the Tannenberg League.

This could not really diminish the distance between the *völkisch*-religious camp and Ludendorff. His wife's "German theosophy," constructed upon popularized natural science and religious speculation, rejected *a priori* any rapprochement with other groups not because of their foreignness—the primary opposition between the "alien faith" and "blood-conditioned faith in God"[46] could perfectly well have been agreed upon—but because of its inventor's intolerance. Moreover, Ludendorff's financial means made it possible to spread his wife's ideas—along with countless books in two in-house newspapers, the *Deutsche Wochenschau* (*German Weekly Outlook*), 1925-29, and *Ludendorffs Volkswart* (*Ludendorff's National Guardian*), 1929-31)—in a way that no one could compete with him. This not only stirred up envy; among the *völkisch*-religious, there was widespread doubt whether questions of faith had any importance for the Ludendorff couple at all. The chief cause of their success as publicists was the struggle against Jewry, Freemasonry, "Jesuitism,"

|46| *Blutmäßige Gottglaube*, i.e., religious faith proper to those of a specific origin. (*Ed.*)

and capitalism along with spreading fanciful tabloid reports about the supposed murder of great Germans (Luther, Lessing, Mozart, and Schiller).

If the *völkisch*-religious appear even from a sympathetic point of view, like "a peculiar confusion of strange men, communities, and

efforts" (which they were), this should not lead us to infer the poverty of interwar *völkisch*-religious ideas as such. We have already mentioned in connection with the German Christian groups that there were significant individual representatives of this school of thought, as well as that of the neo-pagans. These persons, however, had good reasons to avoid entering the subcultural milieu of the *völkisch*-religious organizations. Along

LUDWIG KLAGES

with the above named Hauer and Mandel, we must mention the philosophers Ernst Bergmann and Ludwig Klages. The sharpness, with which Klages repeatedly spoke against certain fundamental *völkisch* ideas, makes it difficult to include him in this context. Yet, on the other hand, his ideas and those of his followers had considerable influence on the movement as a whole. At least, the title of his principal work, *Der Geist als Widersacher der Seele* (*The Spirit as Adversary of the Soul*), was adopted as a kind of slogan.

Moreover, *völkisch*-religious ideas contributed to the readiness of the educated middle class to accept *völkisch* thought processes in general. The writings of Lagarde and Langbehn still enjoyed wide distribution; the novels of Dahn were printed in large numbers; and best-selling *völkisch* authors of the

ERNST BERGMANN

Wilhelmine period, like Hermann Burte,

continued to exert influence. Younger men such as Gustav Frenssen, Jakob Schaffner, Hans Grimm, Erwin Guido Kolbenheyer, or Hans Friedrich Blunck were among the most successful writers of the 1920s and early 1930s. Their books were often not even considered "political," since they largely suited elevated contemporary taste.

HANS FRIEDRICH BLUNCK	GUSTAV FRENSSEN	ERWIN GUIDO KOLBENHEYER

Although there had been deeply pessimistic opinions in the ranks of the *völkisch* after the end of the war, they held fast to a belief in the race's eternal power of renewal: *finis Germaniae* must not mean *finis Germanorum*. It was also for this reason that the reserve with which Spengler's diagnosis was greeted was so considerable. Chamberlain, for instance, criticized not only Spengler's ignorance of the racial factor, but also that *Decline* was spreading hopelessness. He (and with him the Bayreuther Kreis) insisted that Germany and the Germanic nations were called upon to usher in a new age. For *völkisch* circles, Chamberlain was a sort of "anti-Spengler," and the *Foundations*, even after his death in 1927, went through several new editions. Chamberlain, who joined the Vaterlandspartei during the war, and, after the collapse, went over to the National Socialists very early on, also formulated a domestic program that most of the *völkisch* would have supported. The program included dictatorship, an authoritarian state structure, reorganization of society based on a corporative model, exclusion of Jews from all public offices, and limitation of their economic and social influence.

An important factor favoring the cultural influence of the *völkisch* was also their authors included especially gifted popularizers like Hjalmar Kutzleb or Jörg Lechler. They transposed not so much concrete religious or political ideas as *völkisch* historical thought, which worked with a core set of interpretations. In the Weimar period, these interpretations were practically a general possession of the Right, but especially of the Conservative Revolution. This *völkisch* historical thought shared certain aspects with traditional models of interpretation, especially, the Borussian School of historiography, but leaned toward an anti-statist way of looking at things. That explains its affinities to "Greater German" historiography, but, above all, their proximity to interpretations widespread in the Deutsche Bewegung and later among the protagonists of democracy and liberalism in the 19th century. Only the knowledge of these roots allows one to understand why most *völkisch* writers positively viewed the origins of German history under Saxon rulers, but saw the unfolding of power under the Hohenstaufens negatively; why they sympathized with humanism, the Reformation, and rebellious peasants, but, at the same time, regretted the failure of the latest attempts at reform; why they considered the Peace of Westphalia a disaster, but the revolt of Brandenburg-Prussia—legitimate; why they celebrated Bismarck's founding of the Reich, whereas, at the same time, they called for the work to be completed in a Greater German State.

The question of origins remained more important for the *völkisch* than an overall image of history. And whereas one can find quite a few departures from the model of history sketched above, on this point, all reflections were subject to one basic dogmatic assumption: the "superiority of the Germanic race." Already at the end of the 19th century, *völkisch* authors developed a variant of the "diffusion theory" (also often found elsewhere), according to which all culture had a common origin and had been spread across the earth by identifiable "carrier groups." In Gobineau, we already see this idea connected with the assertion that the "Aryans" were this carrier group. However, it was the intensive debate about the original homeland of the Indo-Germansß that first lead to the solidification of this train of thought. While most scholars accepted the first location in Asia, the *völkisch* saw this as an unacceptable attack on the dignity of their ancestors and asserted a Nordic origin. In his 1891 book, *Tuisko-Land: der arischen Stämme und Götter Urheimat* (*Tuisko-Land: The Original Homeland of*

GUSTAF KOSSINNA

the Aryan Tribes and the Gods, Ernst Krause (under the pseudonym Carus Sterne) developed the thesis— to great acclaim— that the Aryans inhabited the polar region before the Ice Age and only afterward reached Europe and the other continents in long migrations. The conviction that the North, and thus Scandinavia and a greater part of Germany, comprised some of the original homeland of the Indo-Germans—and that the Germans as the principal Germanic nation were thus autochthonous—may have been more important than such speculations.

Practically all *völkisch*-oriented presentations of prehistory—from Gustaf Kossinna to Ludwig Wilser and beyond—adhered to the "Nordic" thesis. Since the 1920s, Hans F. K. Günther, in particular, linked this concept more closely with the results of racial anthropology and tried—in widely distributed books—to prove that Nordic blood was, if not exclusively, then at least mainly responsible for great cultural creations. The nordische Bewegung (Nordic Movement), co-initiated by Günther, not only aimed at a closer cultural connection to the Scandinavian countries; it also sought to Nordicize the German population, threatened by racial mixture, by eugenic measures and the exclusion of Jews from the national community. Along with Günther, Ludwig Ferdinand Clauss, a "racial-psyche researcher," Berhard Kummer, a *völkisch*-religious theoretician, and author Hans F. Blunck exercised decisive influence on the nordische Bewegung. Here as well, we must not conclude from the limited ability of the Nordische

Gesellschaft (Nordic Society), founded 1921, to exercise influence that the corresponding lines of thought were also without influence. The central element of these was the "yearning for the North," which, since Romanticism, was among the most stable factors in German thought.

A rather remarkable variant of the idea of the Nordic origin of all culture was the assertion of a "Nordic Atlantis." Helmuth Wirth was

LUDWIG FERDINAND CLAUSS

undoubtedly one of the most important representatives of this concept. He believed that the "white wedge" of the Nordic race originated in today's polar region, and that this "ruling and culture-bearing stratum" had, since Noah's flood or the quaternary age, migrated to all the coastal regions of the Atlantic Ocean in order to found new civilizations. Wirth was probably strongly influenced by the so-called *Ura-Linda Chronicle*, a forged Friesian manuscript of the 19th century that also included the tradition of an early Germanic "Atland."

Other *völkisch* authors, such as Karl Georg Zschaetzsch, Albert Herrmann, and Heinrich Pudor, expressed comparable opinions. They considered Helgoland a remnant of the submerged Atlantis. Moreover, Atlantis played a considerable role, by means of Ariosophy, for authors such as Peryt Shou, Hermann Wieland, Rudolf John Gorsleben, Herbert Reichenstein and the inventor of the "World Ice Theory," Hans Hörbiger. On the other hand, the astrological hypotheses of a rebirth of Atlantis through "vril," the "original cosmic power," were rather marginal.

The ideas presented here may appear bizarre, and the number of their adherents must not be overestimated. Yet undoubtedly the influence of Wirth and others clearly spanned beyond sectarian circles. Moreover, one could be quite far removed from any expectation of an

"Atlantid Renaissance" and still consider the "Germanic resurrection" necessary. Based on considerations of a "racial hygiene"—approved by many doctors, anthropologists, and biologists to settlement projects— there was a broad repertoire of attempts to apply these ideas practically. Geopolitics, too, which blossomed after the war under the leadership of Karl Haushofer and his school, belongs in this context, although spatial and racial thought were never quite congruent. *Völkisch* ideas in a wider sense influenced artistic projects of the 1920s, where we might least of all expect such a background. The "Atlantis House," constructed by the Bremen patron of the arts Ludwig Roselius in the Boettcherstrasse, was expressly indebted to Wirth's ideas in its symbolism. The Folkwang Museum, opened in Essen by Karl Ernst Osthaus, a promoter of Henry van de Velde and modern art in general, not accidentally bore the name of a palace of the Germanic god of springtime, Freya. The stately buildings of the Hamburg architect Fritz Höger, including the famous Chile House, were conceived as expressions of the "Nordic" spirit.

One must not be misled in other respects by the whimsical traits of the *völkisch* worldview. The groups consciously used all contemporary methods of propaganda. Some of the publishing houses closest to the *völkische* Bewegung, including J. F. Lehmann in Munich, reached—with a combination of irreproachable technical literature (in the field of medicine, in their case) and ideological publications—a public much larger than the narrow *völkisch* circle. Even archaeophilia could accompany the use of privately produced films and slide shows. The *völkisch* clearly understood the necessity of these media to form the raw material of the "*Volk.*" It did

**JULIUS FRIEDRICH
LEHMANN**

not shake their faith that it was only possible to restore the alienated Germans to themselves by luring, convincing, or forcing them "to start all over."

5.2 SECOND GROUP: THE JUNGKONSERVATIVEN

The term Jungkonservativen, "young conservative," arose immediately after the end of the war, paralleling the combination of "conservative" and "revolutionary." It was accepted slowly, however. Only in the second half of the 1920s were those groups regularly called "young conservative" that represented a "rejection of the mass- and party-states of West European democracy, social renewal along corporative lines, independent, responsible, and personal leadership in political life, the struggle against the Versailles Treaty, and the so-called fulfillment politics."[47]

Among all the currents of the Conservative Revolution, the Jungkonservativen were the most influential. Their connection to the literary and artistic world, important personalities in government, the military, and business explain some of their impact. There was no Jungkonservativ Partei (Young Conservative Party), however; forming discussion circles around various journals and their leading contributors was more typical. These also had access to the larger organs of the Right (*Deutsche Allgemeine Zeitung* or *Tag*), but they primarily benefitted from relationships with the most influential publishing houses that can be ascribed to the Conservative Revolution (Hanseatische Verlagsanstalt, Langen-Müller, and Diederichs).

Gewissen, the journal that was so important for the origin of the Jungkonservativen camp, had to get by without such support. Instead, it had a certain organizational backing from the Juni-Klub (June Club), founded in the spring of 1919. If Moeller was the "secret King"

---

[47] MaxHildebert Boehm, "Jungkonservative," letter to Brockhaus, in *Grosser Brockhaus*, v. 9 (Leipzig: Brockhaus, 1930), 512.

of the *Juni-Klub*, then Heinrich von Gleichen was his "Chancellor." One reason for the growing influence of both not only on the club but on *Gewissen*, was Eduard Stadtler's frequent absences, giving lectures across the entire Reich and being only nominally its editor. Another cause lay in Stadtler's conception oriented toward agitation and day-to-day politics. The club and the journal were not the proper forum for the latter, and Moeller and von Gleichen were more interested in clarifying questions of principle.

The ideas about the regenerating community put forward both in the Juni-Klub and in *Gewissen* corresponded to many *topoi* of cultural criticism that developed since the end of the 19th century. They were

confident enough to declare themselves the heirs of all valuable ideas in conservatism, liberalism, and socialism and to reject any suspicion that they sought the restoration of previously existing conditions. Rather, "formal democracy" was to be replaced by a "national democracy" characterized, with an explicit appeal to Spengler, as "Prussian socialism," elsewhere as "organic" or "German socialism."

EDUARD STADTLER

Despite reservations about counter-revolutionary and national-revolutionary endeavors, the circle around *Gewissen* was firm in maintaining that the existing system would collapse and bury both liberalism and Marxism beneath it. It was difficult to say precisely, however, who would be the subject of the overthrow, among whom the "social revolution as national revolution" was to take place. One imaginable model for the construction of a new type of revolutionary formation might have been fascism. But only after the March on Rome was any interest taken in or benevolence shown toward the Italian movement by those close to *Gewissen*. Moeller's formula "*Italia docet*" can only be understood in light of the interpretation of fascism dominant in this circle, namely, as a kind of continuation of the *Risorgimento* by other—contemporary—means.

In any case, the combination of "revolution from above" and "revolution from below," successfully practiced by Mussolini, seemed promising to the members of the Juni-Klub. They speculated successively about the commissarial dictatorship of Noske, then of Stinne. In the autumn of 1923, von Gleichen visited Munich several times in order to hold talks with Gustav von Kahr, to whom many looked for a "March on Berlin." After its failure, all eyes were on Hans von Seeckt, at least for a short time, when executive power was transferred to the German Army in November of 1923.

After all these hopes were shattered and the Republic, contrary to all expectations, stabilized, there was a crisis in the Juni-Klub. Obviously, a "heroic democracy"—that wanted to rise up under the black flag against its liberal oppressors—did not exist. The forces in Der Ring (The Ring)—which, like von Gleichen, hoped for a classic statist solution to the political crisis and preferred stricter metapolitical work—now gained influence. The group that was "young conservative" in the stricter sense—the term appeared in *Gewissen* on October 29, 1923 for the first time—already had, by founding the political college, a kind of training school for the right-wing intelligentsia. *Die Neue Front*, a volume edited by von Gleichen, Moeller, and Boehm (referred to in the pages of *Gewissen* as "the book of our movement") established a clear programmatic accent. The fact that Stadtler was among the contributors, but not the editors of *Neuer Front*, was probably an early sign of the distance between a more "young national" and a more "young conservative" wing.

The content of the new term "Jungkonservativen" was strongly determined by the new definition of "conservative" that Moeller van den Bruck had formulated in his book *Das Dritte Reich*. Despite the great influence Moeller exercised, the Ring movement lacked homogeneous unity. Along with ideological differences, generational differences also played a role. Von Gleichen belonged to the older group that could exercise greater influence merely because of its social position. In an article for the 28th issue of *Gewissen* (July 14, 1924) entitled "Upper Stratum and Leadership," von Gleichen not only introduced a change of course in respect of Young Nationals like Stadtler, but also marked a shift away from social-reform tendencies. *Gewissen* was no longer to rely on mobilizing the masses, but on "assembling the elite." They promoted a line that Walther Schotte, one of von Gleichen's new confidantes, later formulated in the following way, "We are political, but are not engaging in politics."

To this consciously elitist "conservatism of personalities" corresponded the idea that one must find "an exemplary German solution to the fundamental problem of all politics," namely, "how the masses can be excluded by historically justified, politically limited force." Heinz Brauweiler, one of the leading theorists of the corporative state, developed a corporative model for *Gewissen*, which, in contrast to earlier ideas, was strongly oriented toward the preservation of private property.

The clearer reorientation of the journal and Ring movement as a whole finally led to an open conflict. The meeting of the Juni-Klub as early as April of 1924 established that there were strong tensions within the organization based on different judgments about what the task of the national opposition should be. Reconciliation between Jungnationalen (Young Nationalists) and Jungkonservativen turned out to be impossible, and the "crisis of the national opposition" ascertained by Stadtler in the summer of 1924 corresponded to a crisis in his own position within *Der Ring*. His contributions to *Gewissen* gradually diminished throughout 1925, and by the end of that year, he lost the leadership of the journal. Thus, von Gleichen's line totally triumphed; he dissolved the *Juni-Klub* and, in its place, founded the Deutscher Herrenclub (German Gentlemen's Club) in November of 1924.

Moeller was the only one in a position to prevent these developments, but for reasons of health, he could no longer intervene.

He suffered a nervous breakdown in the autumn of 1924 and was constantly under doctor's care afterwards. On April 30, 1925, he took his own life. *Gewissen* remained under von Gleichen's leadership until the end of 1928. Already on January 1, 1928, however, the first issue of a new journal entitled *Der Ring* appeared. Shutting down *Gewissen* cannot be satisfactorily explained by the personal and ideological quarrels among its leadership; it was also connected to a change in circumstances. The paper's influence up until the middle of the 1920s had less to do with the regularly exaggerated publication figures (rather than the 10 to 30 thousand copies often estimated by the publishers, the true figures were probably more like four thousand) than with the intellectual influence it exerted. Even Thomas Mann was a subscriber for a time. He wrote to Heinrich von Gleichen in July of 1920: "I have just renewed my subscription to *Gewissen*, a paper that I am always glad to see and that I mention to everyone with whom I discuss politics as incomparably the best German paper."

Political developments left behind the assumption of the Republic's speedy breakdown and did away with the idea of a great national and social balance. Similarly, the time for aan ideological society (*Weltanschauungsgemeinschaft*)[48]—like the Juni-Klub was meant to be—also seemed to have passed. Moeller's elitist demand that *Gewissen* should be the "representative of a spiritual-intellectual Right, a Right which does not even exist yet" hardly seemed convincing after his death and under changed circumstances. Von Gleichen, therefore, based the Herrenclub more clearly on traditional, especially English, models and did so without ideological cohesion. In its place, he sought to create the widest possible catchment area, including, in principle, all of the upper middle class, but, primarily, the nobility insofar as it was oriented between conservatism and liberalism.

Der Ring served as a powerful link between the local societies of the German Herrenclub. Its weekly publication is said to have begun

---

|48| *Weltanschauungsgemeinschaft*. Literally, a "world-view community." (*Ed.*)

with 2,000 copies of each issue, and only with effort managed to increase the figure to 2,300 or 2,500 by 1931. The figure may have risen to 6,000 only during the von Papen era. What *Der Ring* lacked in brilliance and surprising *volt faces* as compared to *Gewissen*, von Gleichen tried to make up for with ideological consistency and the building up a solid base of contributors. Along with Boehm and Schotte, the most important contributors were Hans Bogner, Karl Eschweiler, Julius Evola, Edgar Jung, Leonore Kühn, Karl Christian von Loesch, Heinrich Rogge, Friederich Schmid Noerr, Wilhelm von Schram, and Ferdinand von Stumm. Von Gleichen was also concerned with overcoming the notorious mindlessness of an organized party-political conservatism. This conservatism suspected little or nothing of the intellectual assistance that the intellectual life of the nation offered even before the war that it preferred to ignore. This "assistance" meant the impulses that came from art (Stefan George and his circle) as well as Lebensreform (Jugendbewegung). Above all, von Gleichen wished to point to Moeller, whose Young Conservatism had overcome the Old Conservative *attentisme*[49], as well as the senile philosophy of cultural pessimism so prevalent in the postwar years.

In view of this conception of conservatism, it only made sense for the Ring movement to reject "organological" total systems as well as restorationist concepts. The tradition, on which they wanted to rely, reached back into the 19th century, but only in terms of the current, whose origins are to be sought in Romanticism and Prussian Reform. Baron von Stein was explicitly taken as a model. Many contributions that dealt with clarifying the essence of the conservative worldview took the position of claiming the mission of refounding the state and wanted to renew the classical conservative *topoi*: structure, responsibility of the elites toward the divine and natural law, defense of the people as the reference point of political order, recognition of social evolution when this is consistent with the laws of "life."

|49| An opportunistic wait-and-see attitude. (*Ed.*)

Insofar as the Ring strove for the "regeneration of a truly conservative Right," only the DNVP came into consideration as a possible partner for negotiation. Their attitude toward the new party leader, Alfred Hugenberg, was, however, ambivalent. Von Gleichen understood how to prevent him from influencing the Ring or the Herrenclub, which resulted, in turn, in Hugenberg (who already had negative experiences in the financing of the Juni-Klub) denying any further support.

The Ring wanted, above all, never to submit to *raison de parti.* This explains their brusque turn against German Nationalists when this party—together with the Stahlhelm and National Socialists—agitated against the Young Plan[50] and did not shrink from attacking Reichspresident Paul von Hindenburg. The reason for this behavior lay not only in respect for Hindenburg's person, but was also linked to the consideration of Jungkonservativen of the presidential office as the starting point for a "revolution from above." They did not want to declare themselves "in agreement *per se*" with "the method of calling up the masses, stirring up Acheron." (Already in February of 1929, they stated apodictically "that this system [The Weimar Republic—*Ed.*] was at an end.") The Ring, therefore, advocated extending the powers of the highest political office. In its strengthening, they saw the only possibility for a "constitutional reform in the sense of securing our political life that wants out from between the Scylla of dictatorship and the Charybdis of mob rule." It is hardly unexpected that from the summer of 1930, Carl Schmitt's writings, especially his theory of "Guardians of the Constitution," was repeatedly attested in favor of this concept (of strengthening the presidency—*Ed.*).

The political reform sought by the Ring movement provided for a quasi-monarchical Reichspresident, the disempowerment of the Reichstag along with the formation of a second chamber, a kind of

---

|50| The Young Plan of 1929 was a program for Germany to pay World War I reparations following the Dawes Plan of 1924. (*Ed.*)

upper house. The equal right to vote was to be replaced by a "plural-vote" system, giving those with responsibility an additional number of votes. Very much in the line of conservative thought was also the clearer separation of state and society, the latter to be protected by a corporative reordering and a strengthening of self-administration bodies.

The orientation toward Hindenburg within the Ring movement contributed to a relative openness toward the Brüning cabinet and the idea of a "constitutional democracy." One reason for this sympathy may have laid in von Gleichen's and Brüning's personal acquaintance from the era of the Juni-Klub. It was probably more important that von Gleichen saw in Brüning (and even more in Kurt von Schleicher) the man who, supported by the president's trust, would be able to carry out a revolution from above.

With certain inevitability, this assessment strengthened their mistrust toward parties they thought unable to constructively solve fundamental political problems. This explains not only the continuing skepticism toward the Deutschnationale Volkspartei, but also the reserve toward all efforts to create new conservative formations. Von Gleichen considered hopeless the attempt to use the secession of a few German Nationalists, due to Hugenberg's confrontational course, in order to form the Volkskonservative Vereinigung (National Conservative Union), later—the Volkskonservative Partei (National Conservative Party), despite the fact—or because of it— they were trying to implement the ideology of his late friend Moeller van den Bruck. Criticism grew once again because of the Popular Conservatives' consistently positive attitude toward the Brüning administration. The Ring already turned against it, because it did not fulfill the hopes they placed in it and, once again, got "stuck on parliamentary birdlime."

Since Moeller's death, the Ring greatly distanced itself from his ideas not only in regard to domestic and social policy but also on foreign policy. There, a desired Eastern orientation, even a tactical alliance with the Soviet Union, played an important role. The group still opposed *"doctrinaire-alliance* politics" and considered winning back German sovereignty as the most important goal, but, in fact, was more inclined to a Western orientation. Even if they considered the *rapprochement* with Great Britain favored by Brüning to be illusory, a compromise with Germany's "hereditary enemy" France seemed possible. The relations between the two nations, however, should be placed on an entirely new basis of forming a "Western Front" against Bolshevism in order to overcome purely negative anti-Versailles politics. Concessions expected from Paris for such a turnabout were considerable, since it amounted, in fact, to their abandonment of Poland as France's satellite in the East.

In comparison to *Gewissen*, questions of foreign policy played a subordinate role for *Der Ring*. Domestic politics came to the forefront precisely in the final phase of the Weimar Republic. Thus, von Gleichen stated *à propos* of nationalist agitation against the Young Plan:

> From the standpoint of conservative politics, we must wish success on the holding of a referendum, so that the crisis of a bad system may be intensified, and the path cleared for responsible leadership to give to the people what belongs to the people and obtain for the state what belongs to the state.[51]

The desired "crisis" did not, however, lead to the emergence of the conservative "man of the people" from whom one hoped a turnaround. Rather, by sharpening the political situation following the "earthquake victory" of the National Socialists in the Reichstag elections of September 14, 1930, the question arose whether the sought crisis, in fact, tended toward healing, and whether collapse was not to be expected.

|51| *Der Ring* 42 (October 13, 1929): 785.

What seemed to justify the relative optimism of *Der Ring* was the assumption that not only the President but, above all, the Reichswehr allied with the paramilitary organizations could be considered guarantors of the state. Von Gleichen and his collaborators also believed that the von Paper cabinet installed in July of 1932 could carry out a corresponding policy. Especially for Schotte, who was active as an advisor to the Chancellor and wrote a programmatic book called *The New State*, it was evident how strong von Papen's conception agreed with that of *Der Ring*. They shared the government's elitist gesture, provocatively emphasized that they represented the "leading stratum," and that *Der Ring* was "a journal consciously intended for the upper stratum" that maintained relations with the leading authorities in politics, diplomacy, the army, and the economics. There was a certain concern about the insufficiency of the "perl basis" in the government, but this was drowned out by principled approval of the "new state."

The assumption that von Papen's ideas were realizable also relieved von Gleichen from the always-somewhat-agonized refuge among the German Nationalists. Finally, the desired "party-free cabinet" seemed to exist. This cabinet—through a Conservative Revolution—would make the choice between chaos and dictatorship unnecessary and open the way for great constitutional reform. This was an illusion that they were only ready to give up after the events in January of 1933.

Developments in the final phase of the Weimar Republic led also to a *rapprochement* between von Gleichen and some Jungkonservativen dissidents who, after Moeller's death, had not openly broken with the Herrenclub but maintained a certain distance from it. This group found its own political home in the Volksdeutscher Klub (German National Club) and the Jungkonservativen Klub. While the Volksdeutscher Klub gained considerable influence in constructing a network in the political and metapolitical realm through its connections to parliamentarians, administrators, and leaders of Jugendbewegung, but, above all, through its close personal amalgamation with the Deutscher Schutzbund (German Protection League) and the highly influential

Verein für das Deutschtum im Ausland (Union for Germanness Abroad), the Jungkonservativen Klub, which considered itself in many ways the continuation of the Juni-Klub. Originally intended as a recruitment device for the Herrenclub, the Jungkonservativen Klub never succeeded in attracting a large membership. It is all the more remarkable that Edgar Julius Jung—the only representative of the Jungkonservativen who might have been in a position to take Moeller's place—appeared in its ranks.

Following his completion of secondary school, Jung took up the study of law in Lausanne, but returned to Germany when the war broke out. He volunteered, was deployed to the Western front, later served in the German Air Force, and was discharged with the rank of Lieutenant following the German collapse. He completed his studies by 1922 at the Universities of Würzburg and Heidelberg, but at the same time actively participated in the hostilities that followed the end of the war. He joined the Freikorps Epp, which helped to overthrow the Bavarian Soviet Republic. After the occupation of his native Palatinate region by the French troops, he formed a secret organization, the Rheinisch-Pfälzischen Kampfbund (Rheinish Palatinate Combat League), which in January of 1924 carried out the assassination of Franz Josef Heinz-Orbis, president of the separatist Palatinate Republic. Because of his involvement, Jung had to flee to Bavaria—where, however, no prosecution of him was undertaken, since the authorities had accused Heinz of high treason and considered his shooting an act of political self-defense.

Jung settled in Munich as an attorney. He had earlier found a political home in the Deutsche Vaterlandspartei. Following the conclusion of the treaty of Locarno[52], he distanced himself from the National Liberals and gradually lost all interest in political activity. He saw his place where the "spiritual preconditions of a German rebirth were being created."

---

[52] Postwar territorial settlement (1925) between Weimar Germany, WWI victors, and new Central and Eastern European states.

In the mid-1920s, Jung joined the conservative-club movement and quickly became the most important programmatic thinker within this school of thought. For him, the "conservative revolutionary principle" presupposed the existence of metaphysically justified, supra-individual values as the basis of all community:

> *The impulse to preserve these [values] at any price can be called "conservative." Insofar as previous generally valid value judgments are apt to engender a false attitude toward these highest values, we are in favor of a 'revaluation of all values.' If this revaluation is synonymous with an overthrow of all things, then we might be called revolutionary. Our justification is: that one must, from the deepest will to preservation—destroy.*[53]

These statements come from a book that made Jung famous overnight. It appeared in 1927 under the clearly Nietzschean title *Die Herrschaft der Minderwertigen* (*The Rule of the Inferior*). This formulation already signalized that the work was fundamentally a critique of parliamentarism and democracy. During his student years in Lausanne, Jung had attended Vilfredo Pareto's lectures; Pareto's idea of the circulation of elites had strongly influenced him. Later he studied Robert Michels and Alexis de Tocqueville intensively. In the development of the Weimar Republic

OTHMAR SPANN

Jung saw his assumption confirmed that "liberalism" was in no

---

|53| Jung, Edgar. *Die Herrschaft der Minderwertigen* (Deutsche Rundschau: Berlin, 1927), 52.

position to create a political system that could satisfactorily solve the problem of selecting the leadership stratum. In his opinion, the equalizing produced by the "ideas of 1789" as well as by the objective tendencies of industrialization led to the incompetent—the "inferior"—taking the lead and destroying any great order.

Die Herrschaft der Minderwertigen was not, however, merely cultural criticism using Spengler as a starting point; Jung also intended it as an encyclopedia of the counter-Enlightenment, as a foundation for "a new conservative ideology." In three hundred pages, he attempted to make as comprehensive an analysis as possible of all portions of social life and to outline the necessary changes. But he seems to have quickly sensed a certain insufficiency to his own presentation. For this reason, he reworked the first version of *Die Herrschaft* over the following two years and published the second edition in 1930, which had nearly doubled in size. More significant than the increase were the substantive changes that Jung had made. If he had spoken in 1927 of the need for a "new nationalism," now the "Reich idea" stood at the center of his political conception: "a new order, starting with the Central, Near Eastern, and Near South-Eastern region and from there continuing to the outer boundaries, in the form of a league of European nations." Jung had come to the view that one could not merely keep Germany in mind, and that not the "Jacobin nation" but the "*Volk*" must be the basis for new political formations on the continent. With different motives than von Gleichen but with a similar conclusion, Jung expressed skepticism about the idea of "organic democracy" as originally favored by the Jungkonservativen and turned instead toward the idea of an "authoritarian state."

These ideas were clearly influenced by the "universalism" developed by the Austrian philosopher and economist Othmar Spann. From Spann, Jung also took the ideas of "estate" and "cooperative," along with the conception of a "weighted franchise." He combined corporativism with the conviction, inspired by Leopold Ziegler and Nikolai Berdyayev, that a "new Middle Ages" would succeed Enlightened modernity as a consequence of the Conservative Revolution, which would "erect God a new altar."

When the second edition of *The Rule* appeared, the Weimar Republic was already in its death agony. It was happening too early, in Jung's opinion, who watched concernedly as events came thick and fast, and forced their way toward a point that had nothing in common with the ideas of revolutionary conservatism. The expectation that Brüning would delay the catastrophe long enough for their own forces to form was dashed as quickly as the early optimism that Jung harbored in view of the "national conservatives (Volkskonservativen). He could neither realize his claim to a leading position within the framework of the new party nor the idea of transforming it into a "conservative-revolutionary" movement. His strong reservations—shared by all Jungkonservativen—against parties only temporarily receded behind the need to organize a political force.

Prior to this goal, all of Jung's efforts ultimately failed, even though he felt himself called to great tasks and was inspired with "burning ambition." One of his closest friends, Rudolf Pechel, even

RUDOLF PECHEL

perceived "daemonic" traits in him. Pechel was publishing the *Deutsche Rundschau (German Outlook)* since 1919, which, next to *Gewissen* and *Der Ring,* was among the most important Jungkonservativen organs, but functioned more as a forum than as a programmatic journal. Pechel regularly opened the *Rundschau's* pages to Jung and also released *Die Herrschaft der Minderwertigen* in his publishing house. He was among the most influential minds in the network of the right-wing intelligentsia of the Weimar Republic, and gave Jung access to contacts in the industrial sphere. He did not, however, share Jung's optimism from the beginning of the 1930s that it would be possible to exclude the National Socialists, or use them for the ends of the Conservative Revolution.

Jung's estimate of National Socialism was highly ambivalent. Although in his view the NS movement was the "sum of two liberal tendencies," nationalism and socialism, he also considered the NSDAP a resistance movement against the Versailles Treaty and the degeneration of the parliamentary system. Yet the organic state he wished for could hardly be created by "popular *condottieri*" (*Volkscondottieri*) such as Mussolini and Hitler. Its realization would require the rule of a real elite.

The question Jung posed was about the source of these forces. He never conclusively answered. He was probably thinking of a commissarial dictatorship based on the president's emergency powers. This also explains his turn toward von Papen. His idea of the "new state," obviously inspired by Jung, remained unrealizable, especially since the leadership of the armed forces declared themselves in December, 1932 unable to maintain a cabinet in the face of the masses.

Although Jung had placed himself several times in the tradition of the idea of revolutionary conservatism developed by Moeller, there were (along with many points of agreement) also clear differences between the two. The greatest may have been the explicit and, over the course of time, more prominent Christian character of Jung's conception of the Reich, which gave him the reputation of being among the representatives of political Catholicism. Although this denominational classification was incorrect, it had a certain plausibility.

In fact, a certain reserve toward the idea of the Reich corresponded to Jung's deeply Protestant-influenced conservatism. Even Moeller, despite the book title *Das Dritte Reich*, was concerned with the Germans' tendency to live in "ghibelline mystical self-deception." He was inclined to identify the Reich with the state that founded in the positive assessment of the content of the Prussian tradition. In contrast, greater German orientation not only of a part of right-wing Catholicism but even more in Jugendbewegung during the 1920s, contributed to the development of a specific Reich ideology quite substantially.

Among its most important elements—along with the idea of a political union of all Germans and border-area work (*Grenzlandarbeit*)—were reviving the notion of Central Europe and, above and beyond that, the idea of a geopolitically- and historically-based German claim to leadership on the continent. This ideological superstructure received a powerful stimulus. It can be seen also in the significance that the term "New Reich" assumed in the poetry of Stefan George. Several members of the George-Kreis (George Circle) laid a wreath on the grave of the Hohenstaufen Kaiser Freidrich II, whose ribbons bore the inscription: "To its Kaiser and Hero—the Secret Germany." This symbolic act expressed something of the specific pathos that the Reich idea gained at this time, especially when divorced from the identification between Reich and nation and associated with a "Ghibelline" perspective.

The overlap between this sphere of influence and the more specifically Christian sphere was the rule rather than an exception. However, the "anti-secular front" expressed reservations about instrumentalizing religion for purely worldly ends. The concept "anti-secular front" came from Wilhelm Stapel, who was, along with Moeller, von Gleichen, and Jung, the fourth leading figure among the Jungkonservativen of the Weimar Period. Stapel received his doctorate in 1911 with a dissertation in the field of art history. As for his political orientation, he originally leaned toward liberalism, albeit in the special form it had taken in Germany with Friedrich Naumann. In 1911, his idea of the necessary "national-social" equilibrium led him to Ferdinand Avenarius and the Dürer League; a year later, he became editor of Avenarius's journal *Der Kunstwart*—a position he kept until 1917. As a consequence of a quarrel with Avenarius, Stapel followed his long-cherished wish for practical work by assuming leadership of the Hamburger Folksheim, dedicated to the education of working-class youth.

At this point, Stapel had already been in contact with the German National Commercial Employees' Association, who were looking for an editor-in-chief for their new journal, *Deutsches Volkstum* (German

Nationality). In the autumn of 1919, Stapel took over the position. He made the paper, founded two years previously, into the leading organ of the conservative-revolutionary tendency. By this time, he largely shed his older liberal views. Like most Jungkonservativen, however, his attitude to the Republic was somewhat elastic. Far from any thoughts of restoration, he hoped, as Moeller and Stadtler had at first, that the revolution might have a cathartic effect on the nation: it could help organize the future nation-state in the direction of "German socialism." It was his disillusionment about the harsh conditions of the Versailles Treaty and the colorlessness of the new political class that led Stapel into principled opposition.

Many of his thoughts in the 1920s centered upon a critique of "Western" and "formal" democracy, which he, too, wanted to replace with a "national" and "organic" variety. But, in contrast to most Jungkonservativen, Stapel attempted several times a systematic outline for its foundation. His critique of parliamentariansm—as well as the idea of a presidential constitution, graduated suffrage, and corporative representation—stood at the center.

In the crisis of the Weimar Republic, Stapel momentarily thought that the "Popular Conservatives"—he laid claim to the party label— might be suited to realize this program with the help of Brüning (who supported *Deutschesolkstum*). But he was quickly compelled to see that his program possessed no sufficient anchorage among the masses. This led Stapel to a cautious *rapprochement* with the National Socialists. Like many supporters of the Conservative Revolution, he thought it possible to use Hitler's base in order to achieve his own goals; ideologically, he had principled scruples about considering the nation "the ultimate and greatest."

This specific reservation had a Christian, or, more precisely, Lutheran, basis. Although Stapel was no theologian, he studied theological questions intensively and subtitled his principal work, *Der christliche Staatsmann* (*The Christian Statesman*), 1932, with "Eine

Theologie des Nationalismus" ("The Theology of Nationalism"). In contrast both to the idea of an entirely worldly liberal state and the traditional conservative idea of the Christian state, here Stapel developed the vision of a future *Imperium Teutonicum* that—standing in the tradition of the old Reich—would reshape the continent, but also bring his own spiritual principles to bear.

He asserted that the Germans had a special mission based on their "*nomos*," which bestowed upon them the duty to bring a new order to the world. This idea, whose analogy with Israel's claim to chosenness is obvious, also explains Stapel's hostile attitude toward Judaism. In the Jews and their own *nomos*, he saw a metaphysical opponent of Germanness, the only one that could be taken seriously on a fundamental level. Stapel was no biological determinist, however. For a long time he did not wish to doubt that a Jew could join the German *nomos*, but by the end of the 1920s, he championed segregating these two peoples.

Only in April of 1926, after Albrecht Erich Günther joined Stapel in editing *Deutsches Volkstum*, did the quality of the journal, and hence

ALBRECHT ERICH GÜNTHER

its influence, grow perceptibly. Günther was almost 10 years younger than Stapel. His witty essays contrasted clearly with the rather paedogogical sounding expositions of Stapel. Günther published only a very few independent writings, such as the apolitical *Totem: Tier und Mensch im Lebenszusammenhang* (*Totem: Animal and Man in the Context of Life*) and, later, a slim volume entitled *Der Geist der Jungmannschaft* (*The Spirit of the Crew*).

Günther was strongly interested in political practice and believed that a new kind of political movement must be created in order to fight the liberal state and replace it with something better. Immediately following the end of the war, he got in contact with the Hamburger National Communists led by Fritz Wolffheim and Heinrich Laufenberg; later he was in close touch with the circle around the National Revolutionaries Ernst and Friedrich Georg Jünger as well as Ernst Niekisch. At the end of the 1920s, Günther took sides on behalf of Landvolkbewegung until he realized that it, too, was hopeless. His attitude toward National Socialism wavered. In 1931, he refused Rudolf Hess's challenge to himself and Stapel to join the party, but also published a book entitled *Was wir vom Nationalsozialismus erwarten* (*What We Expect from National Socialism*) in the spring of 1932. In this volume, 20 personalities from the Jungkonservativen and National Revolutionary Right explain their attitude to National Socialism which—like that of Günther—mostly amounted to cautious benevolence. Yet Günther still hoped, with the help of the NSDAP, to build that "authoritarian state" that so glaringly contradicted the National Socialist idea of the state. Ultimately, his skepticism seems to have gotten the upper hand. On January 26, 1933, he spoke to Major Erich Marck, one of Schleicher's advisors, to try to convince the Chancellor General that the putsch was necessary as the only way of preventing a National Socialist takeover of the government.

Already in 1924 in a review of Moeller's *Das Dritte Reich*, Stapel expressly affirmed Moeller's view that conservatism and revolution, preservation and change formed a unity, and that all truly revolutionary men had been conservative. And Günther may have succeeded in accurately formulating the Jungkonservativen main concern with his statement that conservatism was not to be understood as "a holding on to what existed yesterday, but as a life based upon what is always valid."[54] In spite of this, it is obvious that within the radius of *Deutsches Volkstum*, at least for polemical reasons, the terms "conservative" and "nationalistic" were interchangeable. Perhaps, the origin of the Deutsche Handwerker Vermittlung (German National Commercial Employees' Association) in the *völkisch* "German National" movement

---

[54] Albrecht Erich Günther, "Wandlung der sozialen und politischen Weltanschauung des Mittelstandes," in *Der Ring* 22 (May 30, 1931): 409.

of the prewar period played a role, but a more important factor may have been that Stapel and Günther wanted to distance themselves from the direction taken by the Berlin Jungkonservativen. Only thus can the fierce polemic against the von Papen cabinet be explained, along with the urgently expressed wish "that Mr. von Papen and his Hugenberg and Herrenclub appendix might clear the field." The above-mentioned "unity" of preservation and renewal could not be attained under existing circumstances, which was decisive for the reserve with which the term "conservative" was used.

With a circulation of between 3,000 and 5,000, *Deutsches Volkstum* was comparable to *Der Ring,* but never wielded similar influence. This

was certainly not because of the journal's quality, which included many prominent minds from the conservative-revolutionary camp among its contributors. These were Günther's brother Gerhard, who also wrote books, Max Hildebert Boehm, Heinz Brauweiler, Heinz Dähnhardt, Hans Grimm, Hans Schwarz, Hjalmar Kutzleb, Gustav Steinböhmer, Hermann Ullmann, and August Winnig. Besides these, there were scholars such as the theologians Hans Asmussen, Emanuel Hirsch, and Karl Berhard Ritter, the historians Hans Bogner and Otto Westphal, along with the jurists Ernst Rudolf Huber and Carl Schmitt. Stapel was in close contact with the latter since the beginning of the 1930s.

If one can observe a certain overlap between Jungkonservativen on the pages of *Deutsches Volkstum,* this goes in spades for *Tat.* Along with the explicit references to Spengler and Moeller van den Bruck, we also find the notion that the National must determine all politics through "class character (*klassenmäßig*) compared to other nations."[55] Founded in 1909 as a monthly publication by the brothers Ernst and August Horneffer, it was originally meant as an independent organ for Nietzscheans and various autonomous religious groups. Only three years later, Eugen Diederichs acquired it, aligning it with his publishing program. Among Lebensreform and broadly *völkisch* journals, *Tat* occupied a special place because of its high quality, but it lacked any larger significance either before or after the World War.

This changed when in October of 1929, Hans Zehrer became its editor. Zehrer volunteered as soon as he turned 18, shortly before the end of the war. Later, he took a role in defeating the Spartacus uprising and in the Kapp Putsch. He left the military early in 1920 and took up the study of medicine and psychology at the University of Berlin. After five semesters, he switched to theology, history, philosophy and economics, finally leaving the university without any degree.

On October 1, 1923, Zehrer joined the *Vossische Zeitung*. As its foreign correspondent since May of 1925, he became one of the most respected journalists of the Weimar years. Up to this point, he took no clear political position. He saw himself as a member of the war generation, and considered the struggle against the Versailles Treaty non-negotiable. Yet his attitude toward the Republic was rather unclear, and a principled opposition to the parliamentary system—undetectable. This changed at the end of the 1920s, when Zehrer came into contact with Diederichs and began his collaboration with *Tat*. Considering his connection with the *Vossische Zeitung* and publisher Ullstein, he did not come out openly until after Diederichs death. Only in October of 1931, after leaving the *Vossische Zeitung*, did Zehrer sign his name as Editor of *Tat*. By then he was already the unchallenged leader of the so-called *Tat*-Kreis (*Tat* Circle). His

---

|55| Eschmann, Ernst Wilhelm, "Die Wandlungen des Nationalen," *Die Tat* 22 (1930): 560.

anti-capitalist, anti-liberal, and anti-parliamentary ideas, his vision of the "third front" besides the previous liberal front—which would carry out national-social reconstruction based upon the middle class and its elite—became the journal's official program.

Zehrer characteristically changed the subtitle of *Tat* from "a monthly for the future of German culture" to "a monthly for shaping a new reality." The unhurried, educational contributions disappeared along with the vestiges of Jugendbewegung. In their place, there appeared massive politization and prophetic air, treatises of dozens of pages long with statistical data, borrowing from modern disciplines such as sociology. The entire publication was bound up with a claim of being able to foresee Germany's further development and solve future problems.

Zehrer attracted a group of contributors. They were personally connected to him and supported his intentions of making *Tat* into an organ of the politically homeless right-wing intelligentsia that did not

WERNER BEUMELBERG

feel as part of the Republic. At the same time, this intelligentsia was not among its enemies to the Right or Left, with the possibility of becoming vectors of the "Conservative Revolution." These included business journalist Ferdinand Friedrich Zimmermann (pseudonym: Ferdinand Fried), educator Horst Grüneberg, military specialist Friedrich Wilhelm von Oertzen, along with the still quite young university assistant Ernst Wilhelm Eschmann (pseudonym: Leopold Dingräve), a disciple of the sociologist Alfred Weber, and Giselher Wirsing, who came from the circle led by economist Carl Brinkmann. Future novelist Carl Rothe was a rather marginal figure. Zehrer also attracted Paul Fechter, Alfred Kantoriwicz, Count Brockdorff-Rantzau, Hans-Joachim Schoeps, Heinrich Hauser, Werner Sombart, Ernst Saemisch, Werner Beumelberg, and Friedrich Sieburg.

The *Tat*-Kreis, in the stricter sense, was formed by Zehrer, Zimmermann, Eschmann, and Wirsing. They essentially contributed to making *Tat* the most important German political monthly publication between 1929 and 1932. Domestically, they set their hopes on the catalytic effect of the Great Depression starting to emerge, which would have to create the conditions for a "total" reordering of Germany. The middle classes were to bear the necessary transformations, thrust into a revolutionary role, because they would otherwise have to fear being crushed between the "masses" and "capital" in a liberal system. Without any precise idea of the state being developed, the future system was characterized as elitist, Caesarist, "national-democratic," to be merely prepared for by a commissarial "dictatorship."

Not by accident, this direction is reminiscent of Carl Schmitt, to whom Zehrer and Grüneberg, especially, referred often. They borrowed his idea that *auctoritas* (the Reichspresident) and *potestas* (the Reichswehr) would "complete the *Volk* community" from above that was already emerging at the base. The new state was to impose the primacy of politics against the supremacy of society, and also be sovereign in respect to the economy. Fried's skepticism toward the free market led to ideas of a corporative system, which he thought of as anti-capitalist and sealed off from the global economy. The "autarchy" he promoted was, however,

| ULRICH BROCKDORFF-RANTZAU | ALFRED KANTORIWICZ | HANS ZEHRER |

not merely meant in the economic sense, since Wirsing—the foreign policy expert of the *Tat*-Kreis—was simultaneously developing a variant of the Central Europe Model popular in Germany. Wirsing was thinking of joining together the states of "inter-Europe" in a federation with "anti-capitalist and anti-imperialist" Germany, and, above all, using the Southeast of the continent as an agrarian resource base for the German industrial state. Fried's theses found support in Wirsing and also by Eschmann's sociological studies. Most notably, he spoke out in favor of a reorganizing society along professional lines, referring to Pareto, Michels, and the experience of fascist Italy.

Between 1929 and 1932, *Tat's* circulation rose from 1,000 to over 30,000 copies. Its impact and the influence of the *Tat*-Kreis derived mainly from their function as a "gathering spot for a younger national movement." In spite of this, their immediate political effectiveness must be judged skeptically. Zehrer's basic thought—the formation of the "third front" from the Strasser wing of the NSDAP, Landvolkbewegung, Churches, Youth Movement, and trade unions—had any prospects of success only in the brief period of Schleicher's government.

The connection between the *Tat*-Kreis and Schleicher[56] and the Reichswehr leadership was built up after 1929 by Oertzen and Hellmuth Elbrecher, who was a dentist at that time. The latter belonged to the wider *Tat*-Kreis, but was long-impaired by the rejection of von Papen, the "representative of the capitalist rump," by Zehrer and his followers. Advisory meetings were probably held between Zehrer and Schleicher; how much influence they may have had is difficult to say. Zehrer's notion—that a "brain trust" could be placed at Schleicher's disposal, and the Chancellor-General thus be led in Zehrer's own direction—proved to be illusory.

|56| Kurt Ferdinand Friedrich Hermann von Schleicher was the 23rd Chancellor of Germany. (*Ed.*)

Although the *Tat*-Kreis was able to earn quite an unusual level of significance for the young generation, it succeeded neither in developing influence on the masses (*Tägliche Rundschau* newspaper, acquired in autumn of 1932, stagnated at 10,000 printed copies) nor in the organizational capture of the "third front" (its readership of 800 or 900 was insufficient for this). *Tat*-Kreis basically failed in the effort to draw in the Left, just as Schleicher had done.

If the Jungkonservative Bewegung has been presented here mainly on the basis of the journals *Gewissen, Der Ring, Deutsche Rundschau, Deutsches Volkstum,* and *Tat,* this is because of the influence exercised by these journals. This is also the case because their leading contributors— Moeller van den Bruck, in many respects, von Gleichen, Jung, Stapel, Günther, Zehrer, and the narrower *Tat*-Kreis—were among the leading figures in this school of thought. Characteristically, the editors of the journals mentioned were all members of the Association of German Periodicals since 1921. This Association also included other organs, such as the *Süddeutsche Monatshefte (South German Monthly),* edited by Cossmann, a journal widely read by the Jungkonservativen. However, because of its close connection with the idea of monarchy, it did not really belong in this domain. Similar remarks apply—if for different reasons—to two other journals that were not members of the Association: *Abendland (Occident)* (1925-30) and *Europäische Revue (European Review)* (1925-36), edited by Karl Anton Prinz Rohan.

Abendland was, first and foremost, an organ of West German right-wing Catholicism, for which Hermann Platz, influenced by *Renouveau Catholique,* played an important role. The idea of linking German renewal with Europe as a whole lay at the core of the *Abendland*-Kreis (Circle). In this context, the League of Nations' ideas about order were considered "liberal," and, therefore, rejected as unsuitable. Instead, the Circle demanded reorganization along the lines of tradition. This led to clear skepticism toward the working form of political Catholicism, especially the Zentrumspartei, and also to reflection upon the idea of the Reich. One of the important authors in this context was historian

Alois Dempf, who published his book *Sacrum Imperium* in 1929; he also had a positive view of Spann's idea of the corporate state. We must not underestimate the influence of the occasionally attested "genius" of Carl Schmitt.

These positions and the profession of a "conservatism of the new generation" can make the group associated with *Abendland* seem like a Catholic wing of the Jungkonservativen. Yet, as stated in its self-evaluation, one can really only speak of a *rapprochement*, not of membership in the full sense. The same is true, for different reasons, of the direction represented by Karl Anton Prinz Rohan. At first, he was one of the contributors to *Abendland* and even later held fast to his benevolent attitude toward the efforts of this journal, but increasingly distanced himself from its political line.

Rohan was without a doubt one of the most famous and original conservative publicists of the interwar period, marked by his origin in the grand nobility of Europe, but also by his interest in the artistic avant garde. Already in 1922, Rohan founded the Deutscher Kulturbund (German Cultural League) in Vienna. In 1924, it became a member of the larger Fédération des Unions Intellectuelles, which was based in Paris and promoted the intellectual and spiritual unity of Europe as a step towards its political unity. Rohan was able to win extraordinary support for the Kulturbunde as well as the Federation both in terms of financing by the influential industrial and political authorities and in terms of the readiness of prominent scientists, writers, and journalists to cooperate.

Both factors also played an important role in the success of his journal *Europäische Revue*, founded 1925, which was meant to serve the Federation's goals with different means. The *Revue*'s circulation never surpassed 2,000, but it was certainly one of the most high-brow publications of the 1920s and 1930s. We can only describe it as an organ of the political Right in a limited sense. Many other leading minds of the Conservative Revolution besides Rohan also published here (Hugo von Hofmannsthal was its *spiritus rector*; others included Karl Wolfskehl and Friedrich Gundolf from the George-Kreis, Leopold Ziegler, Edgar J. Jung, Ernst Wilhelm Eschmann, Hans Rothfels, Heinz O. Ziegler) and intellectual representatives of fascism (Pierre Drieu la Rochelle, Julius Evola, Giovanni Gentile, in a certain sense Henri Massis and Jacques Bainville, later, Marcel Déat), but also liberals (Alfred Weber, Hermann Graf Keyserling, Willi Helpach, José Ortega y Gasset), socialists (Emile Vandervelde, Handrik de Man), and even Soviet authors (Lev Shestov), not to mention the large number of industrialists (Robert Bosch, Werner von Schnitzler), scientists (Carl Gustav Jung) and artists (Max Beckmann, Le Corbusier, Henry van de Velde) who fundamentally did not belong to any political camp at all. Carl Schmitt characteristically declined to cooperate, because he did not wish to participate in a debate, which, from his point of view, was anachronistic.

Rohan's openness to various political positions, but also for the currents of artistic Modernism, cannot deceive us as to his obvious taking sides. Early on, he developed the idea that the collapse of parliamentarism and the belief in progress during the First World War, along with the threat of Bolshevism, would pave the way for a "traditionalist" youth in Europe. His irritating benevolence in view of the anti-liberal traits of the Soviet system was probably owing to a certain intellectual coquetry; his admiration for Mussolini's Italy must be taken more seriously.

Rohan, though, like the other Jungkonservativen, was inclined to make up for himself an image of fascism that only partly corresponded to reality. Thus, corporatism fascinated him, as well as the reestablishment of state authority, the dynamics of the movement and the aesthetic orientation toward antiquity; but his inclination to make politics dependent upon religion[57] and embed it into the great tradition of the Reich idea found no support in Mussolini's practical

---

|57| Literally, "to bind the Political religiously" (*das Politische religiös zu binden*). (*Ed.*)

politics. If for no other reason, fascism could only be considered a step on the way to the future political order of Germany. Max Clauss, who as Executive Editor, played a decisive role along with Rohan for the direction of the *Europäische Revue*, argued that the thorough nationalizing of the peoples had indeed been a necessary process, but this must be succeeded by the "disenchantment with nationalism" and the "educating of the nation into a Reich"—the transnational, structured community of the total European sphere.

An emphatic idea of the "Reich" was widespread in the Catholic intelligentsia and Jugendbewegung, gainining special radiance since the end of the 1920s. Yet its importance must not be overestimated. And the *Europäische Revue* along with *Abendland* always stood at a certain, if not unbridgeable, distance to journals that were Jungkonservativen in a narrower sense. There was also a conspicuous lack of exchange between the *Revue*, *Der Ring*, the *Deutsche Rundschau*, *Deutsches Volkstum*, and *Tat*. The significance of the denominational difference from the main camp made itself felt here. It even affected the influence exercised by Othmar Spann, one of the most effective authors and, above all, teachers and public speakers of the Conservative Revolution.

Starting with Aristotle and the teachings of Thomism, Spann developed a "holistic" worldview that claimed to make all elements of existence comprehensible and clarify their interrelations. With reference to politics, this meant that the community as a whole, and not the individual, was fundamental—the original reality from which all else derives. Spann saw such wholeness in the historically evolved classes, all the way up to the highest, namely, the state—but also operative in natural peoples. Already in his book *Der wahre Staat* (*The True State*), 1921, Spann offered a foundation for his political philosophy, which would develop considerable influence in the following years. Along with various groups of the Austrian Right, who especially took up corporative ideas, and Sudetan German autonomous associations in Czechoslovakia (the Kameradschaftsbund [Comradeship League], later the Sudetendeutsche Partei [Sudetan

German Party]), Spann's influence in Gemany reached all the way to the National Revolutionaries and Jugendbewegung, although they were endorsed mainly by the Jungkonservativen. Jung went the furthest, taking up Spann's philosophical and theological positions. Otherwise, such an endorsement was restricted to the "organological" aspects of his teaching, familiar already from neo-Romanticism.

While the corporative state established in 1934 in Austria by a cold-blooded *coup d'état* strongly relied on Spann's ideas, his influence in the German Reich was limited. This fact might be explained by the lack of any journal widely noticed outside Austria. The series *Die Herdflamme* (*Hearthfire*) edited by Spann, which provided an encyclopedic treatment of everything that required notice in the system of "universalism," was unable to fill this gap. Perhaps, Spann's attempt at complete intellectual penetration triggered that sentiment against "pure theory" that is so typical for conservative schools of thought.

But in a certain sense this also repeated a schism earlier exemplified by the division between the Deutsche Bewegung and Romantic conservatism. The distance was no longer as great as in the 19th century, but the Catholic wing still oriented itself toward the great "Reich" and "aristocracy," while the Protestant wing considered "organic democracy" and the "state" as its central points of reference. Common to both was the idea that a corporative reordering of society was necessary, as well as a certain pathos of order.

5.3 THIRD GROUP: THE NATIONAL REVOLUTIONARIES

The word "nationalism" always has a pejorative undertone. This has never prevented individuals and small groups from making a kind of honorary title out of it. The most famous example may be the French man of letters Maurice Barrès, who quite consciously called himself a "nationalist" in order to draw a sharp contrast with the timid bourgeois "patriot." He imbued the concept with that aggressive trait that won intellectual appeal even before the First World War. Barrès became the model of a nationalist of the new type, and even found imitators outside France, such as Gabriele D'Annunzio and Enrico Corradini in Italy. But the resonance of nationalism was essentially weaker there. After all, Italian nationalism did not have the stimulus that the French felt through their military defeat in 1871, and that kept the wish to avenge themselves and humiliate the victorious enemy alive in the country for decades.

BRUNO ERNST BUCHRUCKER

What we have observed about Italy could also be said of Germany before the war. However, it is revealing that in a 1911 lecture, Moeller van den Bruck already pointed to the necessity of a modern nationalism that would encompass and mobilize the entire nation. A good argument can be made that Moeller was alluding here to Barrès, whose artistic preeminence was as well noted in the Reich as his significance as the intellectual leader of the *revanche* party. But the idea of taking French nationalism as a model in Germany first acquired force after the collapse. The parallel between the situations of 1871 and 1919 was striking, and, under the circumstances, it seemed quite promising to choose the path that the French nationalists had so successfully trod. Specifically, this meant:

◊ Strongest inner concentration of all forces within the "national community" and anathematizing all opposition that stood in the way of these efforts.

◊ Preparing the nation for the second armed conflict.

◊ Searching for allies in the struggle against the guarantor powers of the Versailles Treaty.

154

Many aggravating traits of the national-revolutionary movement in the 1920s and 1930s seem much less surprising when they are compared with the neo-Jacobinism and national socialism in prewar France. This goes not only for the commitment to "militarism" but also for the activism of the early period. At the beginning, there was the suppression of leftist uprisings by the Freikorps, then—border fighting in the Baltic states and in armed resistance to the occupation of the Ruhr; then, following the failure of the Kapp Putsch, came the phase of individual acts of terror, reaching a high point with the murder of Foreign Minister Walther Rathenau; finally, it ended in 1923 with two failed attempts at a "national revolution": the Buchrucker and Hitler-Ludendorff Putsches. The same analogy applies to "National Bolshevism" that grew in appeal especially in the last years of the Weimar Republic. The readiness of national revolutionaries to cooperate with the USSR was not merely a copy of the successful exploitation of Soviet military aid by nationalists such as Kemal Atatürk and Chiang Kai-shek, it was also reminiscent of the French reconciliation with its "hereditary enemy," Great Britain, since the 1880s, as well as with the main ideological opponent of the Third Republic, tsarist Russia.

We can see that this use of France as a model is not simply an *ex post facto* assertion in a statement by Ernst Jünger, who had a kind of copyright on the party name "nationalist":

> *I only became a nationalist under the influence of France, and especially thanks to reading Barrès immediately following the First World War; Barrès really inspired me. It was he, who said 'I am not national; I am a nationalist.' I immediately adopted this.*[58]

Jünger was not among the national revolutionaries of the first hour. He first joined the movement around the middle of the 1920s,

---

|58| Julien Hervier. *Entretiens avec Ernst Jünger* (Paris: Gallimard, 1986), 23.

when their boom times seemed to be over. Yet he was less concerned about the possibilities for action than a nationalist "worldview." This distinguished Jünger sharply from the national-revolutionary scene, which continued to exist despite the defeats of 1923. Secret political tribunals[59], especially the "Organisation Consul," which originated in the Marinebrigad Ehrhardt[60], continued to exist. Yet without the cover provided by state authorities that they enjoyed in the immediate postwar period, they were unable to exert much influence.

What until then may well have been an advantage—the lack of any ideology proper to themselves—now proved to be a disadvantage. This explains the speed with which Jünger rose to become the central figure of a "new nationalism." He considered nationalism not only a necessary but a healthy fever, which had seized everyone who wanted to contribute to the resurgence of Germany; like Barrès, he also considered it the necessary consequence of the nihilistic position, into which modernity got itself through its own broken promises. If one were no longer able to believe in the worldy religion of progress, and if the self-evidence of the older ways of life could not be recovered, only the opening ahead (*die Öffnung nach vorn*) remained. Nationalism must itself be modern if it wanted to be effective. It had been born from a mechanized war and had to prove itself in a technological world. In spite of this, the modernism of nationalism must not result in adding but one more illusion to those of modernity:

> *We, nationalists, believe in no universal morality.*
> *We do not believe in any humanity as a collective*
> *being with a central conscience and a unitary justice.*
> *We believe instead that truth, justice, and morality*

|59| *Feme- und Geheimbünde* were shadowy private tribunals within political parties or movements that decided on the murder of political opponents and the punishment of traitors in the ranks. (*Ed.*)

|60| The Freikorps were formed by Captain Hermann Ehrhardt.

are strongly conditioned by time, place, and blood.
We believe in the value of the particular.[61]

Here, in nationalism's renunciation of 18th- and 19th-century universals, an "old truth" was rediscovered. Yet this did not happen through the nostalgic return to the healthy world of the past—rather, through a new kind of thinking that made use of rationality as a method, without underestimating the power of the irrational and without the illusion that all knowledge can be made accessible to everyone. Jünger thus postulated anew what Barrès had characterized as *le sens du relatif.*

FRANZ
SCHAUWECKER

Until the middle of the 1920s, Jünger advocated an altogether conventional idea of the "Fatherland." Only his increasing interest in politics led him beyond this point. After a short interlude in the Freikorps Rossbach, he joined the Stahlhelm in 1925. In September of that year, he became a contributor to *Standarte* (*Stanard*), a supplement to *Stahlhelm-Zeitung* (*Stahlhelm Times*). He thus came into contact with a circle of young men, including Helmut Franke, Franz Schauwecker, Friedrich Wilhelm Heinz, Wilhelm Weiss, and Wilhelm Kleinau and, later, Friedrich Hielscher as well, who were all—in ways different than Jünger—marked by the postwar period. Something of the violent atmosphere of the revolutionary years 1919-23 survived here.

In this milieu, there was, along with the understandable demand for recognition of the front soldiers, a diffuse mixture of vengefulness,

---

|61| Ernst Jünger, "Das Sonderrecht des Nationalismus," *Publizistik* (1927), 280.

peasant romanticism, and conspiracy. But it was only through Jünger that a consistent nationalist—or more exactly, national revolutionary—ideology was formed. Much was already anticipated by Stadtler, Moeller, and others from the Juni-Klub Circle. Yet it was Jünger who took hold of nationalism anew and first lent it the dynamism that characterized it in the second half of the 1920s, just as the Republic seemed to have come to rest and was to make it a political and intellectual power.

It was in no way clear what the nationalists sought exactly, but Franke's postulate that the Stahlhelm must be made into the kernel of "German fascism" would have probably met with general agreement. By "fascism," however, they understood not a copy of the Italian model but a national variant of the anti-parliamentary movement that was then gaining influence in many countries. Jünger spoke of the emergence of a certain new "breed of man among all the nations of Europe." The war destroyed the old optimism of the Enlightenment and scientific positivism; the front generation was announcing its right to shape the world according to its will. The young "recognized their own style" in the great battles. War was their father, and they wanted to measure the political order as well according to warlike virtues. Their state of the future would be characterized, first and foremost, by four traits: it would be "national, social, defensible, and authoritative." They affirmed dictatorship as a means but not as the goal.

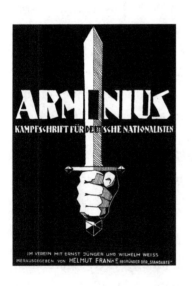

The new warlike nationalism was, despite all its pathos about actions mostly a literary phenomenon. Its protagonists had their own newspapers, like the above-mentioned *Standarte*. It was soon, however, considered unacceptable by the leadership of the Stahlhelm; then came the paper *Arminius*, followed by *Der Vormarsch* (*The Advance*) and *Die Kommenden* (*The Coming Ones*). Most of these organs were short-lived, and the number of subscribers—small; they never enjoyed sufficient financial support. In spite of this, nationalist ideas penetrated the Jugendbewegung and defense organizations as through a capillary system. However, there were strong reservations about the bourgeois Right among the national revolutionaries, and a clear affinity for the program of the National Socialists.

This relationship was never without tension, and it was just as the NSDAP began its triumphant march through parliament that Jünger intensified his criticism of Hitler and the party to the point of an open break, and then gradually withdrew from all direct political activity. Only a part of the national revolutionaries followed him on this path. Some resigned, others joined Hitler's National Socialism or that of his untalented rivals, a third group switched to the side of the man that, with a certain justification, has been called Hitler's evil twin: Ernst Niekisch.

ERNST NIEKISCH

Niekisch belonged to the early nationalists as little as Jünger, and his development toward this position was incomparably more difficult and surprising than that of Jünger. Niekisch originally belonged to the SPD and already before the war had certain prospects of an administrative career. In the revolutionary phase (1918), he turned away from the "mainstream" Social Democrats and played a role in the radical Left in Bavaria. His position as president of the central council (*soviet*[62]) of the first Councilor Republic in Munich earned him two years in prison. After his release in the summer of 1921, there were few signs of a break with

---

|62| In Russian, *soviet* means "council." (*Ed.*)

his political past. Niekisch, who meanwhile joined the Independent Social Democratic Party, returned to the SPD after the ISPD dissolved itself. However, his ambition was not satisfied with party and trade-union work. His ever-stronger doubt concerning the viability of key left-wing ideas was an additional factor. In his 1925 essay "The Path of the German Workers to the State," he already demanded that "the idea of Social Democracy, before it can take over the state, must first immerse itself in the national element."

The publication of this piece triggered a certain unease among the social democratic leadership and led to conflict between Niekisch and the party in the middle term. His inaction—in dispelling the suspicion that he had drifted into National Socialist waters and preventing the division—can probably be explained by his failure to gather a broader following for his ideas within the SPD. Neither getting in touch with the earlier followers of "war socialism" associated with The Bell nor the enthusiasm of the so-called Hofgeismar direction amongx the Young Socialists could really give him a power base. The alternative—leaving the party and joining the Alte Sozialdemokratische Partei (Old Social Democratic Party), a regional splinter group especially strong in Saxony—proved to be a mistake as well. After the group's crushing defeat in the Reichstag elections in the spring of 1928, Niekisch

PAUL WEBER

concentrated exclusively on his activity as a publicist, which would simultaneously create for him an independent political formation, the Widerstandsbewegung (resistance movement).

This name goes back to the monthly journal *Resistance*, founded in 1926 by Niekisch—initially with the help of some Young Socialists, then with another Social Democratic dissident, August Winnig, and finally from January 1931, with the illustrator

A. Paul Weber—originally characterized as an organ "for national revolutionary and socialist politics." Especially with the funds provided by Hamburg wholesale merchant Alfred C. Toepfer, Niekisch was able to engage in propaganda that stood in clear contrast to the actual influence of his position in German public life at the end of the 1920s and beginning of the '30s. Apart from a few defensive organizations, especially Oberland, the nationalist wing of Jugendbewegung and some of the Landvolkbewegung there was hardly any clearly delineable political current indebted to Niekisch's ideas. Niekisch, however, did not consider mass effectiveness necessary, but believed in a modified version of the Leninist cadre principle: that a "nationalist minority" would be in the position to prepare the overthrow and then strike the decisive blow.

If 1926 can be considered the turning point in Niekisch's thought, it is because from this point onward, he shed all remnants of his earlier social-democratic position. This had two principal consequences: the gradual break with the idea that the proletariat would have to be integrated with the nation and prepared for its role as a vector of a national revolt, and the turning away from "fulfillment politics" toward the Entente powers. Authoritarian leadership within and an external alliance with the Soviet Union now seemed to Niekisch the only possibility for throwing off the fetters of the Versailles Treaty and the liberal "system." If the first point of this program would have been agreed to by most of the German Right, Niekisch was almost entirely isolated by the second.

Even though similar thought had been repeatedly expressed since the end of the First World War, this is still applicable. These variations of "National Bolshevism" differed from the efforts of individual communists—finally, of the entire Kommunistische Partei Deutschlands (German Communist Party)—to exploit nationalism for their own goals, in that its supporters assumed tactical cooperation, that is, they wanted the energy released by the Bolshevik Revolution to be channeled into a new struggle against the Western powers.

Unlike the practical collaboration in the military sector supported by the leadership of the Reichswehr and certain politicians, and unlike the revival of Bismarckian Eastern Policy wished for by a fraction of conservatives, the true National Bolsheviks counted on a revolution in Germany, but were prepared to accept this if it formed a precondition for the resurgence of the Reich.

The "Germanic-Slavic Bloc" projected by Niekisch was intended to be a power-political factor of outmost importance, because of its geopolitical position and economic and demographic weight. Niekisch was not afraid that the incomparably larger Russian segment might overwhelm the smaller German counterpart. He believed in a qualitative superiority of Germany in the "*völkisch*" sense, and assumed that the Prussian achievement could be replicated on a large scale: as with the Medieval colonization of the East, the Slavic elements were to be led and integrated.

Although Niekisch claimed to be a political realist, the great importance of historical-philosophical speculation for his orientation can hardly be ignored. In a pamphlet of the Widerstandsbewegung he stated:

> *The resistance movement is opposed to the ideas of the West as such, regardless of what form they influence Germany's fate. The uprising against the idea of Roman rule, against Roman law, against the ideas of 1789, ideas of civilization, individualism, liberalism, democracy, against the bourgeois view of the world and economy—all this we consider the necessary condition of Germany's struggle for liberation. The rejection of Europe's goods is not mere lip service, but is also a willingness to draw the consequences from this position in all their scope and severity. The resistance movement demands, among other things, a decisive turn to the East, creating relationships with all oppressed*

peoples, and kindling irredentist struggles in all states in which the German nationality is muzzled. Getting the nation, especially the youth, used to a simple life of discipline and duty, maintaining defensive capability by all means, abdicating the principle of private property in the sense of Roman law, limiting the right to dispose of one's property, rejecting the capitalist form of economy and society, comprehensive, well-prepared, and ruthless withdrawal from the global economy with all its consequences.[63]

Although nowhere else was the anti-Western, anti-Liberal, and anti-Roman ideology of the German path ever so brilliantly and emphatically expressed, and although Niekisch succeeded in winning over the leading minds of the nationalist intelligentsia to *Widerstand*—Ernst and Friedrich Georg Jünger, Franz Schauwecker, Friedrich von dem Reck-Malleczeven, Hugo Fischer, Ernst von Salomon, Alfred Baeumler, Arnolt Bronnen—this program remained without a large following. Not even under the conditions of the Great Depression did the Spartan and necessarily agrarian Germany that Niekisch demanded,

ERNST VON SALOMON

or the vision of a collectivism based on the Stalinist model, become more appealing. And the constantly mocked "horror of the East," a deeply rooted fear of Russian Bolshevism, could not be overcome by references to the inevitability of uniting with the Soviet Union against the Versailles powers.

Niekisch's isolation did not dissuade him from his opinions. The growing power of the NSDAP with its strong

---

|63| Leaflet *Die Widerstandsbewegung* (Nürnberg: Moser, 1930).

anti-Communist program was something of an irritation. Yet the Widerstandsbewegung remained convinced that once the base became disillusioned with the Führer's corruption—Niekisch's brochure *Hitler, ein deutsches Verhaengnis* (*Hitler: A German Disaster*) was meant to enlighten them on this point—the National Socialist masses would go

over to National Bolshevism. Because of the Berlin transport workers' strike supported by both Communists and National Socialists, there was rejoicing about "National Bolshevism as a political reality." The latter would impose itself against Hitler's legalism as well as against the internationalism of the Communist leadership, which refused to understand the connection between the class struggle and the German struggle of liberation.

ARNOLT BRONNEN

The assurance—with which Niekisch pronounced his political diagnoses—was frustratingly disproportionate not only to his overall lack of political influence but even to his ability to integrate into his movement certain individual national-revolutionary groups, which formed since the end of the 1920s with goals similar to his own. Their reservations can be explained, first of all, as competing claims to

leadership. Friedrich Hielscher, for instance, from the Jünger brothers' and Schauwecker's Kreis (Circle), developed an alternative concept with the contrast between imperialism and nationalism at its core. A worldwide insurrectionary movement was to arise against alienation by the West with its eternally materialistic and leveling culture. Hielscher also believed in the significance of class-based factors that put Germany on the side of other proletarian

RICHARD SCHERINGER

nations. And, like Niekisch, he wished to agitate among workers and peasants in favor of a socialist revolution; but the model of the Soviet Union was not the decisive factor for Hielscher. For him, the alliance with the peoples of Africa and Asia played a decisive role. He wanted to support them in their anti-colonial wars of liberation that must necessarily be directed against the Entente powers.

FRIEDRICH HIELSCHER

Hielscher had—even more so than Jünger or Niekisch—concentrated on the political metaphysics that could help redesign the German state, determined by "inwardness" *and* the "will to power." Hielscher tried to sketch out its outlines in his main work, *The Reich*. What is striking is not so much its apodictic quality (which characterizes all national-revolutionary writing) but the bizarre line of argument and its religious, or at least pagan, connotations. This says nothing about Hielscher's influence, however, even though between 1930 and 1933 he only possessed a primitive and hardly noticeable organ, also called *Das Reich*; Mohler counted him among the leading constituency-forming minds among the national revolutionaries, and even his opponents acknowledged his charisma.

Apart from Hielscher's influence, there were, above all, two factors that prevented Niekisch's Widerstandsbewegung from being the only representative of the national revolutionary idea in the final phase of the Weimar Republic. First, there was the aversion of many nationalists toward the kind of theoretical National Bolshevism that demanded unconditional application, but was never able to clearly state the basis for its hopes for a coup. And second, it was doubtful that Niekisch, with his admiration for the Soviet Union and Lenin, on the one hand, and his firm rejection of the Kommunistische Partei Deutschlands, KPD, on the other hand, was ready to follow through consistently to the end of the path he initiated.

Along with National Bolshevism in the specific sense, at the beginning of the 1930s, there were also individuals and groups that can only be called, in contrast to the main current, "national communist." They, too, recruited mainly from the youth leagues. Their leading figures were Josef "Beppo" Römer—an officer of the Freikorps Oberland, who took part in the assault at Annaberg[64], the fighting in the Ruhr, and the march on the Feldherrnhalle[65]; Richard Scheringer—a lieutenant in the Reichswehr, accused of forming National Socialist cells; furthermore, Bruno von Salomon, who had connections with Landvolkbewegung and the nationalist youth leagues; Bodo Uhse, Friedrich Lenz, Werner Lass, Karl O. Paetel, Fred Schmid, Hans Ebeling, and Harro Schulze-Boysen. Many of these men were disappointed followers of Hitler (Römer, Scheringer,

BODO UHSE AND BRUNO VON SALOMON

von Salomon, Uhse, and, in a certain sense, Lass). Because of the NSDAP's attentism[66], they either wholeheartedly took the side of the Kommunistische Partei Deutschlands (Römer, Scheringer, von

|64| Part of the Third Silesian Uprising (1921) of ethnic Poles against German rule in Upper Silesia. On May 21-26, 1921, German Freikorps units pushed back a Polish advance at Annaberg, a hill southeast of Oppoln.

|65| That is, the Hitler-Ludendorff Putsch of November 9, 1923.

|66| The party's abjuring of revolutionary methods following the failure of the Hitler-Ludendorff Putsch. (*Ed.*)

Salomon, and Uhse) or pled for a closer working association, in which subordination, not only of tactics but strategy would be in effect.

KARL O. PAETEL

The influence of the National Communists, even when they directly supported the party—as was the case with Römer's journal *Aufbruch* (Departure)[67]—remained narrowly circumscribed. With its emphatically national party line of the early 1930s, the KPD wanted to expand its middle-class clientele, just as it simultaneously tried to win over the rebelling farmers. Yet greater independence of the mistrustfully-watched renegades was not in its interest. The periodicals of the larger national communist sphere, such as Lass's *Umsturz* (*Overthrow*) and Lenz's and Ebeling's *Vorkämpfer* (*The Pioneer*), had absolutely no influence on the party line. The KPD was scarcely impressed, even when they adopted Marxist analysis. Direct action propagated by former officers and Freikorps men was unable to get a purchase under existing circumstances, especially since they were reluctant to return to individual acts of terror.

OTTO STRASSER

As it became clear that the KPD was no more serious about its "Programmatic Statement on the National and Social Liberation of the German People" of August 24, 1930, than it had been with its Schlageter Course of the mid-1920s initiated by Radek, a fraction of the National Communists returned to their starting position. This applies especially to the above-mentioned Gruppe Sozialrevolutionärer Nationalisten, GSRN

|67| The title, literally "the breaking up," refers to "breaking camp" just before advancing against an enemy.

(Group of Social-Revolutionary Nationalists) that first assembled in May of 1930, around Paetel's youth league journal *Die Kommenden*. At this time, Paetel was a sympathizer of the NSDAP's left-wing and believed it was possible to bring the party back to its position of 1923-24, i.e., to abandon the legality course and replace it with the building up of a military organization. Paetel thus supported Otto Strasser's splinter group, Kampfgemeinschaft Revolutionärer Nationalsozialisten (Fighting Community of Revolutionary National Socialists). The latter, for its part, also adopted National Bolshevik arguments), but finally considered "National Socialism without Hitler" the wrong option.

The Kampfgemeinschaft Revolutionärer Nationalsozialisten turned away completely from the NSDAP to the KPD. They even took up class-struggle slogans, but foisted an "idealist" interpretation upon them, as did practically all National Bolshevik groups. In the winter of 1932, Paetel made an attempt—fruitless, of course—to establish his own National Bolshevik Party. The *Nationalbolschewistische Manifest (National Bolshevik Manifesto)* he published shortly afterward, in the same month Hitler came to power, indicated where the essential distinction between National Communists and National Bolshevists lay. Despite certain remaining reservations, the former completely gave up on any thought of a third front between capitalism and Communism and went over to the Communist side. National Bolsheviks, on the other hand, held fast to their vision of a *Volk* uprising that would find Communists, National Socialists, and revolutionary nationalists side by side.

National Bolshevism was, in many respects—in any case, more strongly than the warlike Rousseauism of Ernst Jünger and the circle around *Standarte, Arminius,* and *Vormarsh (The Advance)*—the consistent completion of nationalism, insofar as the thought of national liberation was given *absolute* precedence over all other political, economic, religious, and ethical considerations. The primacy of foreign policy led not only to the demand for liberating the Entente's "colony"[68] from its yoke, but also proposed an anti-imperialism that demanded that all oppressed nations together break the iron ring of the Western powers. Such assumption of a position hitherto considered "left-wing" was typical not only for the nationalists but for the Conservative Revolution as a whole; here, it reached its most extreme point. And this was not the case of changing sides, but, rather, followed a political idea—oriented toward Machiavelli not by accident. It was confident enough to enter into an alliance with the Soviet Union and Communism, since "National Bolshevism, above all, meant revolutionary action. Everything else is the question of our own intensity and national (*volkhaft*) force."[69]

The willingness to accept socialism or Communism looking toward nationalism was akin to being ready for a revolution for the sake of the nation—an assessment of the situation that made a break from the traditional Right unavoidable. Bronnen summarized a view common to all circles and alliances by saying, "[T]he new nationalism must walk over the corpse of the old one."[70] This was congruent with the perception that the national movement of the immediate postwar period, as of the earlier Wilhelmine Right, had failed. And, above all, it was senseless to place their hopes in the Reichswehr; not a Putsch, but a revolution by the workers, farmers, and nationalist intelligentsia must be the goal.

Revolutionary nationalism was not necessarily anti-democratic, but was certainly anti-parliamentarian. Its key problem was that it was not in a position to unleash any revolutionary force. Even contemporary observers came to the conclusion that this worldview was unsuited to become the ideology of a mass movement. It was the fact that National Revolutionaries were consistent that prevented their effectiveness.

|68| That is, Germany.

|69| Artur Grosse, *Nationalbolschewismus II* 2 (1931), 21.

|70| Arnoldt Bronnen, *O.S. Roman* (Berlin: Rowohlt, 1929), 353.

Fertile soil was indeed prepared for the idea of nationalism as a worldly religion—as for the idea of a German socialism. But there was as little sympathy for decisionism that did not flinch from admiring Lenin's revolutionary massacres as there was for the idea of transforming a modern industrial society into a warrior state or a copy of Stalin's Russia. For a certain time, it seemed sensible to employ "nationalism" or the "new nationalism" as an umbrella concept for all conservative-revolutionary currents. However, this kind of identification could not be long-lasting, even though it was the National Revolutionaries who most clearly formulated in a single *aperçu* the uneasiness that was the decisive factor for the entire Conservative Revolution: "The present has no form...."

5.4 FOURTH GROUP: THE LEAGUES

When Max Scheler asserted in a 1922 essay that the Jugendbewegung of the postwar period was an "international phenomenon," he meant that the pathos of youth and the generational struggle were helping to shape rather different political, social, and artistic currents. Its aggressiveness, Scheler said, is quite distinct from the escapist tendency that had characterised the Wandervogel, and even in Germany the youth were becoming more activist and strongly influenced by something one might call the search for an "unequivocal (*einsinnig*) style of life."

In fact, the search for a "new style," the "will to form" was the most obvious feature of this phase in Jugendbewegung, denoted by the hitherto altogether unknown adjective *bündisch*.[71] The change first became clear in outward appearance: the Youth Leaguists put aside the anarchic elements of the Wandervogel, no longer going about in hordes, but marching as a unified body, in step and to

---

|71| From *Bund*: league, association, alliance; as odd-sounding in German as "leaguish" would be in English. (*Ed.*)

the accompaniment of music. They made their clothing more alike, similar to military uniforms or costumes. Their emblems became less playful and lost all reminders of pennants or ribbons that designated schoolboy associations, becoming more martial and mysterious. Camping out and expedition-like trips abroad only began at this point.

The origin of the "new style" cannot be explained without reference to the influence of scouting, always rejected by the older Youth Movement. Although there were early attempts to alter Anglo-Saxon scouting in the direction of national pedagogical traditions, the gap between scouts and Wandervogel became unbridgeable in the prewar period. The reason for this was, first, a very different attitude toward the idea of self-education and, second, to premilitary training.

The importance of boy scouts for military auxiliary services during war essentially contributed to its crisis after the end of the Kaiserreich. Under new conditions, not only the memory of a "military" past became an obstacle, but also—the international orientation, very emphatic in scouting. As a consequence of this, several small groups opposed the largest German scouting organization when they tried to reorganize, and finally had to leave it.

Bund deutscher Neupfadfinder (New League of German Scouts), BNP, founded by these rebels in January of 1921, was the starting point for changes that affected the entire Yough Movement in the Weimar period. The program developed in the publications of Der weiße Ritter (White Knight Publishers) and, especially, by the leader of the BNP, Martin Voelkel, played a decisive role in this process. Voelkel, a Protestant Minister, was strongly influenced, along with his associates, by Jungkonservativen thought, especially Mann's *Reflections of a Nonpolitical Man*. Voelkel sought, above all, to renew the idea of the Reich. In it, metaphysical, in part, decidedly Christian notions of the *Sacrum Imperium* were merged with Stefan George's vision of a "New Reich."

In an essay from this time, Voelkel wrote:

> We are not concerned about the external form
> of this Reich, about its possibilities within the
> historical constellation, and how well it suits
> domestic and foreign political demands, doctrines,
> and programs. Rather, we penetrate to the true
> realities, to the original material as experienced by
> the youthful spirit, and rate them according to their
> essential significance and inner necessity for us and
> our nation.[72]

It becomes obvious that Voelkel saw in the Reich less a concrete form of political order than a "myth," i.e., not an illusion, but a political ideal that could mobilize the efforts of youth and give the youth leagues a goal and the nation—an opportunity for renewal.

The scouts' call to unite Jugendbewegung did not succeed, but the new "leaguish" worldview penetrated people's minds, not least favored by the practical merging of elements from the Wandervogel (youthful autonomy, election of leaders) and scouting (a more disciplined appearance, organized camps, increasing emphasis on physical fitness). Since the older groups in Jugendbewegung did not disappear, reservations about "scouting" remained, just as there was repeated criticism of the individualism of those more strongly rooted in the prewar tradition. Still, the new form became so strongly pronounced by the middle of the 1920s that the term *bündische Jugend* (league youth) gained general currency.

It was at this time that the first impulse toward reform began to lose force. Voelkel withdrew, but not before proposing the formation of a *Hochbund* (super league) that would join the various leagues

---

|72| Martin Voelkel, "Die Wiedergeburt des Reichsgedankens aus dem Geist der Jugend," in *Hie Ritter und Reich: Gesammelte Aufsätze* (Berlin: Der weiße Ritter, 1923), 47.

under a single leader and an advisory panel (*Reichsthing*). Along with the idea of a super league, clarifying the relationship between age groups within the league played an important role. Voelkel expressly rejected the idea of a lifelong league, preferring a restriction to the boys' section (*Jungenschaft*) of 10-18-year-olds and the young men's section (*Jungmannschaft*) of 18-25-year-olds. The boys' section would maintain the traditional program of trips, camping, and games. The older section would be educated in a more political fashion through military training, year-long volunteer programs, and "border camps."

Just as the idea of a general merger was rejected—to which the autonomy of the individual groups would be sacrificed—so was the sense of this division misunderstood in most leagues. There were still attempts to create umbrella organizations, however: most successfully in the form of the Deutsche Freischar (German Volunteers) founded in 1926, as the Bund der Wandervögel und Pfadfinder (League of Wandervogel and Scouts). But no convincing solution to the age-group queston was found. The inauguration of a "labor service" which could assume the educational function of military service met with great practical difficulties. Hopeful attempts were made in the form of the Boberhaus Camp held every year since 1927. But this initiative—which originated with Helmuth James Graf von Moltke and Eugen Rosenstock-Huessy—meant to employ young academics, young farmers, and young workers together, did not become a model as was hoped. Without support from the authorities, not much could be achieved. Until the spring of 1931, however, the government strictly rejected the idea of a labor service. Only under the influence of the Great Depression, which affected young adults more than anyone, did they decide to change course, leading to the first regulations concerning a "voluntary labor service" that was supported mainly by the various youth leagues.

The conflict over the position of adults that recurred since the beginnings of the Wandervogel was settled by the leagues at the end of the 1920s not through integration, but in a typical fashion: when the younger members split off. Two new "energy organizations" played a decisive role in this. The first of these was the Graues Corps (Grey Corps) founded in January of 1930 under the leadership of Swiss Alfred "Fred" Schmid—perhaps, the most restrictive unit among all the leagues. Elegance in clothing and demeanor, deliberate member selection not only according to character, but also according to aesthetic criteria, tough athletic demands, and the originality in the group's typical forms of expression, especially songs and megaphones, all fit the unconditional alignment toward the leader.

Schmid was, therefore, conscious that the existence of the Grey Corps depended entirely on his person, and accepted that it would crumble with his own biographical distance from youth. This attitude

distinguished him from Eberhard Koebel, known by the traveling name "Tusk." From the end of the 1920s, he sought to achieve an inter-league unity for the youth. The "d. j. 1. 11" or deutsche Jungenschaft vom 1. November (1929)—(autonomous) German youth of November 1, 1929—that he created never came close to this goal. Yet Tusk left an impact through the revolutionary style of his journals and travel reports, through the costume he invented for members, the blue "Juja" (youth jacket), the "Kohte" imported

EBERHARD KOEBEL

from Lappland as a group tent, insignia design, and the grey-and-red youth-league flag. Ultimately, Koebel failed due to opposition from the older members of the national leadership. However, his ideas had such lasting influence that the viewpoint of the youth leagues changed after the spring of 1930, and older elements almost entirely disappeared.

For all the differences between Schmid and Koebel, they both agreed that the time of youth must be a "politically protected area," i.e., that those coming of age must not be overwhelmed with ideology. On this point they were in agreement with a large majority of those in the youth leagues, who always emphasized the necessity of political education, but meant by this a kind of basic instruction on political order, economics, and society. Here, there was something of the Wandervogel's reservations about any form of indoctrination and something of the ideal of a *"Volk* community" that was to be shaped in a preliminary fashion in the youth league.

This reserved attitude distinguished the majority of youth leagues from the minority that understood itself as unconditionally political. Yet these, too, rejected any direct relationship with political parties. The most important of these groups was founded in 1921: the Jungnationaler Bund ("Young National League") that originated as the youth organization of the DNVP, the Adler und Falken ("Eagles and Falcons"), the Schilljugend ("Schill Youth," originally, the Sturmvolk [Assault *Volk*]) as well as the Geusen (Beggars[73], later known as the Freischar Junger Nation [Voluneer Brigade of the Young Nation]). The Geusen originated as a splinter group of the Fahrenden Gesellen—

HARRO SCHULZE-BOYSEN

Travelling Companions (founded 1910), a hiking club of the Deutschnationaler Handlungsgehilfen-Verband (German National Association of Commercial Employees), which, in the postwar period, may also be considered among the political leagues.

The conviction of living in a "time of preparation" was stronger here than in other groups of Jugendbewegung. These groups were meant to prepare for the

---

|73| *Die Geusen*, a name drawn from Dutch history. In 1566, a group of about 250 Calvinist noblement marched upon the palace of Margeret, Duchess of Parma to present a list of grievances against the Spanish throne. Margeret was alarmed by their large number, and a councillor reassured her by saying: "Have no fear, Madame, they are nothing but beggars (*gueux* in French)." The insult was remembered and later taken up as a badge of honor by the Calvinist Party.

second option of resorting to arms both theoretically (schooling) and practically (paramilitary games). The attitude toward the Republic was not merely latently hostile (the case with many youth leagues) but openly so, suggesting an approach to *völkisch* groupings, and, later, to national-revolutionary groupings. The enthusiasm for the *Volk* and everything *Volk*-oriented (*volkstümliche*)—that was as typical of the youth leagues as an avowal of "greater German" sympathies— involved at least a cultural obligation to care for all ethnic Germans within and without the Reich's borders, as well as a political obligation toward ethnic Germans in Austria, which intensified into an open and intransigent nationalism. They turned decisively against the common youth league formula "for us, the nation is not the measure of all things."

Influenced by the great economic and political crisis of the end of the 1920s, nationalist youth leagues were able to register an increase in significance, but without being able to influence the overall movement to the degree they had hoped. Once the requirement of party-political neutrality in the youth leagues began weakening, and leaders or ex-leaders publicly came forward with their positions. Most activism focused on the new Right, i.e., those small parties such as the Christlich-Sozialer Volksdienst (Christian-Social People's Service) or the Volkskonservative Partei (Popular Conservative Party) that were close to the ideas of the Jungkonservativen. When the old demand for a German socialism became louder once again, this "socialism as a life feeling" was clearly distinct from the concrete plans of the nationalist leagues.

The ideas of Ernst Niekisch and Ernst Jünger (who, for some time, exercised a kind of sponsorship of the nationalist youth leagues and functioned as the nominal editor of the weekly *Die Kommenden*) were in their ranks, first and foremost. But the more radical versions also played a decisive role. The nationalist youth leagues, in turn, provided an essential part of the national revolutionaries' "mass" base. In the Aktion der Jugend (Youth Action) against the Young Plan promoted by the *Widerstands-Kreis* (Resistance Circle), it was they who held most of the demonstrations. This did not lead to a resounding success, and both Jünger and Niekisch turned away from the youth leagues after a time, disillusioned. Harro Schulze-Boysen (*Gegner—Opponent*), Werner Lass (*Der Umsturz—The Overthrow*), and Hans Ebeling (*Vorkämpfer—The Pioneer*) led National Revolutionary groups that were of no significance to the movement as a whole. They came from the youth leagues themselves, and, since the beginning of the 1930s, demanded proletarian mobilization as well as a more or less consistent attachment to the Soviet Union for the sake of "creating a unified front of all oppressed classes and nations."

The offer to ally themselves with the Communists often resulted from disappointment that the NSDAP made no move toward assuming the function of mass exponent of social-revolutionary nationalism attributed to it. Hitler and those around him were always skeptical of any cooperation with the "Young Nationalists." The efforts of the Schill volunteer brigade and the Geusen to form closer contacts regularly failed because the leagues—even when they accepted the NSDAP's version of National Socialism, like the Geusen—refused to submit to or be dissolved into the Hitlerjugend (Hitler Youth). The alternative of joining the left-splinter group of the Strasser-wing failed because of the latter's insignificance.

WERNER LASS

At the end of the Weimar Republic the youth leagues, despite their small membership of never more than 40,000, had become a generational phenomenon. The number of critics, who originally believed in the "mission of the young generation" and now complained of their indecisiveness, grew simultaneously. They regularly failed to perceive that the limits of all politization of the youth leagues was determined by the age of the members and their lack of interest in an ideology. Experience was the decisive factor, not the interpretations being offered. Most of those in the leagues were satisfied with the lines from George's *Stern des Bundes* (*Star of the League*) as an explanation of what they felt:

> *Whoever has circled the flame*
> *Remains the flame's satellite!*
> *However he wanders and revolves:*
> *Wherever its brightness reaches him*
> *He never errs too far from the target.*
> *Only when his gaze loses it*
> *His own shimmer deceives him:*
> *He lacks the law of the middle*
> *He drives on scattering into space.*[74]

The youth leagues not only lacked a coherent worldview but also a theory. A few thinkers who emerged from the Jugendbewegung, however, created a kind of "league doctrine." The most famous was undoubtedly Hans Blüher. In the prewar period, Blüher wrote the first history of the Wandervogel and later wrote a two-volume work, *Die Rolle der Erotik in der männlichen Gesellschaft* (*The Role of Erotics in the Male Society*), which appeared in 1917 and 1919. The male league (*Männerbund*)—the state-forming function of which was first discovered by the ethnographer Heinrich Schurz—was at the center of his meditations. Blüher took up this thesis and built a bridge between the earlier forms of the male league—in archaic societies, in the Spartan cosmos, among the Knightly orders of the middle ages, and the officer corps of the Prussian Army—and the new youth movement. Although there had been girls in the ranks from the beginning, the question of the sexes had always played an important role along with that of age groups. The continuing reservations about

HANS BLÜHER

|74| Stefan George, *Der Stern des Bundes* (Munchen: Küpper und Bondi), 84.

the feminine element in many Wandervogel organizations is as striking as the fact that all elite groups such as the Graues Corps or the d. j. 1. 11 strongly displayed the characteristics of a male league.

Schurtz's thesis was that the male league represented a special form of age grouping. turned this completely around, saying that the male league breaks through the horizontal stratification of age groups as a vertical order. This is an interpretation, the significance of which can only be rightly understood when *Die Rolle der Erotik* is seen in the larger context of Blüher's works. Already in a paper that appeared shortly before the second volume, *Führer und Volk in der Jugendbewegung (Leader and People in Jugendbewegung)*, he treated various aspects of the themes "elite and the masses," "commander and his following," and directed his gaze to league formations, in which charisma and voluntary obedience of the "leading man" played a decisive role. But this only carefully hinted at his real purpose. After all, in his scandal-arousing history of the Wandervogel, he already asserted that sublimated homosexuality is what gives the league cohesion. It enables the young men to orient themselves toward the leader, the Male Hero. Thus, it creates—on a small scale— what is accomplished on a large scale when the male league prepares to form a state, insofar as homosexuality expressly disregards the need for procreation and the rearing of the young.

Blüher's theory of the significance of male-male Eros is linked to his view that the occurence of the *typus inversus* (the "invert," or homosexual—*Ed.*) in history is vulnerable to considerable "periodic fluctuations," but in the present is being strengthened. This would lead us to expect the emergence of a new, both anti-bourgois and "anti-feminist" position, following a certain interpretation of the Platonic Eros, free of Wilhelmine clichés concerning relations between the sexes and directing women to a sphere separate from that of men and (especially) from the public sphere: "The male league is more important. The family goes without saying; the male league, however, requires affirmation."[75]

---

[75]   Hans Blüher, "Was ist Antifeminismus?" in *Gesammelte Aufsätze* (Jena: Diederichs, 1919), 91.

Blüher's line of argument—strengthened by other rather surprising readings for a man of the Right in the area of sex—unleashed considerable irritation and angry polemics. This did not prevent his writings from exercizing influence, quite the reverse. They were intensively discussed in the first years after the war, especially in the youth leagues. Linked to this reception, we should mention Herman Schmalenbach's sharp criticism. Schmalenbach also came through the Wandervogel, but, unlike Blüher, had received considerable academic training. He was among the disciples of Georg Simmel and belonged to the larger George-Kreis, as is apparent in his extensive 1922 essay, "Die Kategorie des Bundes " ("The Sociological Category of the League"). Schmalenbach focused on the voluntary character of the league in a very different manner from Schurtz or Blüher. Thus, he could place the league in the context of relationship forms developed by Ferdinand Tönnies—"community/society"—and assert, in contrast to Tönnies, that it was not community, but the league that was the form of human grouping that relied on emotion.

Community, on the other hand, knows all kinds of ways of objectively binding the individual, only not by contract or enlightened self-interest like society but by descent or the ritual assumption of obligation. Much like Blüher, Schmalenbach emphasized the importance of charisma for the leadership of the league. Thus, he reduced the "objective" character of gathering a league that Schurtz's analysis asserted for primitive societies. He also rejected any limitation of the league phenomenon to the *male* league.

Unlike Schurtz or Blüher, Schmalenbach, a "man of letters," disputed the possibility of a clear sex-specific classification. Research of the specifically male and female factors was necessary, but could not be achieved with the available sociological means. Despite this reservation concerning the possible consequences, Schmalenbach's text also included a practical aspect. Like many others, he was convinced he was living in a transitional age and believed that a chaotic time of a new beginning was at hand. This would lead to the return of conditions unseen in Europe since the age of migrations.

The warrior bands that traveled around towards the end of antiquity were still "leagues," the Medieval states arising out of them were "communities," and the modern states were "societies." Their collapse was due at any moment:

> *In the end, even the external bands are increasingly broken. The barbarians break in in resolute masses. "League"-like ('Bund'hafte) late age and "league"-like antiquity merge in the last syncretism, in which the blood is renewed for some, for others—made supple. A broad ditch, in which the world slowly comes to rest, divides two cultures, of which the newer (but built upon the older) slowly blossoms into the "Middle Ages."*[76]

The expectation of renewal through the leagues could hardly be found in Jugendbewegung but rather in the "paramilitary leagues." Between the two formations, there certainly were similarities, and a group like the Schill voluneers could rightly claim to be the "link between the paramilitary movement and Jugendbewegung."[77] This self-description was all the more easy in that the league arose from the Freikorps, just as conversely, members of the Wandervogel played a considerable role in the volunteer ranks. Otherwise, the paramilitary leagues were clearly distinct from those of the youth movement. This was not only due to the age difference but also the difference in the goals they pursued.

---

[76]   Herman Schmalenbach, *Die Soziologische Kategorie des Bundes* (München: Meyer & Jessen, 1922), 105.

[77]   Werner Lass, *Die Freischar Schill. Ihr Werden und Wille* (o.S. [Blatt 3] in Zs: Die Kommenden, o. J. [1930] Flatrchheim).

Apart from the Roter Frontkämpferbund (Red League of Frontline Fighters)—which was never anything but a project of the KPD and was outlawd in 1929 because of its criminal activities—practically all paramilitary leagues of the Weimar period, especially the Jungdeutscher Orden (Young German Order), the Wehrwolf (Werewolf), and the Wiking (Viking), Ekkehard, and Oberland Leagues, were on the political Right. They developed from the Freikorps and were also striving for an "unequivocal form of community" during the civil-war years. Their character as leagues was explicable from the dissolution of the old army and the traditional hierarchy with it, on the one hand, and from the strengthening ties to the leader of the unit, the exclusively male community, and the consciousness of general hostility, on the other.

Stabilizing the Republic in the 1920s caused the Freikorps disappearance. Insofar as they tried to continue the struggle against the new order with terrorist means, they fell victim to state prosecution; insofar as they abandoned armed struggle, they saw themselves confronted with the question of why they existed. The leaders fluctuated, therefore, between reconstructing them as traditional veterans' associations based on the model of the Stahlhelm and founding activist paramilitary leagues that operated on the edge of legality. The numerical strength of such groups fluctuated greatly, from the barely 500 men of the Oberland (1930) to the 30,000-40,000 members of the Wehrwolf, to the nearly 100,000 of the Jungdeutscher Orden.

If members of these organizations were interested in justifying their existence, it was not difficult to take over the male-league concept, which, above all, justified understanding politics as an exclusively male domain. But we can only speak in a qualified sense of accepting Blüher and Schmalenbach. Schmalenbach's text was at a level unsuitable for immediate ideological use; Blüher's theses had to be shorn of their sexual aspect, the offensiveness of which threatened to discredit the entire concept of the male league. New approaches came mainly from the ranks of the National Revolutionaries and the Jungkonservativen, who, unlke the völkisch, put little hope in the initiative of the Volk. In their view, the Volk needed a male vanguard in order to be brought into the proper form. Albrecht Erich Günther and Alfred Baeumler, especially, promoted equivalent theses. They were concerned about dedicating the youth association to the idea of the male league. Student associations and armies were to form their starting point and create a state appropriate for the male league. The idea of the new state of male leagues, "the central idea of which seeks none other than transforming functional democracy into a leadership-democracy (Führerdemokratie)," was widespread in the ranks of the Conservative Revolution and found an organizational starting point in the Bündische Reichschaft, founded in 1930 by Kleo Pleyer. The Reichschaft, an elite combination of elders from the Jugendbewegung, seriously considered consistently reordering the totality of the political constitution and economy with the help of the "league."

At the end of the Weimar Republic, one could, in fact, get the impression that youth-league formations were the last remaining factor maintaining stability amid the general dissolution. Even the parties of the "Weimar Coalition"—fundamentally pacifist and quite alien to such conceptions—tried to immitate this model of their opponents: the SPD and the Zentrumspartei, in a strange coalition with the Jungdeutscher Orden of the Left-Liberal Deutsche Demokratische Partei, founded a "Reichsbanner Schwarz-Rot-Gold (Black-Red-Gold)" youth league. Influenced by the Great Depression, the government, as already mentioned, abandoned its earlier opposition to labor service, labor camps, and settlements.

Many hoped that the "fraternal-national sentiment" could be renewed through the leagues in the midst of a collapsing mass society. Others, however, believed that the way was being prepared in the leagues for a new mentality and an altogether new form of collective life:

> Egotism seemed to be getting the upper hand,
> and fear for one's personal fate pressed everyone

183

downward into inaction and silent despair. Now suddenly the very excess of distress is transformed into its opposite. Gloweringly, resolutely, perhaps without much hope, but convinced "it is worthwhile," the first century joins combat. It is worth it to fall as "us" (wirhaft); it is not worth living egotistically (ichhaft). And already after the first street battle the pioneers have thousands and hundreds of thousands behind them. Only courage in the face of death saves man from his Ego. Only from the blood of the fallen arises the new We.[78]

5.5 FIFTH GROUP: THE RURAL POPULATION

The peasantry has often been considered instrinsically conservative as the part of the population that naturally rejects change. A fundamental perseverance can be asserted in view of their bond with the earth and landscape, with tradition and custom. But with respect to politics, this assessment is doubtful. The peasants have often formed a revolutionary power, and not only in German and even European history. Peasant revolts have played an important role in historic development all the way into the modern age.

The rural-population movement in the closing phase of the Weimar Republic fits into this scheme quite well. We must first recall, however, the memory of the Peasants' War of the 16th century or the self-assertion of Frisians, Stedings, and Dithmarschers. It is more obvious, therefore, to understand the rebellion of the rural population in the context of the Great Depression, which, since the end of the 1920s, had contributed so greatly to destabilizing the Weimar Republic, and the first signal

---

|78| Fritz Künkel, *Grundzüge der Politischen Charakterkunde* (Berlin: Junker und Dünnhaupt, 1931), 114..

of which, long before Black Friday, lay in the rapidly worsening condition of the farmers.[79]

The unrest that seized Western and Northern Schleswig-Holstein, parts of Lower Saxony, East Prussia, and Silesia began with a

demostration by more than 140,000 farmers in the district capitals of Schleswig-Holstein on January 28, 1928. The farmers protested the dire situation on many farms and the inaction of the political class. Such marches, often performed in silence, were a common method of passive resistance among farmers, along with boycotting farm auctions, distraints, or refusal to pay taxes. A purchasing-and-delivery strike that lasted nearly a year forced the city of Neumünster to return a black flag seized during a violent demonstration on August 1, 1929. This was the alarm bell for the opening phase of the so-called Landvolkbewegung.

Demonstrating farmers attached a sombre banner with a white plow and red sword to the handle of a straightened scythe, thus creating a powerfully expressive symbol that forged a connection between the farmers and other groups of the Conservative Revolution. The circumstances surrounding the origin of the flag leave no doubt that the color black was, as often happened in the immediate postwar years, at first a spontaneous expression of despair. Thus, the "Black Flag Song" went:

|79| *Bauer* is translated as "peasant" when it refers to an earlier time in history, and "farmer" when refering to the modern era. (*Ed.*)

Black is care, black our bread.
And black is the flag of the farmers' distress.
Black is the earth under the plow
And the farmer goes about in black mourning.

We plow and sow and build without rest—
We harvest and do not know to what purpose.
For what we gain with our strength,
Is taken from us and carried away.

What the taxes leave for us to live on,
Is extracted from us in the form of interest!
And what we sell earns us nothing,
Farming be damned!

Now we are exhausted—we do not wish to go on,
We are a dispairing army of farmers;
Black is care, black our bread
And black the flag of the farmers' distress.

Landvolkbewegung arose in reaction to the idleness and the decline of the traditional representation of their corporate interests (the Kleinbauernverband [Small Farmers' Union], Bauernverein [Farmers' Union], and Landbund [Land League]) in Schleswig-Holstein. Although they never created entirely permanent structures, there was, from the beginning, a program that went beyond the demand for concrete aid to farmers. Corporative ideas played a role, but also the plea for autarchy and protective tariffs, along with demands for the nullification of the Versailles Treaty, especially the war-guilt clause and reparations. The accusation of corruption against a "system" that had, for 10 years, waged war on its own people quickly joined the protest.

Early on, the Deutschnationale Volkspartei, DNVP, and various small *völkisch* groups thus placed their hopes in the rural population and the possibility of instrumentalizing it. But the participation of the German Nationalists in the government disspointed its followers among the farmers, because the minister had not done enough for the interests of agriculture. The loss in the elections of 1928 of nearly one third of the votes that the Deutschnationale Volkspartei had received in Schleswig-Holstein in 1924 was not made up for by the foundation of new parties claiming to represent the interests of the countryside. The rather democratically oriented Deutsche Bauernpartei (German Farmers' Party) and the conservative Christlich-Nationale Bauern- und Landvolkpartei (Christian National and Rural People's Party) were left far behind, with 0.7 and 0.2 percent of the vote, respectively.

One reason for this lay in the southern and central German origin of these groupings. Yet the conviction among the rural

population of Schleswig-Holstein that any form of "party-politics" was inherently evil and must be fought on principle may have been more decisive. In the second phase of development beginning in the summer of 1929, Wilhelm Hamkens and Claus Heim came forward: two men, whose status was essentially determined by their personal integrity and charisma.

WILHELM HAMKENS

Already since January of 1929, the farmers possessed an organ of their own in the paper *Das Landvolk* (*The Rural Volk*), published in Itzehoe. Its increasing influence can be seen in the fact that the originally weekly paper was soon published almost daily, gaining nearly 10,000 subscribers. No suitable editor, however, came from the ranks of the farmers. Consequently, Bruno von Salomon, a journalist from the circle of new nationalism, was appointed to the leadership of *Das Landvolk*. The course followed by Salomon, with the support of a few like-minded comrades such as his brother Ernst, Herbert Volck, and Friedrich Wilhelm Heinz, was oriented toward consistently mobilizing the farmers in order to overthrow the existing order. The national revolutionaries expressly wanted to use dissatisfaction with existing conditions as the vehicle for political goals that went well beyond concrete improvements.

Hamkens saw the problematic character of this tendency but did not want to lose such gifted agitators. These men could be sure not only of support by activists from the Bündische Reichschaft around August Georg Kenstler and from his journal *Blut und Boden* (*Blood*

CLAUS HEIM

and Soil), but also a certain backing from Heim, who had earlier considered the partial arming and military organizing of the farmers' resistance movement. While Hamkens was sitting out a jail sentence and thus could exercise no influence on the movement, Heim prepared eight bomb attacks with the support of national revolutionary circles and combat organizations (especially Viking and Wehrwolf), carried out between April 6 and September 6, 1929.

The attacks were only against property, but the effect was not what had been hoped. Large parts of the rural population expressly condemned the actions and governmental organs proceeded even more harshly than before against the farmers' leaders. Between September 9 and 11, 1929, the police arrested Heim and 34 other persons; a year later, on October 31, 1930, Heim was sentenced to seven years imprisonment in the Altona "bomber trial."

Landvolkbewegung was thereby beheaded. In Heim, the farmers lost their most talented leader, and Hamkens, released in the meantime, was unable to fill the gap. The farmers' bitterness against the government and the existing economic order remained, but had little to do with being ready for revolution. Their dissatisfaction led rather to the NSDAP exercising influence on the rural population. Originally, the National Socialists had poor prospects with the farmers; the German Nationalists, the *völkische* Bewegung, the Tannenberg League, and even individual activists from Jugendbewegung enjoyed significantly greater success in this area. But now the National Socialists were victorious, not least demonstrated by the results of the Reichstag elections of September 14, 1930, in which the NSDAP enjoyed an above-average increase in its share of the vote in Schleswig-Holstein.

Already in May of 1929, the responsible National Socialist Gauleiter Heinrich Lohse wrote in a letter to the party leadership in Munich: "The rural population is still causing us great difficulties. The danger that these people's stupidity might become dangerous for us is immense."[80] Hitler completely shared this way of thinking and, in connection with his legality course, distanced himself from the bombings. This, once again, led to a quarrel with the National Revolutionaries, who remained sympathetic toward the NSDAP, but now came to the view that Hitler made his peace with existing circumstances or at least had no respect for the "purity of means."

On the other hand, the nationalists were forced to doubt whether their hopes in the Landvolkbewegung were justified. The idea that with his actions, the farmer professed support for the national-revolutionary idea seemed questionable in the very least. At first, the farmers even brusquely rejected an offer of support from Niekisch's *Widerstands-Kreis*. Only after Heim's arrest did relations become closer. Hamken, who, once again, took over the leadership, entrusted Niekisch following the closure of the journal *Rural Volk*, with the editorship of a super-regional informational newsletter. It appeared after December of 1931, under the title Deutscher Landvolk—und Kampfbund (German Rural Volk Fighting League). Niekisch not only came forward several times as a public speaker at meetings of the Landvolkbewegung up until January of 1933, but also worked to set up Heim, in prison since

---

|80| Gerhard Stoltenberg, *Politische Strömungen im Schleswig-Holsteinischen Landvolk 1918-1933* (Düsseldorf: Droste, 1962), 146..

March of 1932, as a symbolic candidate for Reichspresident. Heim had no chance against Hindenburg or Hitler, but his candidacy was a signal to demarcate the position of the national-revolutionary camp.

The *Widerstands*-Kreis succeeded in gathering many more than the 20,000 signatures than necessary. However, they found agreement

9.JAHR BERLIN APRIL 1934 60 Pf.

mainly in the larger cities of Western Germany, not among the rural population of Schleswig-Holstein and not among the other national-revolutionary groups either; after initial hesitation, their "rejection front" stretched from the small Circles of Paetel's Group of Social Revolutionary Nationalists through to the Pioneer Circle all the way to Otto Strasser's *Vorkämpfer*-Kreis (Circle) of Revolutionary National Socialists. They explicitly rejected election participation and dissent of a few militants, such as Bruno von Salomon and Bodo Uhse, originally the leader of his own NSDAP paper, *Schleswig-Holsteinische Zeitung* (*Schleswig-Holstein Times*), also played a role. Impressed by the farmers' refusal to join other revolutionary strata, especially the working class, both of these men changed course and went over to the Kommunistische Partei Deutschlands. For its part, it was trying to win influence over the rural population with its Bauern-Komitee-Bewegung (Farmers' Committee Movement). This organization was formally non-partisan, but was, in fact, required to hew to the Communist line. This forced Salomon and Uhse to support the candidacy of Ernst Thälmann for the President of the Reich. Thus, the final attempt to make political use of the Landvolkbewegung failed.

The contrast of citizen and farmer largely suited the common philosophical basis of the *völkisch* and the National Revolutionaries, and sympathy for the rural population reached far into the ranks of the

Jungkonservativen and the youth leagues. In the very least, the rebelion of the rural population was viewed as, in a certain sense, prototypical for the German Revolution. In the most extreme case, it was seen as the revenge of the "countryside" upon the "city" in the civilizational sense— which paid too little attention to the concrete situation. Idealizing farmers as the "people of the black flag" was destined to fail. In the best case, the farmers' rebellion could still be understood as a provisional stage of "German nihilism" before the great shift.

6

CLIMAX AND DENOUMENT

n the summer semester of 1927, the German Academy for Politics held a conference on the subject "The Problem of Democracy." Among the participants was Max Hildebert Boehm. Boehm, a close associate of Moeller van den Bruck, member of the Juni-Klub, and contributor to *Gewissen*, was, in many ways, a typical representative of the "New Front." He had ties to both the conservatives and socialists, believed in the possibility of a position beyond Right and Left and in constructing a specifically German order for the 20th century that would leave behind the contradictions (*Aporien*) of the bourgeois era.

Immediately after the collapse, Boehm published the *Kleines Politisches Wörterbuch* (*Small Political Dictionary*). Its articles give a certain image of what was, in his eyes and those of his friends, a goal: separating from "conservatism" as a party-political movement and from Wilhelmine nationalism an orientation toward an "organic progress," intended to aid in achieving a truly democratic Constitution for which parialmentarism could serve as preparation, at most.

If we compare these positions with those which Boehm formulated not 10 years later, the distance becomes clear, as well as the extent of his disillusionment. Even before the great crisis, the Conservative Revolutionaries were convinced of the coming collapse of the political and social order. The Republic was unable either to overcome defeat or to integrate the nation upon a new foundation, and one could observe the advance of that "romantic democratism" that devoured the bases of national existence.

Among the speakers at the conference, Carl Schmitt, along with Boehm, could be considered part of the Conservative Revolution camp. But his lecture on the "Concept of the Political" did not concern itself with the contemporary situation at all and remained curiously inconclusive. Like Boehm, Schmitt championed the view recognizing the democratic character of the age was unavoidable, and demonstrated a clear skepticism toward the effectiveness of the parliamentary system. But he rejected the optimistic view that "formal" democracy could be replaced by "organic" democracy. Contrary to Boehm, for Schmitt not the "Volk" but its political "status"—i.e., the state—was of central interest. And beyond all polemics against "liberal"—thus, inexact—ideas, he asked only what was the basis of politics as a "qualifying unity" (*maßgebende Einheit*), which sovereignly differentiates between "friend" and "enemy." Schmitt's tone was incomparably cooler than Boehm's, his argument brilliant and provocative, a signal not only for a change within the conservative-revolutionary worldview but also for a change in the Zeitgeist that began to be dominated by the pathos of "objectivity."

6.1 CARL SCHMITT AND ERNST JÜNGER

Schmitt took part in the First World War as a volunteer, although he was not deployed to the front. His service at General Headquarters and Munich District Headquarters (*Stadt-kommandantur*) made possible his Habilitation[81] in 1916. After the war, he received his first professorship at Greifswald, transferred to Bonn, and finally, following a marriage that failed under scandalous circumstances, arrived at the Handelshochschule (School of Management) in Berlin.

Following the publication of his work *Roman Catholicism and Political Form* in 1923, Schmitt was considered a prominent

CARL SCHMITT

representative of political Catholicism. He did not belong to the Zentrumspartei, however, whose parliamentary activity he rejected. He also did not follow the majority of Catholic theologians and jurists in recognising natural law. He was only selectively influenced by *renouveau catholique,* and this influence had little to do with the reconciling the Church with modernity. His admiration was directed toward the Church precisely insofar as it stood against modernity, insofar as it—unlike the state—still possessed the "capability of form," insofar as it made the "decision"—in the sense of *auctoritas, non veritas facit legem*—possible.

Although early on Schmitt maintained close ties to the Catholic part of the Jungkonservativen spectrum—which formed around the journals *Abendland* and *Europäische Revue*—he remained at a clear distance from their political activity in a narrower sense. Until the beginning of the 1930s, he declined invitations to contribute to its journals. This changed once the political crisis became obvious. There were essentially three viewpoints that he—for the first time, or at least more clearly—brought into the discussion and that found broad acceptance among the Conservative Revolutionary groups:

|81| An academic qualification higher than the doctorate that enables one to hold a professorship at a German university.

◊ Asserting the specific inability of the parliamentary system to be representative: in the second edition of *Die geistesgeschichtliche Lage des heutigen Parlamentarismus* (*The Position of Contemporary Parliamentarism in Intellectual History*)[82] (1926) Schmitt still cautiously argued that parliamentarism could be considered "socio-technically" useful and offered the "minimum of order." At the same time, he observed the decrepitude of its political-theological presuppositions: the faith in discussion, faith in public opinion, faith in the division of power. The age of the masses must find new paths to ensure "the education and forming the popular will," whereby Schmitt acknowledged the clear advantages of public acclamation and charismatic rule over parliamentary proceedures.

◊ Schmitt's meditations on dictatorial power are also to be understood against this backdrop. Already in the treatise he published on this subject in 1921, he not only differentiated between the tradition of the commissarial dictatorship going back to Rome and the "sovereign dictatorship" that resulted from the modern conception of the people as the constitutive power, but he also interpreted the particular prerogatives of the President of the Reich according to article 48 of the Weimar Constitution in the sense of what he later called "dictatorial power." Under the impression of the Reichstag's self-blockade and the growth of radical currents at the end of the 1920s, Schmitt attributed the task of the "guardian of the Constitution" to President of the Reich.

◊ It is part of the peculiar character of Schmitt's constitutional expositions that large stretches of them can be interpreted as attempts to rescue the Weimar Republic from itself. It became clearer from the beginning of the 1930s, however, that Schmitt was pursuing a more distant goal to which

---

|82| Translated in 1988 as *The Crisis of Parliamentary Democracy*.

he finally—after an interpretive U-turn—affixed the label "the total state." In Schmitt's conception, the separation between state and society had been destroyed in the 19th century, because society was trying to conquer the state. But this procedure did not lead to the absorption of the state by society but rather to individual interest groups taking over the state and using its means in the pursuit of selfish interests. There arose the "state of total weakness," which, on the one hand, destroyed every unpolitical (*staatsfrei*) sphere by its "immanent pluralism" and, on the other hand, was ever less capable of carrying out the most important political function—distinguishing between friend and enemy. Schmitt thus thought it proper to work towards the erection of a "total state" of power that could, once again, take over the central task of the state.

Among Schmitt's friends and admirers in the Catholic camp, there were reservations about this idea of the "total state." But Schmitt was hardly to be deterred by that. His increasing self-confidence following his tranfer to the *Handelshochschule* was also explained by his hope of getting direct access to those who hold power. He already prepared various expert legal opinions for the Brüning cabinet, without a permanent relationship growing out of it. Then, at the beginning of 1931, he was approached by the circle of advisors to the defense minister von Schleicher. Closer contact only began after July of 1932, after Schmitt was charged with representing the government in the trial over the "Prussian coup"[83] in Germany's Constitutional Court.

Interestingly, Schmitt was able to impose his conception against the far more ambitious plans of Chancellor Papen—that the Prussian coup was not to be used as the starting point for an alteration of the constitution. In Schmitt's opinion, this could only meaningfully happen in connection with bringing about a state of emergency. Suitable plans,

---

|83|　Chancellor von Papen's coup against the Center-Left administration of Prussia, following which it was directly administered by the central government.

which he worked out for Schleicher's circle, failed due to Papen's clumsiness and Hindenberg's refusal. Even the "constructive vote of no-confidence" designed by Schmitt—a very moderate correction to the constitution—came up against resistence by the Reichspresident, so that Schmitt resigned in December 1932, even before government affairs were transferred to Schleicher.

If the influence of Schmitt's writings remained limited to specialists before the early 1930s, the attention of those with political interests had grown greatly since then. Along with older contacts to groups of the Conservative Revolution, a close, almost friendly relationship with Stapel developed after 1930. That Schmitt shared the Protestant's reservations about the "use of the word 'Reich' that dangerously weakens the state" helps explain this *rapprochement,* along with his continued distance from the Catholic wing of the Jungkonservativen.

The reasons for Schmitt's special influence within the spectrum of the Conservative Revolution—although he did not really come from the same stable—cannot be derived from his general legal or specific constitutional ideas. Instead, it arose from the right-wing intelligentsia's fascination with the formulas he made available and their decisionistic pathos. On October 14, 1930, Ernst Jünger thanked Schmitt for sending him *The Concept of the Political* with the remark that he "values the *word* too greatly not to appreciate the complete assurance, cold-bloodedness, and malice of this thrust that runs through all parries."

While Schmitt was trying to get closer to political action, Jünger—since the publication of his *Adventurous Heart* in 1929—had been attempting to distance himself ever further from political activism. His statement, "Today in society, one cannot concern oneself with Germany"[84] could only be understood as a rejection of all attempts at practical influence. It was also conspicuous that Jünger was removing

---

[84] Ernst Jünger, *Das Abenteuerliche Herz,* in vol. 67 of *Cotta's Bibiothek der Moderne* (Stuttgart: Klett, 1987 [1929]), 94.

all nationalist passages from his works. This process of distancing reached its high point in 1932 with the publication of *The Worker: Mastery and Form.*

The Worker was—like the essay " Die totale Mobilmachung" ("Total Mobilization") that appeared two years earlier—an apocalyptic

ERNST JÜNGER

text. It evoked a crisis that went beyond the concrete political, economic, social, and moral problems and offered "great" solutions. Technocratic models and plans for reorganizing the state and society were booming at this time, since the free play of politics and business was so clearly failing. For the extreme Left, the Soviet Union's recently introduced "Five-Year Plan"[85] served as a model. Certain representatives of the economic profession followed John Maynard Keynes. In Germany, there were non-conformist circles in which leftists, liberals, rightists, social democrats, bankers, conservatives, and national socialists met to exchange ideas.

Their ideas found their way into the Federation of Trade Unions' WTB Plan (named after its creators Vladimir Voitinsky (Woytinsky), Karl Baade, and Fritz Tarnow), in Gregor Strasser's Immediate Economic Program of the NSDAP or the Immediate Program of Günther Gereke, who entered Schleicher's cabinet as Reichskommissar for Employment. Appealing to anti-capitalist sentiment, Strasser was able to make the elections in July of 1932 a triumph for the NSDAP. The president of the General Federation of German Trade Unions, Theodor Leipart, gathered advocates of national autarchy that wanted to unbind the free-trade unions from the grip of the Social Democratic Party. In his famous Bernauer Address of October 14, 1932, he declared that the worker's task was "service to the nation." He spoke

---

|85| Five-Year Plan—a centralized plan for the entire economy of the USSR starting from 1928. (*Ed.*)

of the "military spirit of order and devotion to the whole"[86] that must animate the proletariat in the future.

The suspicion that Leipart was influenced by Jünger's *The Worker* is not far from the truth. The book hit the nerve of the age and went through several editions within a short period. But it also brought forth a series of misunderstandings and sharp rejection. Some considered *The Worker* a plea for Soviet methods, others as an apolitical glorification of technology, and others yet as the result of a nihilistic philosophy of materialism. It was specifically Jünger's followers from the national-revolutionary leagues who were irritated—an irritation hardly to be allayed by reading *The Worker* as a new embodiment of Nietzsche's "superman" or as the program for a "German Bolshevism." This sentiment was only exacerbated by Jünger's affirmation of modernity and hardly relieved by the emphasis upon the inner connection between "total" and "national" mobilization.

ERNST JÜNGER AND CARL SCHMITT

The effect of Jünger's *Worker* was, in many ways, similar to that of Spengler's *Decline*. In both cases, it was specifically the "conservative people that were greatly shocked by it," since they were asked to recognize

---

[86] Heinrich August Winkler, *Weimar 1918-1933: Die Geschichte der ersten deutschen Demokratie* (München: Beck, 1993), 550.

that the "*nomos* of our ancestors had gone out." This similarity was not an accident in that Jünger considered Spenglerian historical thought to be of great importance; Jünger was one of the few in the camp of the Conservative Revolution who was prepared to fundamentally accept Spengler's diagnosis. His demand for "organic construction" was also a consequence of the insight that "culture" cannot be revived and that now civilization must be founded. This paradoxical formula denoted an ultimate possibility of what the Conservative Revolution was striving for.

Jünger thus strongly oriented his work toward the future, but he was not a utopian. Right on the other side, he recongized that Hegel's idea of the "World Spirit" was the godfather to the "mastery" of his "form." Jünger's model of an "organic construction" in the realm of politics was Prussia—this essentially artificial state that stood opposed to the naturalness of the German *Volk* but gave it its final valid form. Once again, this connected Jünger with the program of the National Revolutionaries, who demanded a Third Prussia following that of Friedrich the Great and Bismarck—one that had grown up on the old

JÜNGER FAMILY

soil beyond the traditional borders of Germany but that was modern, almost *avant-garde* in its political style.

The question of how Prussia was to be developed was one Jünger was hardly able to answer in 1932. After his disappointed hopes in the Stahlhelm, the vain attempts to link the youth leagues, and the failure of Landvolkbewegung, in 1930 he considered himself among the "friends of the National Socialist Party." Yet it was precisely Hitler's success and the kind of success that it was that contributed to his growing alienation from the Party.

Jünger's first contact with the NSDAP can be dated to 1923. At that time, he was extraordinarily impressed by Hitler's speaking ability, and immediately following the Putsch, he expressed his respect for Hitler (as well as Ludendorff) for their attempt at an overthrow. Then, however, his view of Hitler changed. Perhaps Hitler's growing self-confidence contributed to the transition from Drummer to Leader (*Führer*). In any case, Jünger was inclined, after he himself turned to politics, to see in the NSDAP merely the "German workers' movement of the future," whose Chairman would be well-advised to follow the suggestions of Jünger and his friends.

Hitler was not prepared to do this. He wanted neither to stick to the original plan for a Putsch nor accept the restriction of his propaganda to "clean methods," as Jünger recommended. Jünger and his circle yearned for a "clean" (but by no means unbloody) struggle, wherein revolutionaries and counter-revolutionaries would face one another openly. This was just as blind to reality as the demand directed at Hitler and his followers to forego, in their confrontation with the Weimar Republic, all slogans ("November betrayal," "stab in the back," "Jewish conspiracy"), which, precisely because they contained simplifications or falsifications, were able to move the masses.

Even as a nationalist, Jünger was an intellectual and suffered from this trait, distanced from real life, from danger, from action. He could cover up this deficiency, but in the end he had only the choice between becoming a professional revolutionary—his sympathy for Trotsky pointed in this direction—or returning to the position of an analyst. Jünger decided in favor of the second possibility, a circumstance that cannot be entirely separated from his refusal to reject Romanticism in principle (although, in many respects, he can be considered a protagonist of anti-Romanticism), as Carl Schmitt had already done in 1919 in his investigation *Political Romanticism.*

In order for the new "form" that Jünger expected to appear, little could be done by the means of politics. Jünger's clear distancing of himself from Hitler's government early on—refusing a seat in the Reichstag and membership in the German Academy of Literature— was of a fundamentally moral nature. Schmitt's political interests in the proper sense, which gave no evidence of sympathy for Hitler or the NSDAP in 1933, explains much about his readiness to come to an arrangement with the new circumstances and his step to join the National Socialists, precisely because he placed no more than political hopes in them.

6.2 A STRUGGLE BETWEEN WORLDVIEWS

Scmitt's and Jünger's attitude toward National Socialism was related to their prominent position but was also, in many ways, typical of Conservative Revolutionaries. The principal reason for their ambivalence was the similarity or equivalence of key formulas used by both sides. The one side, like the other, combatted the "peace of shame" and the "liberal system" and demanded a new national-socialist order in the first postwar years. Thus, it seemed reasonable to explore the possibilities for collaboration.

While a man like Spengler, who knew what was going on in Munich from his own experience, regarded Hitler from the very beginning with considerable skepticism and set all his hopes in the old elites and the army as the guarantors of order, there were, in the Jungkonservativen camp, those who saw in the NSDAP and its Führer an altogether suitable insturment for achieving their own objectives. Already in the spring of 1921, then-mostly-unknown Hitler was invited to a meeting of the Juni-Klub. The question of what impression Moeller van den Bruck, specifically, received on this occasion is difficult to answer. After the Second World War, Rudolf Pechel, who informs us about the meeting, reported that Moeller was appalled by Hitler's appearance, and following a long conversation declined any further meeting with the words: "The fellow just doesn't get it." In any case, no closer collaboration followed, although Hitler originally spoke very positively about the Juni-Klub, and is said to have recognized its function as the intellectual General Staff of the national revolution.

However plausible one finds this testimony, it unquestionably flattered the self-confidence of the right-wing intelligentsia and also

JOSEF "BEPPO"
RÖMER

explains their dwindling interest in the NSDAP as a mass foundation following the failure of the 1923 Putsch. Even among the National Revolutionaries, who took an active part in the uprising (for instance, Josef "Beppo" Römer, Gerhard Rossbach, Kleo Pleyer), the attempted coup was now considered an "altogether secondary phenomenon in the overall framework of the planned 'counter-revolution.'" They held fast to this judgment after the outlawing and refounding of the NSDAP in 1925, because Hitler's decision to pursue the "legality course" made joining forces with the left wing of the Party appear possible at best. This left wing was accepted as part of the overall nationalist movement, but remained without influence on the further development of the Party.

Hitler used this reorganization to eliminate the influence of earlier Freikorps leaders, discipline the *völkisch* free riders, and establish the triviality of all programmatic debates (in which the right-wing intelligentsia was especially interested); he also made it unmistakeably clear that participation was to be allowed only at the price of absolute submission. Those from the Conservative Revolution, to whom Hitler patronizingly offered an alliance, had suitably bitter experiences: Stadtler, for instance, who after his break with von Gleichen, had already in the mid-1920s spoke out in favor of a merger between German Nationalists, paramilitary organizations, and National Socialists. After the failure of the referendum against the Young Plan and the breakdown of the "Harzburg Front" at the latest, he understood that Hitler could not be integrated into any "national opposition." After the Recihstag elections of September 12, 1930, the NSDAP became a political factor of such importance that the Conservative Revolutionaries were forced to make an entirely new assessment of them.

Even in this phase of development, the fundamental rejection of Hitler and the NSDAP was the exception that, wherever it occured, had widely different motivations. These were, for instance, the jealousy of the unsuccessful competitor, as in Niekisch's case, as well as the

FRIEDRICH WILHELM HEINZ

principled, mainly religious reservations of Ewald von Kleist-Schmenzin. Principled opposition was rare among the unconditional joiners. However, even after the failure of the "New Nationalism" project, a few from Ernst Jünger's Circle temporarily (Friedrich Wilhelm Heinz, Bruno von Salomon) and permanently (Wilhelm Weiss, Alfred Baeumler, Hans Schwarz von Berk, Werner Best) went over to the NSDAP; Landvolkbewegung was largely absorbed by it; some secretly took up contact with it (for instance, Friedrich Zimmermann, a member of the *Tat*-Kreis), and certainly a considerable share of the Conservative Revolutionaries voted for the National Socialists during elections.

LAEUEN, SALOMON, HEINZ, JUPP, KREITZ, RADEMACHER, ERNST JÜNGER

Aside from clear opposition or espousal, from the beginning of the 1930s, one encounters two possible attitudes toward Hitler and the NSDAP on the part of Conservative Revolutionaries:

◊ One group, especially among the Jungkonservativen, clung to the idea that the party could be used as an instrument. This position was unquestionably the most widespread and corresponded to underestimating Hitler and his political assertiveness that was also common among the left-wing and liberal intelligentsia. Expectations ranged from wearing out the Party in the final struggle for power to the idea of separating the Führer from his movement (after the revolution), all the way to belief in the diaclectics of the historical process that would result in "democratic madness striving with redoubled force to its completion only to come to an end and be transformed into its opposite—authority."[87]

|87| Hans Bogner, *Die Bildung der politischen Elite* (Oldenburg: Stalling, 1932), 27.

◊ The second group, unlike the first, saw the NSDAP as a possible coalition partner. If among the leadership of Deutschnationale Volkspartei, it was the tactical considerations that had the greatest significance, then among the National Revolutionaries, such as Ernst Jünger, the idea that the Party could be used as a mass foundation and be led by a "grey council of workers and soldiers" from the National Revolutionaries' own ranks played a role at the end of ther 1920s. In spite of all the irritation caused by Hitler's legality course, such ideas survived into the time immediatly before the National Socialist seizure of power. In this respect, the National Revolutionaries were only slightly less naive than the leaders of the League of Beggars, Eidgenossen (Confederates), or the Freischar Schill, who seriously believed that Hitler would place their "young national-socialist movement" on an equal footing with the National Socialism of the Party.

All the Conservative Revolutionary ideas about the NSDAP's usefulness were condemned to failure because of Hitler's strong position within the Party. His demand for absolute recognition of his authority was, in part, based on the defeat of 1923 and his negative experiences with all the political-military action units. It also went back to his principled reservations about the bourgeois Right (including the Jungkonservativen), on the one hand, and his skepticism, based on much experience, regarding the unpredictability of the National Revolutionaries and the German *völkisch* "travelling scholars," on the other.

Hitler may have also been aware that despite formal similarities between his own worldview and that of the Conservative Revolution, there were significant differences. First of all, this concerned historical thinking, an especially important aspect for all right-wing schools of thought. Hitler's ideology and that of the *völkisch* were relatively close, especially with respect to concern with the racial factor in historical development. But the fact that Hitler did not share the widespread high regard for the Germanics, preferring to speak of Aryans in general, and that among these he named the Greeks and Romans as especially excellent representatives, was an indication of profound differences. Hitler regularly expressed his dislike of Germanomania (also widespread in the Party) and criticized especially the corresponding backward-looking aspect of *völkisch* ideology.

Agreement with the *völkisch* in regard to the race question and enmity toward the Jews conversely led to a relatively large ideological divide between Hitler and the NSDAP, on the one hand, and the Jungkonservativen, on the other. There were individuals, such as Stapel, in their ranks. He went beyond having rather vague reservations about the Jews and demanded segregation. Edgar Jung was another case, who came to the conclusion that "the rights of the individual citizen cannot be ranked according to the racial point of view."[88] Criticism of the "childish anti-Semitism" of the National Socialists was at the heart of the Jungkonservativen criticism of the NSDAP. This notion of childishness also led to the mistaken assumption that National Socialist anti-Semitism was only a means of agitation without further importance.

For the Jungkonservativen, the mass-scale nature of the NS-movement was more decisive than reservations about racial ideology. In their ranks, they wanted decisive issues to be resolved "from above," that is, by the elite that represented the nation not only in a political but an intellectual and spiritual sense. A series of philosophical differences regarding how to assess the past as well as cultural and religious traditions necessarily arose from this position.

While the Jungkonservativen saw themselves altogether as preservers, Hitler was increaslingly convinced of the need to make a clean sweep (*tabula rasa—Ed.*) and inaugurate a new age. The rhetoric of self-empowerment exercized a considerable effect on the party elite

---

[88] Jung, *Herrschaft*, 121.

and strengthened their conviction that history must bend to their will. Their sharp criticism of Spengler is, in this respect, revealing. Rosenberg accused Spengler, not only of lacking partisanship and having a concept of race scarcely oriented toward biology, but also of "fatalism." National Socialism, according to Rosenberg, did not rely on what had historically come to be, but was instead a "history-shaping force" in its own right.

Such formulations remind one of the futuristic aspects of National Revolutionary ideology, but here, too, the similarity was not sufficient enough. Hitler's idea of progress was fundamentally liberal-optimistic and had nothing in common with the expectation of National Revolutionaries, who believed the eternal order of things would be reproduced at a higher level in the coming technocracy. In comparison with this fundamental difference, the conflict over the eastward orientation (to which parts of the Jungkonservativen and the *völkisch* adhered, along with the National Revolutionaries) was of secondary importance.

At the beginning of the 1930s, the ideological differences between National Socialism and the Conservative Revolution were sufficiently clear. Those leaders of the NSDAP who emerged from the Conservative Revolutionary milieu—Himmler, for instance, who belonged to the Artam Bund (League) and was interested in *völkisch* esoterism, or the brothers Otto and Gregor Strasser, with their connections to the Juni-Klub, to Spengler and other minds among the right-wing intelligentsia—either learned to show tolerance toward Hitler's sentiments and *raison de parti*, or else left the Party. This did not stop individuals, such as Goebbels who, for a long time, expressed his admiration for Moeller van den Bruck and Ernst Jünger—from recruiting among the Conservative Revolutionaries for the Party. Failure, however, also led to correcting his assertion that they wanted to reach the same goals as the National Socialists.

6.3 CONSERVATIVE REVOLUTION IN EUROPE?

In January of 1931, poet Rudolf Borchardt gave an address ending with one visionary statement:

> *The entire world is becoming torrentially conservative, out of self-protection, to protect its heritage, from a duty to capture once again the elements that have been shaken together, each in a different way, us ourselves—in the most difficult of all: the re-overthrow of the overthrow, the negated and negating negation, the revolution against the revolution.*[89]

In the ranks of the Conservative Revolution, the idea was quite widespread that the entire world, or at least the European world, was being seized with this "revolution against the revolution." Many nationalists hoped that all "proletarian" peoples would rise up under Germany's leadership against the liberal-capitalist West, and were inclined to make use of the "world revolutionary" rhetoric of Communism; Ernst Jünger expressly intended the *Worker* to be a "planetary" figure. Here, too, we see the *völkisch* at the opposite end of the opinion spectrum. In the prewar period, they used propaganda about "racial solidarity" that hardly played any role in the years of the Weimar Republic. The Jungkonservativen held the Center once again. This was not only the case because of the "occidental" perspective of some of its leading thinkers, such as Edgar Jung or Heinrich von Gleichen, but also related to the view among other thinkers that an anti-liberal movement was seizing upon all Europe, and the age of the French Revolution was coming to an end. One of the most important representatives of this position was undoubtedly Rohan, who referred in his writings to ideological tendencies in neighboring lands that were

---

[89] Rudolf Borchardt, *Führung* (München: Georg Müller, 1931-2), 35.

similar to those of the Conservative Revolution in Germany and, in his opinion, were paving the way for a "new, contemporary European way of life."

Rohan's attempt to claim even the Soviet Union for revolutionary conservatism remained ineffectual; more convincing was his effort to include Italy. We have already referred to the widespread interest in the Italian model among Jungkonservativen and National Revolutionaries, yet this remained a distant sympathy. Conversely, early on in Italy individual fascists connected the words "revolution" and "conservative," although this did not become at all important within the official fascist doctrine. All representatives of views similar to those of the Conservative Revolution—for instance, Julius Evola—remained marginal figures, at most tolerated in the framework of fascist "pluralism."

What justified Conservative Revolutionary reservations about fascism was, above all, the cultural distance, the "Latin" element. By contrast, they felt somewhat of a mental affiliation with the neighboring "Germanic" countries. Austria presents a special case, since its leadership and most of its inhabitants considered themselves German. Along with the "Greater German" idea, that of the "Reich" had obvious significance, which lead to the spread of leading Jungkonservativen ideas, without requiring unequivocal ideological partisanship. We have already called attention to the role of the German Nationalists and Christian Socialists in the prewar period and the influence of the Spann school on the corporate state of the 1930s. It remains only to mention that, along with the *völkisch* (who had considerable influence on the intellectual milieu), a rather traditionalist variant of Jugendbewegung existed, rejecting many "leaguish" (*bündisch*) innovations. By contrast, the Heimwehr presented a fighting league that surpassed in importance all comparable organizations in Germany as a factor in domestic politics, as was proven in the *coup d'état* of 1934. The Heimwehr and its leader Rüdiger Fürst derived a claim to help determine the domestic constitution of Austria not only from its function as a frontline combat organization, but also from a peculiar Catholic-tinged ideology of National Socialism.

The situation in Switzerland was clearly different from that in Austria. Yet its withdrawal from the German nation in the 19th century did not prevent the emergence—since before the war, but especially in the crises of the postwar period—of worldviews similar to those of the Conservative Revolution in Germany. This tendency could also be observed in Flanders, where nearly the entire menu of groupings existed, including the youth leagues. Similar grouping in the Netherlands were considerably less strong.

Great Britain, in comparison, seemed wholly untouched, since its victory in 1918 made the conservation of its archaic political order possible. Of course, nationalistic and imperial groups continued to exist within its spectrum. Conservative groupings inclined to dissidence were regularly reigned in (*wieder eingebunden*). Those who, like Oswald Mosley, were interested in further experiment more or less quickly oriented themselves toward the Italian model. Similar remarks could be made concerning France, the importance of which as a political laboratory in earlier times was already mentioned. Yet from the end of the 1920s, a multiform Jeune Droite (Young Right) made its appearance there. This Right, in spite of its autochthonous roots (especially Action Française, also Neo-Thomism and technocratic models), showed surprising similarities with the schools of thought that made up the Conservative Revolution. Neither inhereted enmity nor the difference in the intellectual climate prevented direct influence: within the framework of the youth camp in 1930, Aléxandre Marc met with a number of prominent "non-conformists," including Otto Strasser, Harro Schulze-Boysen, and Ferdinand Fried. Another, Thierry Maulnier, head of the group Ordre Nouveau, wrote a clearly sympathetic foreword to the French edition of Moeller van den Bruck's Das Dritte Reich.

The Jeune Droite in France did not, however, achieve the degree of influence like that of the Conservative Revolution in Germany. It remained an interesting, but rather isolated group within the right-wing intelligentsia, whose members turned toward rather different camps in the dramatic worsening of the situation up to the outbreak of war. In contrast, the Conservative Revolution was able to gain an influence in the last years of the Weimar Republic explicable not least by its agreement with the "new life feeling." Their growing importance even disturbed the Left that was dominant until that point. They were forced to discuss the ideas of this Right. They were prepared to make nuanced judgments: Carl von Ossietzky's statement is well-known. He said that the National Revolutionaries were "light years ahead of men like Hitler and Seldte." And they were even ready for dialogue: in 1929, Ernst Jünger was able to publish a programmatic essay in *Tagebuch* (*Diary*); in 1932, authors of the Conservative Revolution were allowed to speak for themselves in the pages of *Literarische Welt* (*Literary World*). The growing insecurity of the Left was based upon their being forced to recognize how far the real situation had wandered from their own estimates, and that the intellectual Right could employ a "radiation of energy" to which they had no access.

6.4 HITLER AS EDUCATOR

It was not only the Conservative Revolution, however, that made use of this radiation of energy. They had to recognize that their hopes for a "national revolution" (the rural population, the worker, farmer, and soldier under the leadership of the national-revolutionary intelligentsia) or the minimum program of the Jungkonservativen— cold-blooded *coup d'état*, commissarial dictatorship, "organic construction"—remained without a prospect of success. They lacked influence, competent personnel and, determination. The plan of leading "the ideas" to victory "in alliance with real powers" had failed for the time being; in January of 1933, Edgar Jung came to the conclusion that there was "no German Right capable of ruling."

After all, the new regime—inaugurated by Hitler's assumption of the government and the March elections—viewed Jung along with many Conservative Revolutionaries with distrust. It was this current that seemed to be a dangerous competitor to the National Socialists. The National Revolutionaries, especially, were under suspicion, because their ranks contained disaffected members of the NSDAP gathered since the beginning of the 1930s. The fact that Otto Strasser's Schwarze Front (Black Front) used the slogans of the Conservative Revolution led to even more enmity. Already in February of 1933, Gestapo searched Ernst Jünger's apartment for the first time. Arrests (Josef "Beppo" Römer, Harro Schulze-Boysen; only after a certain delay did the same fate befall Ernst Niekisch and the Widerstandsbewegung) or flights abroad (Karl O. Paetel, Otto Strasser) followed. Emigration was sooner or later also the fate of those Jungkonservativen, who were replaced on racial grounds and then disenfranchised (Rudolf Borchardt, Ernst Kantorowicz, Hans Rothfels, Hans-Joachim Schoeps). For the rest—apart from neophytes (Alfred Baeumler, Ernst Kriek, Otto Westphal, Kleo Pleyer, and, in a certain sense, also Friedrich Gogarten, Emanuel Hirsch, Gottfried Benn, and Martin Heidegger)—conformed, chose "inner emigration"[90] or resistance.

GOTTFRIED BENN   **ERNST KRIECK**   **KLEO PLEYER**

As in the population at large, so in the camp of the Conservative Revolution, the largest fraction consisted of those who opted for

---

|90| *Innere Emigration.* The so-called "inner emigration" was a notion describing remaining in Germany after 1933, while being opposed to Nazism. (*Ed.*)

conformity. Motives ranged from opportunism (Karl Anton Prinz Rohan along with a large number of the *völkisch*) over somewhat naive efforts to at least "win this revolution," to the attempt to prevent worse things from happening through active participation. The most remarkable example of this idea came from those National Revolutionaries, who saw in Hitler, at best, the "Chancellor of the transition period," demanded greater ideological consistency, warned the NS leadership of opportunists (*Konjunkturrittern*), or even projected an alternative program for the new regime. Thus Niekisch conceived (in two books published in 1935, *Im Dickicht der Pakte* [*In the Thicket of Pacts*] and *Die dritte imperiale Figur* [*The Third Imperial Figure*]) a politics that outdid anything (openly) demanded by the National Socialists by being more radical.

Carl Schmitt acted with rather different motives. However great a role ambition and weaknesses of character played, we cannot fail to notice that Schmitt, by going over to the National Socialists, was relying on his own theory: in a civil war, he went over to the side of the victors and the only party capable of carrying out its plans that could establish "peace." The "thought of concrete order" that Schmitt developed was still suspiciously close to Jungkonservativen ideas, and the advantage that Schmitt ascribed to the state could not be reconciled with the idea of a "*völkisch* Right."

Already in an essay by Alfred Rosenberg that appeared at the beginning of 1934 in the *Völkischer Beobachter* (*Völkisch Observer*), the formula of the "total state" used by Schmitt and his disciples was strongly attacked, maintaining that only the party could make a claim to being total, while the state must serve the party as a "tool." The attacks that started on Schmitt only reached their high point after he, by justifying the murders of June 30, 1934, performed an important service for the regime.

It is characteristic that Schmitt supported his activities at this time, above all, in the Hanseatic Verlagsanstalt. Its leader, Benno

Ziegler, brought its publishing program much closer to the wishes of the new wielders of power. They could not mislead the NS leadership (any more than Günther's joining the party or Stapel's anti-Jewish journalism) from seeing that it was faced with a kind of subversion aimed at preserving an independent philosophical position, and trying to somehow give National Socialism a conservative underpinning. In 1939, shortly after Stapel and Günther were removed from power, and *Deutsches Volkstum* was *de facto* liquidated, Rosenberg stated that Stapel was a "thoroughly established philosophical opponent of National Socialism in all directions."

Schmitt's or Stapel's efforts to exert influence always occured on the meta-level of political and ideological events. One example of continued conservative-revolutionary influence on the base was the role played by youth-league leaders in constructing the Hitlerjugend. The starting point was the plan of the ambitious "Reich Youth Leader" Baldur von Schirach to make the Hitlerjugend into a state youth organization in the middle term. This was not realizable in view of the Hitlerjugend's short reach, its social structure—a large percentage was working class—and its unclear character as a party organization. After the forceable integration of all non-denominational youth leagues in the summer of 1933, Schirach needed suitable personnel to integrate the mass of new members and win over the younger members ideally for the new state. Thus, former youth leagues formed, under different banners and insignia, Hitlerjugend youth groups, in many cases youth-league leaders became Hitlerjugend leaders, and thus "infiltrated" parts of the Hitlerjugend.

The Reichs Youth Leadership, however, tolerated this only for just so long as the structures of the Hitlerjugend were firmly established, and they had enough power to carry out a thorough purge (mid-1930s). The widespread enthusiasm of many from the youth leagues for a state youth organization as a realization of the idea of a "super league" only found opposition in individuals pulling out as well as in the formation of illegal leagues that were heavily persecuted by the Gestapo with the support of the Hitlerjugend.

In all cases described, camouflage played an important role. For this purpose, the quantity of ideological similarities between National Socialism and the Conservative Revolution could be emphasized. The common admiration for Nietzsche, Lagarde, and Wagner, to some extent even Chamberlain, could be considered a common foundation; but after a transitional phase, the regime lost all tolerance concerning key areas of ideology.

The attempt to style Moeller van den Bruck as the ancestor of the Third Reich especially demonstrates this point. After a short phase of popularity that made even an identification of the Revolution of 1933 with the "Conservative Revolution" seem possible, unmistakable rejection followed. A doctoral dissertation written at the time stated in conformity with the party line:

> *Moeller van den Bruck is no 'prophet and herald of the Third Reich,' but rather the 'last conservative.' From the world of his politics, no path leads to the German future—because no path of his leads to National Socialism.*[91]

Heavy attacks corresponded to this rejection. The Herren-Club and *Ring* were subjected to them since the summer of 1933. Starting wtih 1934, the journal only continued to be published (under the title *Economic Ring*) as an economic newsletter. Deutscher Herrenclub, renamed German Club in 1934, dissolved a year later. The fate of *Der Ring* was, in many ways, similar to that of *Tat*. After Zehrer lost the editorship in August of 1933, the *Tat*-Kreis dissolved, and, in April of 1934, even the subtitle "independent monthly for the

---

|91| Helmut Rödel, *Moeller van den Bruck: Standort und Wertung* (Berlin: Stollberg, 1939), 164.

formation of new reality" disappeared. Giselher Wirsing and Ernst Wilhelm Eschmann took over the editorship. The journal oriented itself largely on the new ideological guidelines. In March of 1939, the last issue appeared; after that, *Tat* was succeeded in a new form and more modern style by *The XXth Century*; in 1944, the worsened military situation required its closure.

Insofar as conformity did not occur from pure opportunism, its borders with the inner emmigration were fluid. It offered much greater opportunities for influence in the first phase after 1933. Famous authors from the field of the Conservative Revolution were able to publish works that circulated widely and were intensively discussed, although their tendency was unambiguously critical of the regime. The most famous example may be Spengler's *Jahre der Entscheidung* (*Hour of Decision*) and Richard Benz's *Geist und Reich* (*Spirit and Reich*), both published in 1933; Friedrich Sieburg's *Germany is Coming* might be named in this context. Whereas Spengler criticized, above all, the illusionary aspect of National Socialism's conception of politics, Benz and Sieburg turned against what they saw as barbaric and unworthy of a civilized nation (*Kulturvolk*): against anti-Semitism as an expression of a "comfortable and thoughtless ostracism" and against the "spiritual tradition and the coming nation drifting apart."

A very early example of disguised debate with the new circumstances was Friedrich Georg Jünger's collection of poems, published 1934 by Niekisch's Widerstandsverlag (Resistance Publishers), among which was a piece with the title "Opium." This piece was used abroad as a sign of free intellectual life. Even more important may have been *On the Marble Cliffs*, published in 1939 by Hanseatische Verlagsanstalt (Hanseatic Publishing House). The author's prominence protected him from measures by the state authorities, who knew perfectly well that the work was a coded overall critique of existing circumstances. Along with these famous cases, there were a few novels written by authors close to the Conservative Revolution such as Werner Bergengruen (*Der Großtyrann und das Gericht* [*The Great Tyrant and the Court*],

1935), Jochen Klepper (*Der Vater* [*The Father*], 1937), and Friedrich Reck-Malleczewen (*Bockelson: History of a Mass Hysteria*, 1937). Although these writings were not able to include any direct attack on the National Socialist system or its representatives, they could be read as "palimpsests" for their hidden meaning.

6.5 RESISTANCE

What distinguished internal emigration from resistance was, above all, the willingness to intervene actively, and this depended decisively upon how one judged the situation. The idea that the "wrong ruler" was in power was widespread among conservative revolutionaries; some of them even believed that "sheer madness" was in power and that "the greatest folly in German history would ensue." But the path to taking action against it was long.

In a sort of intermediate position were those among the Jungkonservativen (Otto Dibelius, Martin Niemöller, Hans Asmussen), who sided with the Confessing Church in the ecclesiastical struggle, but whose goal was not the removal of the regime as such, but the restoration of the freedom of faith communities. For all the personal courage this position demanded, one must distinguish it from resistance in the proper sense, whose aim was to overthrow the system.

MARTIN NIEMÖLLER

Remarkably, the first and, later on, most important actions of the resistance were undertaken by men who had been marked politically by the Conservative Revolution. The plans of Edgar Julius Jung's circle should be emphasized in this context. Jung saw Hitler's assumption to power as a personal blow, not only because he was active in Papen's administration, but also because of an aversion to Hitler, personally, that went back to the days of armed resistance to the occupation of the Ruhrland[92] (*Ruhrkampf*). In Munich, his main base of operations, Jung was considered an especially dangerous enemy.

EDGAR JULIUS JUNG

At first, Jung tried to interpret the goals of the National Socialists as a detour leading to that "conservative" and "Christian" revolution that was the meaning and direction of great change. Yet at the end of 1933, he began to construct a center of conspiratorial activity with his friend Herbert von Bose in Papen's vice-chancellory (but without his knowledge). Jung's and Bose's plan for a *coup d'état* was based on making use of the conflict between Röhm and the military authorities in order, with Hindenberg's backing, to erect a military regime. In mid-June, the action began. In an address to the Marburg University on the 17th, Papen was to give (without realizing it) the signal to strike. Hitler was beside himself over this address, in which Papen warned of the dangers of Byzantinism, voicing clear criticism of the Party's claim to "totality": "The supremacy of a single party in place of the rightly vanished multi-party system"—Jung had Papen say—"appears historically as a transitional condition that is justified only for as long as ensuring radical change demands it and until the new personnel can begin to function." For Hitler, the assertion that National Socialism and the "sort of conservative-revolutionary movement" of the postwar period were equal partners was just as transparent as Jung's attempt to reinterpret the national revolution as a Conservative Revolution

---

|92| Ruhr was one of Germany's main industrial areas. In 1923-25, the area was occupied by France and Belgium when Germany was unable to pay reparations per Versailles Treaty. (*Ed.*)

and commit nationalism to the program of a new Ghibilline Party in Europe that was to prepare the way for a league of all Occidental nations.

The already printed text of the Marburg Address was impounded as soon as its contents became known and broadcast over the radio—forbidden. The word quickly got out that Jung wrote the manuscript, whereupon Hitler ordered his arrest (June 25). Shortly after Bose was murdered as part of the June 30th action, on July 1, 1933, an SS-Guard shot Jung in a wooded area near Oranienburg. The alleged suppression of the Röhm Purge was also accompanied by the first destructive blow to the conservative opposition, to which Schleicher and Gustav von Kahr also fell victim while others, such as Brüning or Gottfried Treviranus, were able to save themselves by fleeing.

In fact, after Hindenberg's death there was no power independent of Hitler left in Germany that might have become the center of resistance. In the following period, a phase in which the National Socialist regime could celebrate its greatest success, and was supported by a broad consensus, opposition was restricted to the narrowest circles—which did not, however, give up. Thus, in the summer of 1933 opponents of the regime began to gather around Friedrich Wilhelm Heinz. He was a man from the National Revolutionary milieu, who received enough experience with the NSDAP during its "years of struggle," and attempted to use the Stahlhelm and its successor organization as cover for a network of conservative opposition. Old alliances from the fighting leagues, especially the Ehrhardt organization, played an important role in this sense. Heinz always asserted that within the framework of the "September Conspiracy" of 1938, an assault corps of earlier Freikorps men gathered in order to storm the Reichschancellery, kill Hitler, and thus carry out a *coup d'etat*.

The background for such extensive plans was the radical change in the situation with the end of "revision politics." Since starting to plan an offensive against the Czech rump state, a new center of resistance formed around Ludwig Beck, Carl Goerdeler, and Ulrich von Hassell. Its immediate goal was the construction of a commissarial dictatorship that would then create the preconditions for a restoration of ordered conditions. In no way did they wish to undo the external successes of the Reich, but they saw in Hitler's lack of accountability and the destruction of the state of law those factors that must be combated on ethical as well as political grounds. They often imagined their New Germany as a monarchy based on the British model, otherwise the plotters' conceptions differed widely. The restoration of parliamentarism favored by Goerdeler met with widespread reservations.

The lack of support for the opposition abroad soon led to the abandonment of all attempts at an overthrow during the early part of the war; the Wehrmacht's unexpected victories led to regime stabilization. Only in 1942 did the resistance (under the circumstances, mainly a military opposition) find new support, which now came from the younger generation of officers. A *Grafengruppe* (group of Counts) formed around Claus Graf Schenk von Stauffenberg and Henning von Tresckow: its members were mostly staff officers influenced by their origin among the nobility, of course, but also by the ideas of the Conservative Revolution.

Stauffenberg was himself shaped by the elitism of the poet Stefan George. For him, as for Tresckow, Fritz-Dietlof von der Schulenburg, Albrecht Merz von Quirnheim, or Cäsar von Hofacker, the idea of "Prussian socialism" inspired by Oswald Spengler also offered an important point of orientation. This explains not only the remarkable openness for cooperation with a part of the left-wing resistance—Stauffenberg considered Social Democrat Julius Leber a more suitable Chancellor than Goerdeler—but also their rejection of restoring the monarchy or the Weimar Republic. Within the larger group of the conspiracy, personal or organizational connections derived from the community of sentiment or leagues of the Conservative Revolution played a significant role. This explains the importance of the large number of former members of the Ehrhardt Brigade, who found their place in counterintelligence and concerned themselves with orienting it toward opposition. It also explains the character of the Kreisauer-Kreis that had plans for constitutional reform, including graduated suffrage and corporative models that were not accidentally reminiscent of Jungkonservativen ideas of the interwar period (since the Circle was a union that also had roots in the Arbeitslagerbewegung, the labor-camp movement[93]).

The July 20, 1944[94] assassination attempt served a practical goal only in a very limited sense, since the conspirators had given up almost all hope of a separate peace with the Western powers (a necessary condition for an orderly retreat from the East). Stauffenburg and Tresckow saw the act, above all, as proof of the moral integrity of the "secret Germany." This formula, whose origins go back to the prehistory of the Conservative Revolution and received its special mark from the George-Kreis, demonstrated the close connection between the resistance and the intellectual heritage of the "German counter-revolution."

6.6 AMBIVALENCE AND SEPARATION

Hitler himself never used the term "Conservative Revolution," although he did speak of the NSDAP being a "conservative-revolutionary party" and that he himself should be considered the "most conservative revolutionary in the world." These offhand remarks cannot, however, deceive us concerning the essential differences

---

|93| The labor-camp movement, or the German work-service movement, was founded by sociologist Eugen Rosenstock-Huessy in the 1920s. It focused on organizing voluntary work-service camps for students and young workers in order to engage them with the community. (*Ed.*)

|94| Famous for the misnamed "Operation Valkyrie" that was to take place after the assassination, the July-20 plot on the life of Hitler meant to take control of Germany and make peace with the Allies. (*Ed.*)

between the Conservative Revolution and National Socialism, which were constantly emphasized both by Hitler and his disciples. For them, the Conservative Revolution was only part of the "reaction" that "with the slogan 'Conservative Revolution' was propagating the restoration of conditions from 500 years ago."

This polemic was directed toward the reservations about modernity, characteristic of all currents of the Conservative Revolution. This suggests the possibility of explaining the relationship between the Conservative Revolution and National Socialism by contrasting Romanticism and anti-Romanticism, with the romantic impulse being decisive for the Conservative Revolution and the anti-romantic counterpart—decisive for National Socialism.

Undoubtedly, there is some truth to this. There was a sharp turn against Romanticism, particularly among the younger intellectuals, who received a certain impression from the Conservative Revolution but then switched over to National Socialism, such as Baeumler and Westphal. The most interesting example of this may be Christoph Steding, a historian, who died young, and whose posthumously published principal work *Das Reich und die Krankheit der europäischen Kultur* (*The Reich and the Sickness of European Culture*) went through five editions between 1938 and 1943.

Steding's starting point was Westphal's thesis on the completion of the power state idea (*Machtstaatsgedankens*) in Bismarck's Reich. He shared Westphal's view that in the middle of the 19th century, a decision for Hegel ("Hegel is the German Idea"), against Catholicism and against Romanticism had to be made in order to make possible German unification. Every recourse to Romanticism seemed, from this perspective, to be a strengthening of the "unpolitical," as a fixation on "culture" and therefor unsuitable for effecting the necessary regeneration.

Although Steding explicitly appealed to Schmitt for this line of argument and his thought was obviously influenced by certain ideas of

Moeller van den Bruck, *Das Reich und die Krankheit der europäischen Kultur* can be read as a comprehensive settling of accounts with the Conservative Revolution: most of its leading minds are subjected to a more (Thomas Mann, Stefan George, Oswald Spengler, also Ludwig Klages) or less (Lagarde, Moeller van den Bruck) strong critique from which even (and precisely) Nietzsche is not exempted.

Steding's book had the effect of a declaration by National Socialist Germany, for it delineated the position that can be considered philosophically consistent. Philosophical consistency was not, however, a high priority for the National Socialist regime. It permitted a certain ideological leeway, particularly for those who disapprovingly characterized Steding as the supporter of a "merely *völkisch*" worldview. Undoubtedly, there was a whole series of prominent scholars who were recognized National Socialists and who began their line of argument with Romanticism. For instance, these were Kleo Pleyer, a historian who, like Steding, was active in the Reichsinstitut für Geschichte des neuen Deutschlands (State Institute for the History of the New Germany), the champion of racial psychology Ludwig Clauss, a student of ancient Germany, Otto Höffler, or anthropologists Otto Huth and Werner Müller, who originally came from the Klages-Kreis, to name a few. But the orientation of their thought—*Volk, Stand, und Bund*— was considered problematic in the very least. An exact presentation of intellectual history during the years 1933-45 would have to trace the hidden and open conflicts between these Romantics and the anti-Romantics, such as Steding, Baeumler, Kriek, and Westphal, and would probably come to the conclusion that the anti-Romantic line eventually prevailed—the faction that saw in Hitler the "World Spirit on horseback."

The followers of the Conservative Revolution could not follow them when it comes to this point, in part, precisely because they tried so forcibly to steer clear of Romanticism and went as far as Ernst Jünger down the path of ruthless acknowledgment of facts. Shortly after Hitler's seizure of power, Jünger found enthusiastic followers in a group of young, radical National Socialists from Austria formed around Edgar Traugott and Meinhart Sild, who read *The Worker* as a manifesto of a new Germany. They got in touch with him, were benevolently received, but observed with increasing bitterness that the author was not prepared to follow their ideological guidelines.

After the appearance of *Marble Cliffs*, Sild and Traugott did not limit themselves to lamenting the break in Jünger's work; their tone even became threatening. Jünger, however, remained sympathetic. He responded to the accusation of insufficient ideological consistency that a straight progression in the direction outlined in *The Worker* was possible, but would "lead to a world entirely of masks and machines." In the letter, where these words occur, sent to Traugott on September 21, 1942, he concludes,

> *Among your remarks, I was struck by the statement that you and your friends value men only in terms of their functional character. But what is important is undoubtedly what is left over when a man is robbed of his function, whether his techno-political function or life as a whole. That is his metaphysical, indivisible and unorganizable residue.* [95]

An awareness of this "residue's" existence was not to be found in Hitler's and his followers' thought.

6.7 SUBSEQUENT HISTORY

If no continuation of the Conservative Revolution was possible after 1945, this can be explained by the way in which Germany was defeated. The Second World War, like the First, was a constitutional war, and

---

[95] Ernst Jünger, letter to Edgar Traugott, September 21, 1942, Ernst Jünger's estate, Deutsches Literaturarchiv Marbach.

the new orders installed in the rump states had to follow guidelines that were not only meant to prevent a revival of National Socialism but also to make it difficult to build upon the specifically German tradition of political thought. In the Federal Republic, there were, indeed, politicians marked by the ideas of the Conservative Revolution (Eugen Gerstenmaier, Hermann Ehlers, Jakob Kaiser), and experienced thinkers, such as Ernst Jünger, Martin Heidegger, and Gottfried Benn exercised considerable intellectual influence, which, to a certain degree, perpetuated this tradition. There were also subterranean effects, but attempts at intellectual organization remained inconsequential. The shock of the collapse was not only political and material but also spiritual and intellectual. A number of the protagonists broke spectacularly with their past convictions. The most famous example may have been Ernst Niekisch, who, leaving prison badly maimed, went to East Berlin to put himself at the disposition of the Socialist Unity Party.[96] Less well-known is the case of Günther Gereke, Reichscommissar for Combating Unemployment in Schleicher's cabinet, who was removed and condemned by the National Socialists and arrested again in connection with the 1944 assassination plot. He became the co-founder of the CDU after the war, served the regional government of Lower Saxony in several capacities, then was banned from his party because of contacts in the East, and ultimately moved to the German Democratic Republic in 1952.

Less noticeable than such spectacular individual cases was the resigned attitude of many, as well as that process in which "westernization" reduced what used to constitute the "psychology of the German idea of the state" to the vanishing point. The Allies explicitly waged war not only against Hitler and National Socialist ideology but against everything they considered part of "Prussianism," "irrationalism," and "authoritarianism." Not a single key idea of the Conservative Revolution—*Bund, Stand, Volk, Reich*—remained above

---

|96| That is, the official Communist Party of East Germany. (*Ed.*)

suspicion. What was able to survive here and there or in the revival of youth organizations fell into a crisis with the cultural break of the 1960s. The lasting displacement of the system of political coordinates leftward led to all worldviews of the political Right being fundamentally under suspicion of "fascism." The protagonists of the Conservative Revolution are officially considered almost exclusively as "pioneers" or "precursors" of the National Socialists.

This form of ostracism has, however, like all forms, sparked unwelcome reactions from those who take an interest in what has been declared taboo as such, as well as from that minority that seeks for a conceivable right-wing position outside the establishment. Particularly the leading figures of the Conservative Revolution, notably Carl Schmitt and Ernst Jünger, have awakened extraordinary intellectual curiosity; the flood of literature about them, as well as about less well-known authors of the Conservative Revolution, is immeasurable. We can also observe that, among the younger generation, attempts have been made to adapt individual concepts from the Conservative Revolution to the changed circumstances and, thus, to revive them. The various attempts at a "New Right" that have appeared since the national-revolutionary beginnings of the 1970s share the fact that they consider the Conservative Revolution an important starting point.

Among the reasons for this continued fascination is skepticism regarding the prospects for success of the Liberal model of society. Its functionality has never truly been called into question during the postwar period, and the collapse of the Eastern Bloc was even able to provide a basis for the idea that we are at the threshold of the "final victory of the West" or the "End of History," whereby all political alternatives have been exhausted. This optimism has already sustained damage, and we are seeing indications of a new orientation emerging that cannot remain without effect in the realm of worldviews.

What makes our current situation (2003) similar to the starting point of the Conservative Revolution is the dissolution of accustomed ideological classifications. From the Left as well as the Right, the justification for these categories is being questioned. Thus, once again, begins the discussion of great political problems, which has always included the relationship between preservation and change. In Armin Mohler's words: "The conservative-revolutionary attitude stands or falls according to the ability or inability to distinguish sharply between what is timelessly valid and what is the passing form of the day."

AFTERWORD
TO THE ENGLISH EDITION

ALAIN DE BENOIST

seem to recall it was Niekisch who called Ernst Jünger "the eye man" (*der Augenmensch*). For me, the eye man was Armin Mohler. In saying that, I am not only thinking of his taste for painting, nor of his surprising knowledge in the artistic domain. Nor am I only thinking of the conversations we had on this subject, nor of a Lovis Corinth exposition in Munich we visited together a good many years ago, nor of a trip I made to Mexico using his article devoted to Mexican mural art (i.e., the works of Diego Rivera, Jose Clemente Orozco, and especially David Alfaro Siqueiros) as my only tourist guide. All of this is bound together, however. If he had not turned toward politics, Armin Mohler would undoubtedly have been one of the foremost art critics of his time. He had a vocation one might call unfulfilled had it not been subject to a kind of transmutation. In fact, it is my conviction that Armin Mohler *looked* at political life and the unfolding of ideologies in the manner of an artist, more precisely of a painter. A system of thought was for him above all a landscape opening up, a panorama offered to the eyes.

Thus, when he considered the Conservative Revolution, it is first of all in order to identify its *Leitbilder*, its "leading images." And in this predilection for painting, at the expense, for example, of music, I also see the source of his "nominalism"—a landscape as an artist represents it always refers to a particular scene, a determinate context. There is no pictographic representation of a "general reality" any more than a science of the total object.

This opposition between music and painting is fundamental. Abstraction on the one hand, even if admirably harmonious; concrete particularity on the other. *A propos* of the Conservative Revolution, Mohler said he preferred to express himself in images rather than concepts. It's the same principle again: images are always concrete and particular, concepts most often general and abstract. *Wider die All-Gemeinheiten* ("Against the generalities"): that is the motto of an artist.[1] But this motto has nothing in common with a mere recognition of any sort of primacy of the aesthetic that would result in an "aesthetization of politics" of the sort only too much talked about. Its significance lies deeper. It is a question of recognizing that all thought is a matter of forms, that all knowledge is a matter of forms, that the very goal of human existence is to give oneself form and look to the excellence of that form. Now, there is no form-in-itself. I sometimes teased Armin Mohler by telling him that denying the existence of general ideas represents one of the most general ideas there is, but on this point, we were in complete agreement. Ideas themselves are a matter of looking. From this we can see how little Mohler was predisposed to adhere to a religion that privileges hearing over seeing—over the icon—or to a philosophy that makes the abstract man, divested of his particular attachments, the center of reflection.

It was precisely looking that allowed Armin Mohler always to go to the essential. This trait always struck me: immediately, he goes to the

---

|1| See Armin Mohler, *Wider die All-Gemeinheiten, oder, Das Besondere ist das Wirkliche* (Kilchberg, Germany: Sinus-Verlag, 1981).

essential. He never lingers over details or frills. In a system of thought, precisely because he looks at it as a landscape, he quickly makes out the lines of force, that is, perspectives. The same goes for his writing: he always has the right word, *le mot juste*—"the right word in the right place." I remember one day he told me the best way to undertand a book was to take no notes and, after closing it, limit oneself to jotting down on paper what one remembers. I never forgot that lesson (which I have considerable difficulty following, however!). From this taste for the essential comes his contempt for worldly conversation and useless discussion. And if he was sometimes a bit rough with this or that person it was because he hated wasting time, and even more when others wasted his.

Another trait of Armin's which always struck me was his independence of mind and rejection of preconceived ideas. Of course, even if our ideas do not form by themselves but are built up from contact with others, there is no true personal thinking that is not to a large extent autonomous. But in Armin Mohler's case, this independence of mind goes beyond the usual case. Not only is he perfectly independent in regard to the dominant ideology, as witnessed by his works in opposition to "re-education" (*Umerziehung*) and "character-washing" (*Charakterwäsche*). The latter was a neologism coined by Caspar Schrenck-Notzing on the model of "brain washing" and used by him as the title of a book and a kind of red thread throughout his works—the trace of a faithfulness to his country of choice—but Mohler is no less independent in regard to the prejudices of those close to him or those who "think as he does." I find this quality still more meritorious.[2] Mohler is not one of those who, faced with a novel event, idea, or situation, reason according to an *a priori* dictated by their belonging to a "family" of some sort. He does not think something because that is "what one must think," but because he has convinced himself of it. Similarly, he has no enemies on principle: only adversaries whose

---

|2| Caspar Schrenck-Notzing, *Charakterwäsche: Die amerikanische Besatzung in Deutschland und ihre Folgen* (Stuttgart: Seewald, 1965).

good qualities he has always been able to recognize and even praise. Whether it is a matter of writing about the skyscrapers of Chicago or the Parisian "Pompidolium" (the Centre Georges Pompidou), in every case, he tries to form an opinion of his own. He publishes articles on Ireland, France, Mexico, and the United States, but never speaks of countries he never visited. He decides on the basis of what he has seen or read, but without presupposing anything. When you add in his extraordinary curiosity, this trait has allowed him throughout his life to discover what most would have passed by: the particular importance of a Hans Blüher or a Friedrich Georg Jünger, the significance of the work of Zeev Sternhell, Panayotis Kondylis, or the Palo Alto School. Such a procedure is that of a scout who marches ahead of the troops: he discovers the paths to be taken before others; he indicates country to be explored.

But it is also the procedure of a solitary man, an *Einzelgänger*. In fact, from a strictly nominalist perspective, what could be more particular than oneself? The scout can go before the troops, but he is not part of them. Mohler is not a man of groups, of parties, of mass meetings. The value of his work comes from its originality, and originality can never serve as a watchword. He is admired and loved, but has no disciples. That is perhaps what permits him to have friends as faithful to him as he himself is faithful in friendship. For between friends, admiration and love can always last without having to diminish, while disciples can only become themselves by betraying their masters.

Finally, Mohler is for all the reasons I have just explained, a man of the real. "Only a monster can permit himself the luxury of seeing things as they are," wrote Emil Cioran.[3] Armin Mohler is such a "monster." No one is more foreign to utopias of every kind than he is. Here as well we rediscover his nominalism, that is, the look that

---

|3| Emil M. Cioran , *Histoire et utopie* (Paris: Editions Gallimard, 1960); *History and Utopia*, translated by Richard Howard (Chicago: University of Chicago Press, 1987).

can only proceed from particular situations, from what we are *hic et nunc*. Ideas themselves do not escape being put into perspective in this way: they are only valid in relation to concrete situations—and the best of them can become crazy or sick. It was also Cioran who said: "In itself, an ideology is neither good nor bad. Everything depends on the moment when it is adopted." Mohler is too careful about contexts, too "consequentialist" as the Anglo-Saxons say, not to adhere to that assertion to some extent. The same goes for enmities. Like his master, Carl Schmitt, Mohler never forgets that yesterday's adversary can become tomorrow's ally: *Agōn*.

I have known Armin Mohler so long—at least thirty years— that I no longer remember the exact circumstances in which I made his acquaintance. It was perhaps some Italian friends who at the beginning of the 1960s, first spoke to me of him. At the time, he was for me nothing more than the author of *The Conservative Revolution in Germany*. His book was a revelation. To be perfectly honest, I must say that at that time, with my hesitant German, the rudiments of which I had only picked up by chance during my travels, I was barely able to read the Table of Contents! But I saw a new landscape spreading out before me: the image of a principled "Right," which was neither liberal nor Nazi—and quite moderately Christian! It was an astonishing discovery. I entered into that universe as if into an apartment that had been furnished in advance according to my tastes. Over the course of the following years, I was to inventory all the furnishings in detail. This took the form of articles, then pamphlets, books, translations. From the beginning of the 1970s, I personally oversaw the publication in France of a translation of Mohler's great work on the basis of the most recent, and therefore most voluminous, German edition. It took me twenty years to realize my aim, which any normally constituted editor would have considered madness. (On this project, I believe I spent more time than I ever devoted to any of my own books). In neighboring countries (I am especially thinking of Italy) the same work played a similar triggering role. Today the authors of the Conservative Revolution are translated and commented upon all over Europe. Do the Germans, who took some time rediscovering them, know that without Armin Mohler, none of this would have happened?

More generally, I wonder whether the Germans today are conscious of the role Mohler played in the diffusion of the political and cultural patrimony of their country within the European "Nouvelle Droite." But it may not be so important to them, for other European countries are more interested in Germany than German is interested in them! But the fact is that Mohler was one of the best ambassadors in Europe of his adoptive country, especially in France, where he spent so many years and knew so many people. His Swiss origin may have facilitated the task by helping him to become a sort of "bridge" between France and Germany. A fragile and insecure bridge, however. Since the time of General de Gaulle, Armin Mohler has given French examples to the Germans, just as I have given German examples to the French. Have either of us been convincing? I sometimes have the impression that France and Germany are destined to love or hate one other without ever succeeding in understanding one another—perhaps simply because the two countries are not of the same *sex*…. However that may be, the fact is that Armin Mohler had an admirable understanding of France. He even wrote several books about it—which have not been translated into French. Permit me to add that he not only knew France better than most Germans, but also better than many Frenchmen. Whether speaking of Rivarol or Joseph de Maistre, Léon Bloy or Sorel or Céline, Clément Rosset or Cioran, he was still always the one with le *mot juste*.

Memories, too, are images. Nearly all the times of my life with which Armin Mohler and his wife were associated have remained in my memory. I think of our common love of the arts, bibliographies, and cats, of an unforgettable conversation on a little square in Innsbruck, on the colloquia that brought us together in Nice, Turin, or Paris, of

Armin's sense of humor, his way of looking at things, our visits to one another, our telephone conversations, his letters where the name of the city or country was invariably written in giant, bold characters on the envelope as if he thought the postal officials were blind!

In the Liebingstraße in Munich, Edith still waits up for her "Arminio" who, like his friend Michel Mourre, loves to work at night. Night—we were all plunged into it ourselves for decades. During that entire time, on the envelopes of my letters, I wrote "West Germany." And then, one day in 1989, I was able to write "Germany"—period. A new age had begun. What happiness to begin a new age together, dear Armin!

ENGLISH-LANGUAGE BIBLIOGRAPHY

PRIMARY SOURCES

Alverdes, Paul. *The Whistlers' Room.* Oxford: Casemate, 2017 [1924].

Binding, Rudolf G. *Equestrian Hymn for My Beloved.* Hildesheim, Germany: Georg Olms Verlag, 2006 [1924].

Benn, Gottfried. *Impromptus: Selected Poems and Some Prose.* Translated by Michael Hofmann. New York: Farrar, Strauss and Giroux, 2013.

Fallada, Hans. *Little Man, What Now?* Translated by Susan Bennett. New York: Melville House, 2009 [1932].

Flex, Walter. *The Wanderer Between the Two Worlds: An Experience of War.* Rott Publishing, 2016 [1916].

Freyer, Hans. *Theory of Objective Mind: An Introduction to the Philosophy of Culture.* Translated by Steven Grosby. Athens, Ohio: Ohio University Press, 1999 [1923].

George, Stefan. *Stefan George: Poems.* Translated by Carol North Valhope. New York: Pantheon Books, 1946.

Jung, Edgar Julius. *The Rule of the Inferior.* Lewiston, New York: Edwin Mellen Press, 1995.

Jünger, Ernst. *On the Marble Cliffs.* Translated by Stuart Hood. London and New York: Penguin, 1984.

Jünger, Ernst. *Storm of Steel.* Translated by Michael Hofmann. London and New York: Penguin Random House, 2016.

Jünger, Ernst. *The Worker: Dominion and Form*. Edited by Laurence Paul Hemming, Translated by Bogdan Costea and Hemming. Evanston, Illinois: Northwest University Press, 2017.

Kantorowicz, Ernst. *Frederick the Second: 1194-1250*. Translated by E. O. Lorimer. London: Constable and Co., Ltd., 1931 [1927].

Klages, Ludwig. *The Biocentric World View*. Translated by Joseph D. Pryce. London: Arktos, 2013.

Klages, Ludwig. Cosmogonic Reflections. Translated by Joseph D. Pryce. Arktos, 2015.

Ludendorff, Mathilde. The Triumph of the Immortal Will. Forgotten Books, 2012. Originally published: 1921.

Ludendorff, Mathilde. *The Origin and Nature of the Soul, Vol. 1: History of Creation*. Translated by Walter Grossinger. Pähl, Germany: Verlag Hoher Warte, 1977 [1923].

Mann, Thomas. *Buddenbrooks: The Decline of a Family*. Translated by John E. Woods. New York: Vintage Books, 1994 [1901].

Mann, Thomas. *Death in Venice*. Translated by Stanley Appelbaum. Mineola, New York: Dover, 1995 [1911].

Mann, Thomas. *The Magic Mountain*. Translated by John E. Woods. New York: Vintage Books, 1995 [1924].

Mann, Thomas. *Reflections of a Nonpolitical Man*. Translated by Walter D. Morris. New York: Frederick Ungar, 1985 [1918].

Moeller van den Bruck, Arthur. *Germany's Third Empire*. London: Arktos, 2012 [1923].

Niemöller, Martin. *From U-Boat to Pulpit*. Chicago: Willett, Clark and Co.,1937 [1934].

Nietzsche, Friedrich. *Beyond Good and Evil.* Translated by Walter Kaufmann. New York: Random House, 1966 [1886].

Nietzsche, Friedrich. *On The Genealogy of Morals and Ecce Homo.* Translated and edited by Walter Kaufmann. New York: Vintage, 1967 [1887, 1908].

Nietzsche, Friedrich. *Thus Spoke Zarathustra.* Translated by Walter Kaufmann, New York: Random House, 1978 [1883-1891].

Nietzsche, Friedrich. *Twilight of the Idols.* Translated by Richard Polt. Indianapolis: Hackett Publishing, 1997 [1889].

Salomon, Ernst von. *It Cannot Be Stormed.* London: Arktos, 2013 [1930].

Salomon, Ernst von. *The Outlaws.* London: Arktos, 2011 [1932].

Schauwecker, Franz. *The Fiery Way.* London: J. M. Dent and Sons, Ltd.: 1929 [1926].

Schmitt, Carl. *The Concept of the Political.* Translated by George D. Schwab. Chicago: University of Chicago Press, 1996, 2007 [1932].

Schmitt, Carl. *Constitutional Theory.* Translated by Jeffrey Seitzer. Durham: Duke University Press, 2007 [1928].

Schmitt, Carl. *Crisis of Parliamentary Democracy.* Translated by Ellen Kennedy. Cambridge: MIT Press, 1988 [1923].

Schmitt, Carl. *Land and Sea.* Translated by Simona Draghici. Ann Arbor: Plutarch Press, 1997 [1942].

Schmitt, Carl. *The Leviathan in the State Theory of Thomas Hobbes: Meaning and Failure of a Political Symbol.* Translated by George D. Schwab & Erna Hilfstein. Chicago: University of Chicago Press, 1996, 2008 [1938].

Schmitt, Carl. *The* Nomos *of the Earth in the International Law of the*

Jus Publicum Europaeum. Translated by G.L. Ulmen. New York: Telos Press, 2003 [1950, 1974].

Schmitt, Carl. Political Romanticism. Guy Oakes, trans. Cambridge, Mass.: MIT Press, 1986 [1919, 1925].

Schmitt, Carl. *Political Theology: Four Chapters on the Concept of Sovereignty*. Translated by George D. Schwab. Introduction by Tracy B. Strong. Chicago: University of Chicago Press, 2004 [1922, 1934].

Schmitt, Carl. *State, Movement, People*. Translated by Simona Draghici. Ann Arbor: Plutarch Press, 2001.

Spann, Othmar. Types of Economic Theory. Routledge, 2012. Originally published: 1921.

Spengler, Oswald. *The Decline of the West*. Ed. Arthur Helps, and Helmut Werner. Translated by Charles F. Atkinson. Preface Hughes, H. Stuart. New York: Oxford UP, 1991.

Spengler, Oswald. *Man and Technics: A Contribution to a Philosophy of Life*. London: Arktos, 2015.

Spengler, Oswald. Prussianism and Socialism. Translated by C. F. Atkinson. 1922. Original publication: 1920. New translation by Donald O. White at archive.org.

Treitschke, Heinrich von. *Treitschke: His Life and Works*. Edited by Adolf Hausrath. Abington: Routledge, 2013.

SECONDARY SOURCES

Adriaansen, Robbert-Jan. *The Rhythm of Eternity: The German Youth Movement and the Experience of the Past, 1900-1933*. New York: Berghahn, 2015.

Balakrishnan, Gopal. *The Enemy: An Intellectual Portrait of Carl Schmitt*. London, New York: Verso, 2000.

Dahl, Göran. *Radical Conservatism and the Future of Politics*. London: Sage Publications, 1999.

Eksteins, Modris. *Rites of Spring: The Great War and the Birth of the Modern Age*. New York: Houghton Mifflin, 1989.

Herf, Jeffrey. *Reactionary Modernism: Technology, Culture, and Politics in Weimar and the Third Reich*. Cambrdige: Cambridge University Press, 1984.

Jones, Larry Eugene. *Edgar Julius Jung: The Conservative Revolution in theory and Practice*. Central European History, 1990.

Laqueur, Walter Z. *Young Germany: A History of the German Youth Movement*. Routledge, 1985. Originally published: 1962.

Magub, Roshan. *Edgar Julius Jung, Right-Wing Enemy of the Nazis: A Political Biography*. Camden House, 2017.

McCormick, John P. *Carl Schmitt's Critique of Liberalism: Against Politics as Technology*. New York: Cambridge University Press, 1997.

McCormick, John. P (Ed.). *Confronting Mass Democracy and Industrial Technology: Political and Social Theory from Nietzsche to Habermas*. Durham, North Carolin: Duke University Press Books. 2002.

Meierhenrich, Jens and Oliver Simons. *The Oxford Handbook of Carl Schmitt*. New York: Oxford University Press, 2017.

Mosse, George L. *The Crisis of German Ideology : Intellectual Origins of the Third Reich*. New York: Howard Fertig, 1964.

Muller, Jerry Z. *The Other God that Failed: Hans Freyer and the Deradicalization of German Conservatism*. Princeton University Press, 1988

243

Norton, Robert E. *Hidden Germany: Stefan George and His Circle*. Ithica, New York: Cornel University Press, 2002.

Stern, Fritz. *The Politics of Cultural Despair: A Study in the Rise of the Germanic Ideology*. Berkeley, Calif.: Unvieristy of California Press, 1961.

Tourlamain, Guy. *"Völkisch" Writers and National Socialism*. Bern, Switzerland, and New York Peter Lang. 2014.

Travers, Martin. *Critics of Modernity*. Bern, Switzerland, and New York: Peter Lang, 2001.

Woods, Roger. *The Conservative Revolution in the Weimar Republic*. London: MacMillan, 1996.

INDEX

#

18th Brumaire 16
"1871, ideas of" 30–33
"1914, ideas of" 68–69, 73–74, 92

A

ABC. *See also* Antibolschewistisches
    Comitee
Abendland Cirlce 149–152, 195
Absolutism 13–16, 21, 36, 41
Action Française 65, 212. *See
    also* Maurras, Charles
Adler und Falken 175
Advance, The. See Vormarsch
Adventurous Heart (Jünger) 198
Africa 165
Ahnen, Die (Freytag) 50
Aktion der Jugend 176
Alldeutscher Verband 72
Allgemeine Deutsche Schriftverein 46
Allgemeiner Deutscher Verband 53,
    100, 110
Alsatian Center Party 87
Alte Sozialdemokratische Partei 160
Altona 188
America. *See* United States, the
amor fati. See Nietzsche, Friedrich
anarchism 82
ancien régime xxiii, 14
Andersen, Friedrich 112
Anders, Günther xxx
Andreas-Salomé, Lou 56

Annaberg 166
Antibolschewistisches Comitee (ABC)
    89–90
Anti-Bolshevik Committee.
    See Antibolschewistisches
    Comitee
antiquity 78
anti-Romanticism. *See* Romanticism
Anti-Semitic Party. *See* Antisemitische
    Volkspartei
Antisemitische Volkspartei 45
anti-Semitism 42–45, 52–53, 59,
    62–63, 72, 82, 84, 87, 99–100,
    113, 119, 208
anti-socialism. *See* socialism
Aquinas, Thomas 152
Arbeitslagerbewegung 223
archaeophilia 124
archeology 49
Arendt, Hannah xxx
Ariosophic Society. *See* Ariosophische
    Gesellschaft; *See also* Ariosophy
Ariosophische Gesellschaft 114–115
Ariosophy 123
aristocracy 24, 29
aristocratic radicalism 58
Aristotle 152
Arminius 159, 168
Arndt, Ernst Moritz 24, 26, 35, 49
art 38, 231–232
Artam Bund 209
Arts and Crafts (Morris) 59
Aryans 39, 115, 122, 208
asceticism 82
Asia 165

Asmussen, Hans 144, 219
Atatürk, Kemal 155
"Atlantid Renaissance" 124
Atlantis 123
Auerstaedt 83
Aufbruch (journal) 167
Austria 20, 26, 29, 35, 46, 51, 53, 61, 153, 176, 212, 226
autarchy 147
authoritarianism 41
Avenarius 140
Avenarius, Ferdinand 60, 140
axial age 10

B

Baade, Karl 199
Baden-Powell, Robert S. 61
Baeumler, Alfred 163, 183, 205, 214, 224–225
Bainville, Jacques 151
Baltic, the xiii, 61, 69, 81, 84–85, 92, 155
barbarism 57
Barlach, Ernst 92
Barrès, Maurice 57, 153–154, 156
Bartels, Adolf xx, 112
Basel, Switzerland 8
Battle of Leibzig 63
Bauern-Komitee-Bewegung 190
Bauernverein 186
Bavaria, Germany 38, 81, 100, 159
Bavarian Soviet Republic 135
Bayreuther Kreis 37–38, 51, 112, 120
Bebel, August 33
Beck, Ludwig 222
Beckmann, Max 151
Beggars, the. *See* Geusen
Benn, Gottfried 9, 214, 227
Benz, Richard 218
Berdyayev, Nikolai 137
Bergengruen, Werner 218
Bergmann, Ernst 119
Bergson, Henri 61

Berk, Hans Schwarz von 205
Berliner Bewegung 45
Berlin, Germany 8, 44, 127, 164, 195
    East Berlin 227
Berlin Movement. *See* Berliner Bewegung
Bernauer Address 199
Best, Werner 205
Bethmann-Hollweg, Theobald von 71
Beumelberg, Werner 146
"beyond Left and Right". *See* ideology
Bible, the 34, 64
    Old Testament 112
biological determinism 49
Bismarck, Otto von 27, 29–33, 40, 54, 101, 104, 121, 162, 201, 224
    Bismarckism 31
    Eastern Policy 162
black flag, the 104
Black Front. *See* Schwarze Front
"blond beast" (Nietzsche). *See* Nietzsche, Friedrich
Bloy, Léon 236
Blüher, Hans xx, xxii, 178–180, 182, 234
Blunck, Hans F. 120, 122
BNP. *See* Bund deutscher Neupfadfinder
Boberhaus Camp 173
Bockelson: History of a Mass Hysteria (Reck-Malleczewen) 219
Böcklin, Arnold 61
Boeckel, Otto 45–46
Boehm, Max Hildebert xix, xxvi, 86, 88, 106, 127, 130, 144, 194
Bogner, Hans 130, 144
Bohemia 61, 92
Bolsheviks and Bolshevism 72, 84, 88, 97, 101, 118, 133, 151, 161, 163, 200. *See also* Antibolschewistisches Comitee; *See also* Communism; *See also* Soviet Union, the
    anti-Bolshevism 88–89
    Bolshevik Revolution, the 11, 71, 84,

88, 161
Bonn, Germany 195
Bonus, Arthur 61, 111
Borchardt, Rudolf xxii–xxiii, 210, 214
Borussia. *See also* Prussia
Borussian School 121
Bosch, Robert 151
Bose, Herbert von 220–221
Bötticher, Paul. *See* Lagarde, Paul de
bourgeoisie xii, 16, 19–20, 60, 75, 193.
    See also class system, the
Brauweiler, Heinz 128, 144
Breuer, Stefan xxiii–xxiv, xxvii, xxix
Brigade, Ehrhardt 222
Brinkmann, Carl 146
Britain. *See* Great Britain
Brockdorff-Rantzau, Ulrich 146
Bronnen, Arnolt xx, 163
Brüning, Heinrich 132, 138, 197, 221
Buber, Martin xxv, 61
Buchrucker Putsch 155
Bund der Landwirte 46
Bund der Wandervögel und Pfadfinder
    173
Bund deutscher Gelehrter und Künstler
    88
Bund deutscher Neupfadfinder 171
Bündische xx, 11
bündische Jugend 87, 172
Bündische Reichschaft 188
Bündische Youth See *bündische Jugend*
Bund, Stand, Volk, Reich 227
Burckhardt, Jacob 19
Burg Lauenstein 73
Burke, Edmund 17
Burte, Hermann 119
Byzantinism 220

C

Caesarism 16, 77–80, 147
Camus, Albert 9
capitalism 20, 60, 146
    anti-capitalism 146

Carlyle, Thomas 65
Carus Sterne. *See* Krause, Ernst
Catholicism and the Catholic Church
    15, 18, 21, 23, 35, 51, 54, 58,
    71–72, 101–102, 113, 118, 139,
    149, 153, 195, 211
    Church Fathers 34
Céline, Louis-Ferdinand 236
censorship 99
Center Party. *See* Deutsche
    Zentrumspartei
Central European Customs Union 69
Central Powers (World War I) 88
Chamberlain, Houston Stewart 39,
    112, 120
China 78
Christendom 25, 35
Christianity xiii, xxiii, 10, 27, 34, 38–
    39, 49–51, 55–59, 82, 110, 112,
    141, 220. *See also* Catholicism
    and the Catholic Church; *See
    also* Protestantism
    Germanization 39, 51, 111
    Orthodox 59
Christian National and Rural People's
    Party. *See* Christlich-Nationale
    Bauern- und Landvolkpartei
Christian-Social Party. *See* Christlich-
    Soziale Partei
Christian-Social People's Service.
    See Christlich-Sozialer
    Volksdienst
Christian Statesman, The (Stapel).
    See Christliche Staatsmann, Der
    (Stapel)
Christliche Staatsmann, Der (Stapel) 141
Christlich-Nationale Bauern- und
    Landvolkpartei 187
Christlich-Soziale Partei 98
Christlich-Sozialer Volksdienst 176
Cioran, Emil 234, 236
civilization. *See Zivilisation*
Civil War (Russian) 84. *See also* Russia;
    See also Soviet Union, the
Class, Heinrich 53

Classics 24
class system, the 14, 18. *See also* bourgeoisie
Clausewitz, Carl von 26
Clauss, Ludwig Ferdinand xx, 122, 225
Clauss, Max 152
Club Movement. *See* Deutschnationale Vereinbewegung
Cold War, the 227
  Eastern Bloc, the 228
collectivism 82
Communism xii, 16, 80, 86–87, 90, 159, 164–168, 190. *See also* Bolsheviks and Bolshevism; *See also* Soviet Untion, the; *See also* socialism
  anti-Communism 85
Communist Youth International. *See* Kommunistische Jugendinternationale
Comradeship League. *See* Kameradschaftsbund
Concept of the Political, The (Schmitt) 198
Congress of Vienna 17, 26
conservatism xxi, 13–14, 17–18, 21, 23, 29, 31–32, 36, 40, 45, 82, 85, 93, 98
Conservative Revolution, the xxi–xxiii, 75, 79, 91, 95–96, 104–107, 141, 146, 150–151, 169–170, 183, 185, 194, 195, 201, 205, 207, 210–214, 217–220, 222–224, 226–228
  groups 109–182
Constituent Assembly 15
Constitutionalism 101–103
Corradini, Enrico 65, 154
Cortes, Donoso xxviii
Cossmann, Paul Nikolaus 149
Cramb, John Adam 66
Crisis of Parliamentary Democracy, The (Schmitt). *See Geistesgeschichtliche Lage des heutigen Parlamentarismus, Die*

(Schmitt)
culture. *See Kultur*
Cunow, Heinrich 70
Czechoslovakia 152, 221

D

Dachau, Germany 60
Dahlmann, Friedrich Christoph 23
Dahn, Felix 49, 120
Dähnhardt, Heinz 144
D'Annunzio, Gabriele 57, 65, 154
Darwin, Charles 47, 50, 93
  Darwinism 59, 93. *See also* Social Darwinism
Däubler, Theodor 92
Dawn: Thoughts on Moral Prejudices (Nietzsche) 56. *See also* Nietzdsche, Friedrich
DDP. *See* Deutsche Demokratische Partei
Déat, Marcel 151
decadence 19, 54, 65, 92
decline 54, 77
Decline of the West (Spengler) 76–79, 200. *See also* Spengler, Oswald
Deed. See Tat
de Gaulle, Charles 236
Dehmel, Richard 92
democracy xvi, 13–15, 18, 20, 24, 40, 57, 60, 78, 126, 132, 194
Democratic Party (U.S.) xvi
Demokratische Partei. *See* Deutsche Demokratische Partei
Dempf, Alois 150
Departure. See Aufbruch (journal)
de-Prussification 93
Der wahre Staat (Spann) 152
despotism 21, 32, 36
Deutschbund 47, 54
Deutsche Allgemeine Zeitung 125
Deutsche Antisemitischen Vereinigung 45
Deutsche Bauernpartei 187

Deutsche Bewegung 11, 24–28, 31, 35–36, 47, 49, 51, 93, 104–105, 121, 153

Deutsche Demokratische Partei 98, 101, 183

Deutsche Fortschrittspartei 44, 51

Deutsche Freischar 173

Deutsche Freisinnige Partei 45, 51

Deutsche Handwerker Vermittlung 143

deutsche Jungenschaft vom 1. November (1929) 174, 179

Deutsche Kolonial-Gesellschaft 53

Deutschen, Die (Moeller) 92, 94

Deutsche Reformpartei 99

Deutscher Glaube (Lagarde) 37

Deutscher Herrenclub 128–129, 131, 134, 144, 217

Deutscher Kulturbund 150

Deutscher Landvolk—und Kampfbund 189

Deutscher Schutzbund 134

Deutscher Schutz—und Trutzbund 99

Deutsche Rundschau 138, 149, 152

Deutsche Schriften (Lagarde) 37

Deutsches Volkstum 140–141, 144, 149, 152, 216

Deutsche Vaterlandspartei 71, 98–99, 135

Deutsche Volkspartei 98–102

Deutsche Wochenschau 118

Deutsche Zeitung 110

Deutsche Zentrumspartei 30, 42, 71, 149, 183, 195

Deutschgläubige Gemeinschaf 115

Deutschgläubige Gemeinschaft 50, 115

Deutschkonservative Partei 45–46, 98

deutschnational 53

Deutschnationaler Handlungsgehilfen-Verband 47, 175

Deutschnationale Vereinbewegung 46

Deutschnationale Volkspartei xxi, 89, 100–102, 131–132, 175, 186, 207

Deutsch-religiöse Gemeinschaft 50

Deutschsoziale Partei 45, 99

Deutschvölkische Freiheitspartei 101

Deutschvölkische Partei 99

Deutschvölkischer Schutz- und Trutzbund 99–100, 110

Dibelius, Otto 219

dictatorship 15–16, 53, 72, 78, 91, 120, 127, 131, 134, 139, 147, 158, 196, 213, 222

Diederichs, Eugen 73, 145

Diederichs (publisher) 125

Dilthey, Wilhelm 24

Dingräve, Leopold. *See* Eschmann, Ernst Wilhelm

Dinter, Artur 113

Dix, Otto 61

d.j.1.11. *See* deutsche Jungenschaft vom 1. November (1929)

DNVP. *See* Deutschnationale Volkspartei

Dostoyevsky, Fyodor xxi, 65

Dreyfus Affair, the 65

Dritte imperiale Figur, Die (Niekisch) 215

Dritte Reich, Das (Moeller) 105–106, 127, 139, 143, 212. *See also* Third Reich, the (Moeller))

Dritte Standpunkt, Der (Moeller) 106

DVFP. *See* Deutschvölkische Freiheitspartei

DVLP. *See* Deutsche Vaterlandspartei

DvP. *See* Deutschvölkische Partei

DVP. *See* Deutsche Volkspartei

DVSTB. *See* Deutschvölkischer Schutz- und Trutzbund

E

Eagles and Falcons. *See* Adler und Falken

East, the 82, 85, 87, 93, 101. *See also* West, the; *See also* Spengler, Oswald

Ebeling, Hans xxii, 166, 177

economic collapse of 1873 44

economics xxvi, 77
Edda Gesellschaft 114
Edda Society. *See* Edda Gesellschaft
Edda, the 64
education 43, 46, 49, 60, 213
Ehlers, Hermann 227
Ehrhardt organization 221
Eichberg, Henning xxv
Eidgenossen 207
Ekkehard 182. *See also* paramilitary
    leagues
Elbe river 72
Elbrecher, Hellmuth 148
elections 45, 102, 133, 160, 187, 189,
    199, 205–206, 213
Elzbacher, Paul 84
empire and imperialism 19–20, 27, 50,
    52, 64, 66, 67, 77, 80, 89, 105,
    164, 169
Engels, Friedrich xxi
England 15, 20, 36, 41, 53, 66. *See
    also* Great Britain
Enlightenment, the xxi, 14, 20–22, 27,
    54, 59, 66–68, 75, 106, 137, 158
  counter-Enlightenment 21, 137
Entente (WWI) 70, 101, 168
Erdmann, Johann Eduard 30
Eros 179
Erste Freideutsche Jugendtag 63
Eschmann, Ernst Wilhelm 145–148,
    151, 218
Eschweiler, Karl 130
esotericism 113
*Essay on the Inequality of the Human
    Races* (Gobineau) 39
eternal recurrence. *See* Nietzsche,
    Friedrich
ethics 21–22, 28, 33–34, 41, 50, 52,
    168
eugenics 47–49
Europäische Revue 149–152, 195
Europe 10, 13, 16, 26, 29, 41, 54, 57,
    61, 66, 77, 85, 149–150, 158,
    162, 210, 221
  Central Europe 17, 35, 74, 76, 89,

140, 148
  Eastern Europe 92, 135
  Northern Europe 92
  Western Europe 17, 20, 22, 33, 74, 76
European Review. See Europäische Revue
Evangelical Church, the.
    See Protestantism
Evers, Franz 92
Evola, Julius xxviii, 130, 151, 211
existentialism 9

F

Fahrenden Gesellen 175
Fahrenkrog, Ludwig 51
Farmers' Committee Movemen.
    See Bauern-Komitee-Bewegung
Farmers' Federation. *See* Bund der
    Landwirte
Farmers' Union. *See* Bauernverein
fascism xii, 10–11, 82, 126, 151, 158,
    211
fatalism 56
Fatherland 70–71, 73, 157
Father, The (Klepper). *See Vater, Der*
    (Klepper)
Fechter, Paul 146
Fédération des Unions Intellectuelles
    150
feudalism 18, 20
Fichte, Johann Gottlieb 26, 47
Fighting Community of Revolutionary
    National Socialists.
    See Kampfgemeinschaft
    Revolutionärer
    Nationalsozialisten
fin de siècle 11, 19, 55
finis Germaniae 120
First Free German Youth Day
    Conference. *See* Erste
    Freideutsche Jugendtag
First World War. *See* World War I
Fischer, Hugo 163
Fischer, Karl 62

fitness 25
Five-Year Plan, the. *See* Soviet Union, the; *See also* Stalin, Joseph
Flanders 61, 69, 212
Fleig, Hans 8–10
Folkwang Museum 124
Forsthoff, Ernst xx
Fortschrittliche Volkspartei 51
Foundations of the Nineteenth Century, The (Chamberlain) 39
France xxix, 14–15, 20–21, 33, 41, 65, 67, 87, 92–93, 133, 154–155, 235
France, Anatole 57
Franco, Francisco xii
Franke, Helmut 157
Franz, Constantin 37
Frauenbewegung 59
freedom 21, 27, 69
Free German Youth. *See* Freideutsche Jugend
Freemasonry 118
Free-Minded People's Party. *See* Freisinnige Volkspartei
Free-Minded Union. *See* Freisinnige Vereinigung
Freie Deutsche Jugend 63, 86
Freikorps xiii, 135, 155–157, 166, 182, 221
Freischar Junger Nation 175
Freisinnige Vereinigung 51
Freisinnige Volkspartei 51
French Revolution, the 13–14, 19, 21–25, 36, 68, 210. *See also* National Assembly, French
Frenssen, Gustav xx, 112, 120
Freya (goddess) 124
Freyer, Hans xix
Freytag, Gustav 50
Friedenspartei 71
Fried, Ferdinand. *See* Zimmermann, Ferdinand Friedrich
Friedrich the Great 201
Fritsch, Theodor 45
Fröbel, Friedrich Wilhelm August 25

"Front Generation" (Jünger) xii
Frontkriegerbund 117
Frontline Fighters League. *See* Frontkriegerbund
Führerdemokratie 183
Führer und Volk in der Jugendbewegung (Schurtz) 179
Fürst, Rüdiger 211
Futurism, Italian xxviii

G

Gasset, José Ortega y 151
Gay Science, The (Nietzsche) 56. *See also* Nietzsche, Friedrich
Gegner (Schulze-Boysen) 177
Geist als Widersacher der Seele, Der (Klages) 119
Geist der Jungmannschaft, Der (Günther) 142
Geistesgeschichtliche Lage des heutigen Parlamentarismus, Die (Schmitt) 196. *See also* Schmitt, Carl
Geist und Reich (Benz) 218
Generation of 1919 86
Gentile, Giovanni 151
geopolitics 124
George Circle. *See* George-Kreis
George-Kreis 140, 151, 180, 223
George, Stefan xxv, 61, 130, 140, 171, 177, 222, 225. *See also* George-Kreis
Gereke, Günther 227
German Age, the 92
German Anti-Semitic Union. *See* Deutsche Antisemitischen Vereinigung
German Believing Community. *See* Deutschgläubige Gemeinschaft
German Colonial Society. *See* Deutsche Kolonial-Gesellschaft
German Communist Party. *See* Kommunistische Partei

Deutschlands
German Conservative Party.
  See Deutschkonservative Partei
German Cultural League. *See* Deutscher
  Kulturbund
German Democratic Party.
  See Deutsche Demokratische
  Partei
Germanen Orden 114
German Faith (Lagarde). *See Deutscher
  Glaube* (Lagarde)
German Farmers' Party. *See* Deutsche
  Bauernpartei
German Fatherland Party. *See* Deutsche
  Vaterlandspartei
German Free-Minded Party.
  See Deutsche Freisinnige Partei
German Gentlemen's Club.
  See Deutscher Herrenclub
Germanic Community of
  Faith. *See* Germanische
  Glaubensgemeinschaft
Germanic Faith Community.
  See Germanische Glaubens-
  Gemeinschaft
Germanic mythology 38, 49
Germanic Order. *See* Germanen Orden
Germanic Shrines (Bonus).
  See Germanische Heiligtümer
  (Bonus)
Germanic-Slavic Bloc 162
German identity and uniqueness
  27, 29, 35, 38–39, 48–50,
  65, 69, 92, 112, 115–116,
  120–123, 208, 211. *See
  also* "German Question," the; *See
  also* nationalism; *See also* nation,
  the
  German Idea, the 224
  Germanomania 208
  German uniqueness 13–67, 20, 22
Germanische Glaubensgemeinschaft 51
Germanische Glaubens-Gemeinschaft
  115, 116
Germanische Heiligtümer (Bonus) 112

German League. *See* Deutschbund
German Movement. *See* Deutsche
  Bewegung
German Mythology (Grimm) 49
German National Association of
  Commercial Employees. *See*
German National Club.
  See Volksdeutscher Klub
German National Commercial
  Employees' Association.
  See Deutschnationaler
  Handlungsgehilfen-Verband;
  See Deutsche Handwerker
  Vermittlung
German Nationalist Protection
  and Defiance Federation.
  See Deutschvölkischer Schutz-
  und Trutzbund
German Nationality. *See Deutsches
  Volkstrum*
German National People's Party.
  See Deutschnationale
  Volkspartei
*German Outlook. See Deutsche
  Rundschau*
German People's Party. *See* Deutsche
  Volkspartei
German Progress Party. *See* Deutsche
  Fortschrittspartei
German Protection and Defiance
  Organization. *See* Deutscher
  Schutz—und Trutzbund
German Protection League.
  See Deutscher Schutzbund
"German Question," the. *See
  also* German identity and
  uniqueness; *See also* Germany
  Greater German solution 27, 51
  Lesser German solution 27, 35, 40
  reunification 9
German Reform Party. *See* Deutsche
  Reformpartei
German Religious Community.
  See Deutsch-religiöse
  Gemeinschaft

German Rural Volk Fighting League.
See Deutscher Landvolk—und
Kampfbund
German Social Party.
See Deutschsoziale Partei
Germans, The (Moeller). See Deutschen,
Die (Moeller)
German Times. See Deutsche Zeitung
German Völkisch Freedom Party.
See Deutschvölkische
Freiheitspartei
German Völkisch Party.
See Deutschvölkische Partei
German Völkisch Protection and
Defiance Organization.
See Deutschvölkischer Schutz-
und Trutzbund
German Volunteers. See Deutsche
Freischar
German Writings (Lagarde).
See Deutsche Schriften (Lagarde)
Germany 20–22, 27, 29, 33, 54, 60, 66,
67, 82, 86, 88, 95, 101, 106, 146,
152, 154, 156, 162, 170, 199,
202, 210–214, 223–226, 236
Federal Republic of Germany 227
German Democratic Republic 227
reunification 26–27, 30–34, 40
unification 224
Gerstenmaier, Eugen 227
Gestapo 214
Geusen 175, 177
Gewissen 90–91, 105, 125–129, 138,
149, 193
Ghibelline 140
Ghibilline Party 221
Gide, André 57
Glatzel, Frank 87
Gleichen, Heinrich von xx, 79, 88, 95,
126, 128, 130–134, 137, 205,
210
Gneisenau, August Neidhardt von 26
Gobineau, Arthur de 39, 121
God 34, 111, 114, 124, 138.
See also Jesus Christ; See

also Christianity
Goebbels, Paul Joseph 209
Goerdeler, Carl 222
Goethe, Johann Wolfgang von 64, 78
Gogarten, Friedrich 214
Goldberg, Jonah xvi
Gorky, Maxim 61
Görres, Joseph 23
Gorsleben, Rudolf John 114, 123
Göttingen Seven 23
Graefe, Albrecht von 100–101
Grafengruppe 222
Graues Corps 174, 179
Great Britain 17, 33, 35, 65–68, 133,
155, 222. See also England
Great Depression, the 147, 163, 173,
183–184
Great Tyrant and the Court, The.
See Großtyrann und das Gericht,
Der (Bergengruen)
Greece 25, 27, 78, 208
Greifswald 195
Grenzlandarbeit 140
Grey Corp. See Graues Corps
Grimm, Hans xix, 88, 120, 144
Grimm, Jacob 23, 35, 47, 49
Grimm, Wilhelm 23
Großraum xxvi
Großtyrann und das Gericht, Der
(Bergengruen) 218
Gründerkrise 44
Grüneberg, Horst 146
Gruppe Sozialrevolutionärer
Nationalisten 167
GSRN. See Gruppe
Sozialrevolutionärer
Nationalisten
Guido von List Gesellschaft 114
Gundolf, Friedrich 88, 151
Günther, Albrecht Erich xx, 142, 144,
149, 183
Günther, Gerhard 144
Günther, Hans F. K. 122

H

Haenisch, Konrad 70, 85
Hamburger Folksheim 140
Hamburg, Germany 84, 161
Hamkens, Wilhelm 187–188
Handelshochschule 195–196
Hannover, Germany 23
Hanseatische Verlagsanstalt 125, 218
Hapsburg Dynasty 26, 29, 35, 46, 54
Hassell, Ulrich von 222
Hauer, Jakob Wilhelm 9, 112, 119
Hauptmann, Gerhardt 57
Hauser, Heinrich 146
Haushofer, Karl xx, 124
Hearthfire (Spann). *See Herdflamme, Die* (Spann)
Hegel, Georg Wilhelm Friedrich 27–30, 35, 40–42, 54, 66, 201, 224
Heidegger, Martin xxiii, xxv, 214, 227
Heim, Claus 187
Heimwehr 211
Heinz, Friedrich Wilhelm 157, 187, 205, 221
Heinz-Orbis, Franz Josef 135
Helfferich, Karl 89
Hellerau 60
Helpach, Willi 151
Helphand, Alexander 70
Hentschel, Willibald 48
Herder, Johann Gottfried 49
Herdflamme, Die (Spann) 153
Herf, Jeffrey xxvii
heroism xii, 179
  heroic realism 10–11
Herrschaft der Minderwertigen, Die (Jung) 136–138, 208
Herzfeld, Hans 41
Hesse, Germany 45, 222
Hielscher, Friedrich xx, 157, 164
Hierl, Konstantin 117
Hildebert, Max 85
Himmler, Heinrich 209

Hindenburg, Paul von 131–132, 190, 220
Hintze, Otto 67, 86
Hirsch, Emanuel 144, 214
historicism xxii, 34
history 49–50, 77, 92, 219
  end of history, the 228
Hitler, Adolf xv, 101, 113, 139, 141, 155, 159, 166–167, 177, 189, 202–208, 213–214, 219, 223, 225. *See also* Putsch, Hitler-Ludendorff
  plan to assassinate 221
  seizure of power 225
Hitler: A German Disaster (Niekisch). *See Hitler, ein deutsches Verhaengnis* (Niekisch)
Hitler, ein deutsches Verhaengnis (Niekisch) 164
Hitlerjugend 177, 216–217
Hitler Youth. *See* Hitlerjugend
Hochbund 172
Hofacker, Cäsar von 222
Höffler, Otto 225
Hoffmann-Fölkersamb, Herrmann 61
Hofgeismar 160
Hofgeismar Circle. *See* Hofgeismar Kreis
Hofgeismar Kreis 86
Hofmannsthal, Hugo von xxii, 57, 105–106, 150
Höger, Fritz 124
Hohenzollern, House of xxviii, 35, 40, 98
Hoher Meissner 63
Holy Roman Empire, the 20
homoeopathy 59
homosexuality 179
Hörbiger, Hans 123
Horneffer, August 57
Horneffer, Ernst 57
Hour of Decision (Spengler). *See Jahre der Entscheidung* (Spengler)
Huber, Ernst Rudolf 144
Huber, Victor Aimé 32

Hugenberg, Alfred xxi, 131, 144
humanism 121
human rights xvii
Humboldt, Wilhelm von 25
Huth, Otto 225
hybridization 48

I

Iceland 49
idealism 27, 39, 46, 49, 71, 74, 86
Idealism (movement) 24, 54, 59, 62, 86
"ideas of 1914". See "1914, ideas of"
ideology 19, 47, 48, 62, 65, 67, 68, 97,
    102, 113, 132, 137, 139, 156,
    158, 163, 169, 174, 177, 208,
    217. See also Right, the
"beyond Left and Right" 95–96, 104,
    106
"Third Way," the 60, 82, 87, 90
Im Dickicht der Pakte (Niekisch) 215
imperialism. See empire and imperialism
Imperium Teutonicum 142
Independent Social Democrats.
    See USPD
individualism xxvi
Indo-Germanic 50
industrialization 13, 16, 48, 60, 137
Innere Emigration 214
intelligentsia 8, 19, 56, 70, 73, 75, 79,
    102, 127, 138, 146, 152, 163,
    169, 198, 204–206, 209, 212
Israel 12, 142
Italia docet 126
Italy xxix, 56, 65, 82, 93, 151, 154, 235

J

Jacobins and Jacobinism xxviii, 15, 21,
    26, 83, 137, 155
Jahn, Friedrich Ludwig 25–26, 50
Jahn, Turnvater. See Jahn, Friedrich
    Ludwig
Jahre der Entscheidung (Spengler) 218

Jaspers, Karl xix, xxvii, 10
Jena, Germany 62, 83
Jesus Christ 34, 112. See also God; See
    also Christianity
Jeune Droite 212
"Jewish Quesiton," the. See Jews and
    Judaism
Jews and Judaism xiii, 35–36, 39,
    41–43, 53, 61, 72, 84, 112–113,
    116, 118, 120, 142, 202, 208. See
    also anti-Semitism
"Jewish Question," the 43, 62
Judaic renaissance 61
Jugendbewegung xx, 37, 58–66, 111,
    130, 134, 139, 146, 153, 161,
    172, 175, 178–181, 189, 211
Juja (youth jacket) 174
June Club. See Juni-Klub
Jung, Carl Gustav 151
Jungdeutscher Bund 86
Jungdeutscher Orden 182. See
    also paramilitary leagues
Jungdeutschland-Bund 61
Jung, Edgar Julius xix, xxii, 130, 135–
    141, 151, 210, 213, 219–221
murder of 221
Jungenschaft 173
Jünger, Ernst xii, xx, xxiii, xxvi, 8–9,
    155–158, 163, 168, 176,
    194–203, 209, 213–214, 225,
    227, 231
Jünger, Friedrich Georg xx, 143, 163,
    218, 234
Jungkonservativen xix, 11, 125–153,
    171, 176, 182, 191, 195, 198,
    204, 208–215, 219, 223
Jungmannschaft 173
Jungnationalen 128
Jungnationaler Bund 175
Juni-Klub xiv, 125, 127–128, 132, 135,
    158, 204, 209
Junker class 29

K

Kahr, Gustav von 127, 221
Kaiser, Jakob 227
Kai-shek, Chiang 155
Kaltenbrunner, G.K. xiii, xv
Kameradschaftsbund 152
Kampfgemeinschaft Revolutionärer
    Nationalsozialisten 168. *See*
    also Strasser, Otto
Kant, Immanuel 66
Kantoriwicz, Alfred 146
Kantorowicz, Ernst xx, 214
Kapp, Wolfgang 72, 155. *See*
    also Putsch, Kapp
Kassel, Germany 63
"Kategorie des Bundes, Die"
    (Schmalenbach) 180
Kathedersozialisten 32
Kemnitz, Mathilde von 117
Kenstle, August Georg 188
Kerensky, Alexander 88
Kessler, Harry Graf 57
Keynes, John Maynard 199
Keyserling, Hermann Graf 151
King Ludwig II 38
Klages, Ludwig xx, xxv, 119, 225
    Klages-Kreis 225
Klagges, Dietrich 113
Kleinau, Wilhelm 157
Kleinbauernverband 186
kleindeutsche Lösung. See "German
    Question," the
Kleines Politisches Wörterbuch (Boehm)
    193
Kleist-Schmenzin, Ewald von 205
Klemperer, Klemens von xxiii
Klepper, Jochen 219
Klinger, Max 61
Koebel, Eberhard xx, 174
Kolbenheyer, Erwin Guido 120
Kommenden, Die 159, 168, 176
Kommunistische Jugendinternationale
    86

Kommunistische Partei Deutschlands
    161, 165–167, 182, 190. *See*
    also Communism
Kondylis, Panayotis xxiii, 234
Konservative Partei Preußens 36. *See*
    also Prussia
Kossinna, Gustaf 122
KPD. *See* Kommunistische Partei
    Deutschlands
Krakow uprising xxi
Krause, Ernst 122
Kreisauer Kreis 223
Kriek, Ernst 214, 225
Kühn, Leonore 130
Kultur 74, 77
Kulturkampf 30
Kulturvolk 218
Kummer, Berhard 122
Kunstwart, Der 60, 140
Kusserow, Wilhelm 115
Kutzleb, Hjalmar 121, 144

L

Lagarde, Paul de xx, xxv, 34–43, 47, 52,
    62–64, 94, 105, 119, 217, 225
Landauer, Gustav xxv
Landbund 186
Land League. *See* Landbund
Landvolkbewegung xx, 11, 143, 148,
    161, 166, 185, 186, 188, 189,
    202, 205
Landvolk, Das 187
Langbehn, Julius 37, 62, 119
Lange, Friedrich xx, 47
Langen-Müller 125
Lappland (region) 174
Lasaulx, Ernst von 19
Lass, Werner 166, 177
Laufenberg, Heinrich 84, 143
Lausanne, Switzerland 135
League of German Scholars and Artists.
    See Bund deutscher Gelehrter
    und Künstler

League of Nations 149

League of Wandervogel and Scout. *See* Bund der Wandervögel und Pfadfinder

League Youth. *See bündische Jugend*

Lebensgefühl 23

Lebensreform 58–66, 85, 113, 130, 145

Leber, Julius 222

Lechler, Jörg 121

Le Corbusier 151

Left, the xiii–xiv, xv, 42, 51, 65, 70, 72, 82, 95–96, 104, 106, 199, 204, 213, 229

nature of 14–15

legislature 41

Lehmann, Julius Friedrich 124

Leipart, Theodor 199–200

Leipzig, Germany 63

Lenin, Vladimir 82, 88, 90, 165. *See also* Communism; *See also* socialism; *See also* Bolsheviks and Bolshevism

Lensch, Paul 70, 86

Lenz, Friedrich 166

Leo, Heinrich 35

Lessing, Theodor xxv

Liberale Vereinigung 51

liberalism xvi, xxvi, 13–14, 18, 21, 23, 29, 33, 36, 41, 44, 51, 57, 64, 82, 85, 88, 90, 93, 97, 126, 146, 228

anti-liberalism 146, 163, 210

Liberal Union. *See* Liberale Vereinigung

libertinism 82

Liebenfels, Jörg Lanz von xx, 50

Liebknecht, Karl 33

Life Reform. *See* Lebensreform

Literarische Welt 213

Literary World. See Literarische Welt

literature 38, 74, 92

Locarno, treaty of 135

Loesch, Karl Christian von 130

Lohse, Heinrich 189

London, England 9, 92

Lower Saxony 185, 227

Löwith, Karl 56

Ludendorff, Erich 117–118, 202

Ludendorff, Mathilde xx

Ludendorffs Volkswart 118

Luther, Martin 35, 54, 104, 112. *See also* Protestantism

M

Machiavelli, Niccolo 28, 41, 58, 169

"*Machtstaat*" 30. *See also* Bismarck, Otto von

"*Machtstaatsgedankens*" 224

Mahler, Gustav 57

Maison, Rudolf 38

Maistre, Joseph de xxviii, 236

Makart, Hans 38

Mandel, Hermann 112, 119

Man, Handrik de 151

"*Männerbund*" 178

Mann, Thomas xx, xxii, 37, 65, 74–75, 78, 91, 104, 107, 129, 171, 225

Marburg Address 221

Marburg University 220

Marc, Aléxandre 212

March on Rome 126. *See also* Mussolini, Benito

Marck, Erich 143

Marinebrigad Ehrhardt 156

Marxism xiv, 88, 126

Marx, Karl 20, 68, 167

Marx, Simon 89

Massis, Henri 151

materialism xxvi, 44

Maulnier, Thierry 212

Maurenbrecher, Max 113

Maurras, Charles xxi, 57, 65

Meinecke, Friedrich 28, 73, 86

Meissner Formulation 63

Meister Eckhardt 64

Merlio, Gilbert xxv, xxvii

metapolitics 103

Metternich, Klemens von 23

Michéa, Jean-Claude xxx

Michels, Robert 136, 148

Middle Ages, the xiii, 49, 76, 181
middle class, the. *See* bourgeoisie
military, the 8, 16, 25, 27, 29, 31, 40,
    67, 71, 77, 92, 99, 145–146,
    154–155, 162, 168, 171, 173,
    176, 181, 188, 200, 207, 218,
    220, 222
    militarism 70, 74
modernism and modernity xxvii, xxvii–
    xxviii, 12, 137, 156, 195, 200,
    224
Modernism (art) 151
Moeller van den Bruck, Arthur xix,
    xxii, 64, 79, 86, 88–94, 105–
    107, 126–127, 130, 132, 134,
    139–140, 143, 144, 154, 158,
    204, 209, 212, 217, 225
Mohler, Armin xi–xviii, xix, xxiii,
    231–237
Mohler, Edith 237
Moltke, Helmuth James Graf von 31,
    173
Mommsen, Theodor 28
monarchy 15–16, 27–28, 40–41, 46,
    54, 69, 97–98, 149, 222
    restoration 97
Morgenstern, Christian 37
Morris, William 59
Moscow, Russia 88
Möser, Justus 21
Mosley, Oswald 212
Mourre, Michel 237
Müller, Adam 23
Müller, Werner 225
Munch, Edvard 57, 61
Munich, Germany 124, 127, 135, 159,
    189
music 38, 74, 171, 232
Mussolini, Benito 139, 151
mythology. *See* Germanic mythology

N

Napoleon I 16, 20, 25, 28, 58

Napoleonic Wars 69
Napoleon III 16
Napoleonism 16
National Assembly, French 14–15, 91.
    See French Revolution, the
National Bolshevik Manifesto.
    See National Bolshevism
National Bolshevism xxv–xxvi, 76, 83,
    155, 162–165, 168–169. *See
    also* Niekisch, Ernst
    National Bolshevik Manifesto 168
National Conservative Party.
    See Volkskonservative Partei
National Conservative Union.
    See Volkskonservative
    Vereinigung
National Constituent Assembly 102.
    See also Reichstag, the
nationalism 19, 25, 42, 53, 58, 64,
    68, 82, 153–155, 205. *See
    also* nation, the; *See also* nation-
    state, the; *See also* German
    identity and uniqueness
    integral nationalism 52
    "new nationalism" xxiv–xxv, xxix
National League. *See* Volksbund
National League for Fatherland and
    Freedom. *See* Volksbund für
    Vaterland und Freiheit
Nationalliberale Partei 40
National Liberal Party.
    See Nationalliberale Partei
Nationalrevolutionäre xx, xxvi, xxviii, 9,
    11, 143, 153–170, 190, 201, 204,
    207, 209, 211, 213–215, 221
National Revolutionaries.
    See Nationalrevolutionäre
national socialism 69–70, 83, 155
National Socialism xx, 8, 113, 139,
    143, 159, 177, 203, 205, 209,
    214–220, 224–225
Nationalsozialistische Deutsche Arbe-
    iterpartei (NSDAP) 101–102,
    133, 139, 141, 143, 148, 163,
    166–167, 177, 188, 190, 199,

202–209, 214, 221–223,
227–228
National Socialist German Workers'
Party. *See* National Socialism
nation-state, the 20, 26–29, 99, 141
nation, the 15, 25, 35–36, 52, 66, 71,
73, 83, 85, 93, 105–106, 118,
122, 130, 140, 141, 152, 154,
161, 176, 194, 208, 212, 218. *See*
also nationalism
age of 93
natural rights 22, 27, 41
Nature Worshipers. *See* Naturgläubige
Naturgläubige 116
Naumann, Friedrich 51, 89, 112
Nazi Party. *See*
Nazism. *See* National Socialism
neo-Idealism 62
neo-Romanticism. *See* Romanticism
neo-Thomism. *See* Thomism
Netherlands, the 175, 212
Neue Kalandgesellschaft 114
Neuer Front 127
Neumünster 185
New Kaland Society. *See* Neue
Kalandgesellschaft
New League of German Scouts.
See Bund deutscher
Neupfadfinder
"new nationalism" xxiv
New Right, European. *See* Nouvelle
Droite
New Right (politics) 64. *See also* Right,
the
Niekisch, Ernst xiv, xx, 9, 143, 159–
165, 176, 189, 205, 215, 218,
227, 231
Niemöller, Martin 219
Nietzsche, Friedrich xiii, xxii, 8, 9, 37,
54–60, 62, 64, 66, 75, 77–78, 85,
94, 105, 200, 217
amor fati 56, 66, 77
blond beast 55
eternal recurrence xxii, 10, 56
influence 56, 64

Last Man, the 55
Übermensch 55
upbringing 55
Night of Long Knives, the. *See* Purge,
the Röhm
nihilism xxii, 54, 59, 106, 107, 191
nobility 32, 79, 129, 150, 222
Nohl, Herman 24
nomos xxvi, 107, 142, 201
Nordau, Max 19
Nordic Faith Community.
See Nordische
Glaubensgemeinschaft
Nordic Faith Movement. *See* Nordische
Glaubensbewegung
Nordicism 115–117, 122–125
Nordic Movement. *See* nordische
Bewegung
Nordic Religious Consortium.
See Nordisch-Religiöse
Arbeitsgemeinschaft
Nordic Society. *See* Nordische
Gesellschaft
nordische Bewegung 122
Nordische Gesellschaft 122
Nordische Glaubensbewegung 115
Nordische Glaubensgemeinschaft 115
Nordisch-Religiöse Arbeitsgemeinschaft
116
North America 93
Noske, Gustav 81, 91, 127
nostalgia 57, 94
Nouvelle Droite (New Right) 228, 236
Novalis (Georg Philipp Friedrich
Freiherr von Hardenberg) 22
NSDAP. *See* National Socialism
nudism 59

O

Oberland 161, 166, 182
Occident. See Abendland Cirlce
occult 115. *See also* esotericism; *See*
also esotericism

Odin Society. *See* Wodangesellschaft
Oertzen, Friedrich Wilhelm von 148
Offenbach, Jacques 43
Old Social Democratic Party. *See* Alte
  Sozialdemokratische Partei
On the Marble Cliffs (Jünger) 218, 226
opera 38. *See* Wagner, Richard;
  See Wagner, Richard
Opponent (Schulze-Boysen). *See Gegner*
  (Schulze-Boysen)
Oranienburg 221
Orden der Nordungen 115
Order of Nordungen. *See* Orden der
  Nordungen
Ordo Novi Templi 114
Orozco, Jose Clemente 231
Orthodox Christianity. *See* Christiantity
Ossietzky, Carl von 213
Osthaus, Karl Ernst 124
Overbeck, Franz 37
Overthrow, The (Lass). *See Umsturz, Der*
  (Lass)

P

Paasche, Hans xxv
Paetel, Karl Otto xx, 166, 168, 190, 214
paganism 49, 56, 57, 112
  Germanic paganism 49, 116
  neo-paganism 114, 119
Palo Alto School, the 234
Pan-Germanism 68–69, 98, 99
  Pan-German League. *See* Allgemeiner
    Deutscher Verband
Pannwitz, Rudolf xxii
Papen, Franz von 130, 134, 139, 144,
  197, 220–221
paramilitary leagues
  61, 134, 205. *See also* freikorps
Pareto, Vilfredo 136, 148
Paris, France 92, 150
parliamentarianism 91, 141
Partei des deutschen Idealismus 86
Partei des Lebens 58

parti de la résistance 16
Party of German Idealism. *See* Partei
  des deutschen Idealismus
Party of Life. *See* Partei des Lebens
Parvus. *See* Helphand, Alexander
Paul the Apostle 34
Peace of Westphalia 121
Peace Party. *See* Friedenspartei
Peasants' War 184
Pechel, Rudolf 138, 204
pedagogy. *See* education
pensée immuable 28
pessimism 39, 57, 64, 130
Pestalozzi, Johann Heinrich 25
Pioneer, The (Ebeling). *See* Vorkämpfer
  (Ebeling); *See* Vorkämpfer
Plato 55
Plenge, Johann 33, 68, 69, 70
Pleyer, Kleo 183, 204, 214, 225
plutocracy 66
Poland 69, 81, 133, 166
polis 25, 28
Political Romanticism (Schmitt) 203
Popular Conservative Party.
  See Volkskonservative Partei
populism 45, 46
*Position of Contemporary
  Parliamentarism in Intellectual
  History, The* (Schmitt). *See Die
  geistesgeschichtliche Lage des
  heutigen Parlamentarismus*
  (Schmitt)
positivism 54, 66
praeceptor Germaniae 37
Preußische Jahrbücher (Treitschke) 40
Preußische Stil, Der (Moeller) 93–94
private property 18
Progressive People's Party.
  See Fortschrittliche Volkspartei
progress, the idea of xvii, xxii, xxvii, 13,
  16, 19, 23, 27, 51, 57, 59, 66, 70,
  78, 107, 111, 116, 151, 156, 193,
  209, 226
proletariat 18, 52, 60
propaganda 61, 72, 80, 88, 90, 124, 161,

202, 210
Protestantism 21, 23, 25, 28, 35, 42, 51, 54, 61, 98, 111–114, 139, 153, 171, 198. *See also* Luther, Martin
Reformation, The 21, 66, 112–113, 121
Providence (divine) 56
Prussia 20, 26, 28–29, 32–33, 36, 40, 42, 53, 79, 81, 85, 93, 94, 139, 162, 202
Age of Reform 26, 32
East Prussia 185
Prussianism xx, 227
Prussian socialism xxvii, 79. *See also* Spengler, Oswald
Prussianism and Socialism (Spengler) 79
Prussian Yearbooks. See Preußische Jahrbücher (Treitschke)
public health 48
Pudor, Heinrich 123
Purge, the Röhm 221
Putsch, Hitler-Ludendorff 101, 155, 202–204. *See also* Hitler, Adolf; *See also* Ludendorff, Erich
Putsch, Kapp 85, 155. *See also* Kapp, Wolfgang

Q

Quirnheim, Albrecht Merz von 222

R

race and racialism xxvi, 39, 42–48, 78, 93, 114, 121–123, 208–209
Radek, Karl 167
radical conservatism 94
Rathenau, Walther 51, 57, 83, 88, 100, 155
Ravensburg, Germany 8
reactionaries xxvi
Realpolitik 28–30, 40
Realpolitik (Rochau) 40

Reck-Malleczeven, Friedrich von dem 163, 219
Red Army, the 81. *See also* Soviet Union, the
Red League of Frontline Fighters. *See* Roter Frontkämpferbund
Red Scare, the xii. *See also* Communism
Reflections of a Nonpolitical Man (Mann) 74–76, 171
Reformation, The Protestant. *See* Protestantism
Reich and the Sickness of European Culture, The (Steding). *See Reich und die Krankheit der europäischen Kultur, Das* (Steding)
Reich, Das (Hielscher) 165
Reichenstein, Herbert 123
Reich Guardian, The. See Reichswart, Der
Reich Hammer League. *See* Reichshammerbund
Reichsbanner Schwarz-Rot-Gold 183
Reichshammerbund 110
Reichsinstitut für Geschichte des neuen Deutschlands 225
Reichstag, the 40, 45, 71, 99, 102, 131–132, 160, 189, 196, 203
Reichsverdrossenheit 42
Reichswart, Der 110
Reich und die Krankheit der europäischen Kultur, Das (Steding) 224–225
religion 9, 22, 24–25, 34, 50, 57, 60, 112, 115–116, 140, 151, 156, 170. *See also* Protestantism; *See also* Catholicism and the Catholic Church; *See also* Christianity
Rembrandt 37
Rembrandt als Erzieher (Langbehn) 37
Renan, Ernst 65
Renouveau Catholique 149
Republican Party (U.S.) xvi
Resistance Circle. *See Widerstands-*Kreis
"resistance" movements 139, 160,

162, 188, 219–224. *See also* Widerstandsbewegung
restauration, royal xxii, xxviii
Reuter, Otto Siegfried 50
Reventlow, Ernst Graf zu 101
revolution 30, 32, 36, 53, 64, 72, 80, 82, 88
Revolution of 1848, the 16–18, 26, 29, 33, 38, 40, 42, 47, 49
Rheinisch-Pfälzischen Kampfbund 135
Rheinish Palatinate Combat League. *See* Rheinisch-Pfälzischen Kampfbund
Right, the xi, xiii–xv, 14–15, 42, 46, 53, 64, 65, 75, 84–85, 95–96, 101–106, 125, 129, 169, 176, 182, 207, 212–215, 229. *See also* ideology
Ring, Der (group) 127, 131
Ring, Der (journal) 129, 133, 138, 144, 149, 152, 217
Ritter, Karl Berhard 144
Rivera, Diego 231
Rochau, Ludwig von 29, 40
Rochelle, Pierre Drieu la 151
Röcken, Germany 55
Rodbertus, Carl 32
Rogge, Heinrich 130
Rohan, Karl Anton Prinz 105, 149, 152, 210–211, 215
Röhm, Ernst 220–221
Röhr, Franz 89
Role of Erotics in the Male Society, The (Blüher). *See Rolle der Erotik in der männlichen Gesellschaft, Die* (Blüher)
Rolle der Erotik in der männlichen Gesellschaft, Die (Blüher) 178–179
Roman Catholicism and Political Form (Schmitt) 195
Roman Priests as Bolsheviks (Ludendorff). *See Rom-Priester als Bolschwisten* (Ludendorff)
Romanticism xxvii, 21–26, 27, 31, 35, 42, 47, 54, 58, 78, 93–94, 106, 123, 130, 153, 203, 224–225
anti-Romanticism 58, 78, 93–94, 203, 224
neo-Romanticism 58, 62
Rome, ancient 66, 163, 208
Römer, Beppo xx
Römer, Josef "Beppo" 166, 204, 214
Rom-Priester als Bolschwisten (Ludendorff) 118
Roon, Albrecht von 31
Roselius, Ludwig 124
Rosenberg, Alfred 209, 215
Rosenstock-Huessy, Eugen 173, 223. *See also* Arbeitslagerbewegung
Rossbach, Gerhard 204
Rosset, Clément 236
Rössler, Constantin 30
Roter Frontkämpferbund 182
Rothe, Carl 146
Rothfels, Hans 151, 214
Rothschild family 43
Rousseau, Jean-Jacques 15, 20, 168
Ruhr, Germany 102, 155, 166
Rule of the Inferior, The (Jung). *See Herrschaft der Minderwertigen, Die* (Jung)
Rural People's Movement. *See* Landvolkbewegung
Rural Volk, The. See Landvolk, Das
Russia xiv–xv, 35, 61, 65, 70–74, 84, 87, 92, 155, 162, 170. *See also* Soviet Union, the
Russian Revolution, the. *See* Bolshevik Revolution, the

S

Sacrum Imperium (Dempf) 150
Saemisch, Ernst 146
Salomon, Bruno von 166, 187, 190, 205
Salomon, Ernst von xx, xxii, 163, 187
sans-culottes 15
Saxony 45

Scandinavia 92, 122
Schaffner, Jakob 120
Scharnhorst, Gerhard von 26
Schauwecker, Franz xx, 157, 163, 164
Scheler, Max xx, 61, 170
Scheringer, Richard 166
Schermann, Ludwig xx
Schill, Freischar 207
Schilljugend 175, 177, 181
Schill Youth. *See* Schilljugend
Schirach, Baldur von 216
Schlageter, Albert Leo 167
Schlegel, Karl Wilhelm Friedrich 23
Schleicher, Kurt von 132, 143, 148,
    197, 198, 199
Schleiermacher, Friedrich 26
Schleswig-Holstein, Germany 185, 186,
    189, 190
Schleswig-Holsteinische Zeitung 190
*Schleswig-Holstein Times. See Schleswig-
    Holsteinische Zeitung*
Schmalenbach, Herman 180
Schmid, Alfred "Fred" 166, 174
Schmid, Friederich Noerr 130
Schmitt, Carl xii, xvi, xx, xxiii, xxv–
    xxviii, 131, 144, 147, 150–151,
    194–203, 215–216, 224, 228,
    235
    "total state" 197
Schnitzler, Werner von 151
Schoeps, Hans-Joachim 146, 214
Schönerer, Georg von 53–54
Schopenhauer, Arthur 28, 50, 66, 78
Schotte, Walther 128, 130, 134
Schram, Wilhelm von 130
Schulenburg, Fritz-Dietlof von der 222
Schultze-Naumburg, Paul xx
Schulze-Boysen, Harro xx, 166, 177,
    212, 214
Schurz, Heinrich 178
Schwaner, Wilhelm 51
Schwarze Front 214. *See also* Otto
    Strasser
Schwarz, Hans 144
scouting 61, 171–173

Second World War. *See* World War II
Seeckt, Hans von 127
Seeley, John R. 65
Seibertz, Norbert 115
Seldte, Franz 213
Semites 39
September Conspiracy 221
sexuality 60, 180
Shaw, George Bernard 61
Shestov, Lev 151
Shou, Peryt 123
Sieburg, Friedrich 146, 218
Sild, Meinhart 226
Silesia (region) 166, 185
Sils-Maria 56
Simmel, Georg 61, 180
Siqueiros, David Alfaro 231
Slavs 93, 162
Small Farmers Union.
    See Kleinbauernverband
Small Political Dictionary (Boehm).
    See Kleines Politisches Wörterbuch
    (Boehm)
Social Age 33
Social Darwinism 47–48, 52
social democracy 30, 44, 62, 68–71, 80,
    160
Social Democratic Party.
    See Sozialdemokratische Partei
    Deutschlands
socialism xvi, 13–18, 29, 33, 44, 58–59,
    60, 69–70, 78–79, 82, 84–85,
    89, 99, 126, 170. *See also* war
    socialism; *See also* National
    Socialism; *See also* national
    socialism; *See also* Communism;
    See also Bolsheviks and
    Bolshevism
    anti-socialism 99
    Russian socialism 61
Social-Revolutionary Nationalists,
    Group of. *See* Gruppe
    Sozialrevolutionärer
    Nationalisten
societas christiana 14

"Sociological Category of the League, The" (Schmalenbach). See "Kategorie des Bundes, Die" (Schmalenbach)
Sohnrey, Heinrich 62
Solidarists 87–93
Sombart, Werner xx, 70, 73, 146
Sonderweg thesis xxiii
Sorel, Georges xxviii, 65, 236
South German Monthly. See Süddeutsche Monatshefte
Soviet Union, the xiv, 8, 76, 84, 89, 133, 151, 155, 163–165, 169, 177, 199–200, 211. See also Communism; See also Bolsheviks and Bolshevism
Five-Year Plan, the 199
Sozialdemokratische Partei Deutschlands 70–72, 80, 160
Spann, Othmar xix, 137, 150, 152, 211
Spartacus Group 71
Spartacus uprising 145
SPD. See Sozialdemokratische Partei Deutschlands
Spengler, Oswald xiii, xix, xxvi, 9, 76–78, 91, 120, 126, 144, 201, 209, 218, 222, 225
Spirit and Reich. See Geist und Reich (Benz)
Spirit as Adversary of the Soul, The (Klages). See Geist als Widersacher der Seele, Der (Klages)
Spirit of the Crew, The (Günther). See Geist der Jungmannschaft, Der (Günther)
SS-Guard 221
Stadtler, Eduard 79, 87–91, 126, 128, 141, 158, 205
Stahlgewitter xii
Stahlhelm 98, 131, 158, 182, 202, 221
Stahlhelm-Zeitung 157
Stalin, Joseph 170. See also Soviet Union, the; See also Communism

Stalinism 163
Standarte 158, 168
Stapel, Wilhelm xix, 10, 141–143, 216
Star of the League (George). See Stern des Bundes (George)
Stassen, Franz 38
state, the 25, 92, 99, 110, 111. See also Volksstaat
Stauffenberg, Claus Graf Schenk von 222–223
Steding, Christoph 224–225
Stegerwald, Adam 89
Stein, Baron von 25–26, 130
Steinböhmer, Gustav 144
Stein, Heinrich Friedrich Karl vom und zum. See Stein, Baron von
Stein, Laurenz von 32
Stern des Bundes (George) 178
Sterne, Carus 122
Sternhell, Zeev xxix, 12, 234
Stoecker, Adolf 44
Storm and Stress. See Sturm und Drang
Strasser, Gregor xiv, 199, 209
Strasser, Otto xiv, xvi, 168, 190, 209, 212, 214
Strauss, Richard 57
Stresemann, Gustav 98–99
Struggle for Rome (Dahn) 50
Strzygowski, Josef xx, 114
Stuck, Franz 38
Stumm, Ferdinand von 130
Sturm und Drang 24
Sturmvolk 175
style 94, 158, 170
Süddeutsche Monatshefte 149
Sudetan German Party. See Sudetendeutsche Partei
Sudetendeutsche Partei 152
Sudetenland 152
super league. See Hochbund
Switzerland 8–9, 56, 61, 212, 236

T

Taft, Robert xvi
Tag 125
Tagebuch 213
Tägliche Rundschau 149
Taine, Hippolyte 65
Tannenbergbund 117. *See also* Erich
  Ludendorff
Tannenberg League.
  See Tannenbergbund
Tarnow, Fritz 199
Tat 9, 144–147, 152, 217
  Tat-Kreis 145–147, 205, 217
TB. *See* Tannenbergbund
Teudt, Wilhelm 112
Thälmann, Ernst 190
Théâtre Français, Das (Moeller) 92
theology 34, 111–112, 142, 145
Third Reich, the (Moeller)) 75.
  See Dritte Reich, Das (Moeller)
"third way," the. *See* ideology
Thoma, Hans 38
Thomism 212
Thor 111
Thus Spoke Zarathustra (Nietzsche) 56,
  66. *See also* Nietzsche, Friedrich
time xxii
Tirpitz, Alfred von 72
Tivoli Party Convention of 1892 45
Tocqueville, Alexis de 19, 136
Toepfer, Alfred C. 161
Tönnies, Ferdinand 180
Tory Party (British) 17
Totale Mobilmachung, Die (Jünger) 199
totalitarianism 15, 107
Total Mobilization (Jünger). *See Totale
  Mobilmachung, Die* (Jünger)
"total state". *See* Schmitt, Carl
*Totem: Animal and Man in the
  Context of Life* (Günther).
  *See Totem: Tier und Mensch im
  Lebenszusammenhang* (Günther)
*Totem: Tier und Mensch im
  Lebenszusammenhang* (Günther)
  142
Traugott, Edgar 226

Travelling Companions. *See* Fahrenden
  Gesellen
Treitschke, Heinrich von 40–43, 52, 65
Tresckow, Henning von 222–223
Treviranus, Gottfried 221
Troeltsch, Ernst 20, 67
Trotsky, Leon xii, xv, xxi, 203
True State, The (Spann). *See Wahre
  Staat, Der* (Spann)
*Tuisko-Land: der arischen Stämme und
  Götter Urheimat* (Krause) 122
*Tuisko-Land: The Original Homeland of
  the Aryan Tribes and the Gods*
  (Krause). *See Tuisko-Land: der
  arischen Stämme und Götter
  Urheimat* (Krause)
Tusk. *See* Koebel, Eberhard
Tyr Circle. *See* Tyr-Kreis
Tyr-Kreis 114

U

Übermensch. *See* Nietzsche, Friedrich
Uhse, Bodo xx, 166, 190
Ullmann, Hermann 144
Ullstein (publisher) 145
Umsturz, Der (Lass) 167, 177
uni-Klub 131
Union for Germanness Abroad.
  See Verein für das Deutschtum
  im Ausland
Union of German Students. *See* Verein
  deutscher Studenten
United Kingdom, the. *See* England;
  See Great Britain
United States, the 72, 92–93
Universal German Writing Union.
  See Allgemeine Deutsche
  Schriftverein
University of Berlin 8, 145
University of Göttingen 34
University of Heidelberg 135
University of Würzburg 135
Ura-Linda Chronicle 123

USPD 71
USSR. *See* Soviet Union, the

V

Vandervelde, Emile 151
Vater, Der (Klepper) 219
Vaterlandspartei 120
vegetarianism 59
Velde, Henry van de 61, 124, 151
Verein deutscher Studenten 46
Verein für das Deutschtum im Ausland
    46, 135
Versailles Peace Treaty xiv, xvii, xxv,
    80–83, 97, 104, 125, 133, 139,
    141, 154, 161, 163, 186
Vico 55
Vienna, Austria 150
Vienna Congress. *See* Congress of
    Vienna
Vitalism 59
Voelkel, Martin 171
Voitinsky, Vladimir 199
Volck, Herbert 187
Volgraff, Carl 19
Volk and *völkisch* 9, 11, 24, 27, 36,
    46–47, 49, 51, 53, 62, 64, 68–69,
    82, 87, 91, 97–106, 100–102,
    109–124, 137, 147, 168, 176,
    183, 189, 190, 194, 201, 205,
    208–209. *See also Volksstaat;*
    See also Volksreligion; See
    also Volksbildung
Volk community 69, 87, 103, 175
völkisch ideology xx, 47–48
völkisch Right 215
Volk education. *See Volksbildung*
völkische Bewegung xx, 11, 46–52, 110,
    113, 124, 189
Völkischer Beobachter 215
Völkisch Observer. See Völkischer
    Beobachter
Volksbildung 25, 46
Volksbund 73

Volksbund für Vaterland und Freiheit
    73
Volkscondottieri 139
Volksdemocratie 83
Volksdeutscher Klub 134
Volksgeist 92
Volkskonservativen 138
Volkskonservative Partei 132, 176
Volkskonservative Vereinigung 132
Volksmonarchie 69
Volks monarchy 69. *See Volksmonarchie*
Volkspartei 45
Volks religion. *See Volksreligion*
Volksreligion 25, 110
Volksstaat 25, 69, 74, 104
Volks state. *See Volksstaat*
Volk, Stand, und Bund 225
Volkstum 114
volonté générale 15
Voluneer Brigade of the Young Nation.
    See Freischar Junger Nation
von Gleichen, Heinrich 129
Vorkämpfer (Ebeling) 167, 177
Vorkämpfer-Kreis 190
Vormarsch 168
Vossische Zeitung 145

W

Waffen-SS 8
Wagner, Adolph 33
Wagner, Richard xxiv, 37–39, 42–43,
    51, 56, 58, 217
Wandervögel xx, 61–64, 87, 170–172,
    175, 178, 181
war guilt xiii
war socialism 70, 82–83, 160. *See*
    also national socialism
Wars of German Unification 69
Was wir vom Nationalsozialismus
    erwarten (Günther) 143
wealth 18, 43
Weber, Alfred 146, 151
Weber, A. Paul 161

Weber, Josef 50
Weber, Max xxvii, 61, 73, 83
Wehrmacht 222
Wehrwolf 182. *See also* paramilitary
    leagues
Weimar Republic, the xxi, xxiii, 57, 82,
    94, 101–104, 121, 131–134,
    136, 140–141, 145, 155, 165,
    171, 177, 183–184, 194, 196,
    210, 213, 222
weiße Ritter, Der 171
Weiss, Wilhelm 157, 205
Wells, Herbert George 57
Werewolf. *See* Wehrwolf
Werkbund 61
Westarp, Kuno Graf von 98
Westphal, Otto 144, 214, 224–225
West, the 57, 82, 85, 87, 93, 101, 221,
    228. *See also* East, the; *See
    also* Spengler, Oswald
What We Expect from National Socialism
    (Günther). *See Was wir vom
    Nationalsozialismus erwarten*
    (Günther)
Whig party (British) 17
White Knight Publishers. *See* weiße
    Ritter, Der
Wideranverlobung 56
Widerstand 163
Widerstandsbewegung 160, 162, 164–
    165, 214. *See also* "resistance"
    movements
Widerstands-Kreis 176, 189, 190
Widerstandsverlag 218
Wiederkehr. See Nietzsche, Friedrich
Wiederkunft. See Nietzsche, Friedrich
Wieland, Hermann 123
Wiking 182. *See also* paramilitary
    leagues
Wilhelm Heinz, Friedrich xix, 157
Wilhelm II 94, 97
Wilhelmine Age 92, 103, 107, 169
Wilser, Ludwig 122
Wilson, Woodrow 82, 90
Winnig, August 86, 144

Wirsing, Giselher 148, 218
Wirth, Helmuth 123, 124
Wirth, Hermann xx
Witzenhausen 115
Wodangesellschaft 50
Wolffheim, Friedrich 84
Wolffheim, Fritz 143
Wolfskehl, Karl 151
Wolzoge, Hans von 112
Women's Movement.
    See Frauenbewegung
women's rights 116
Worker: Mastery and Form, The (Jünger)
    xxvii, 9, 199–201, 210, 225
"World Ice Theory" 123
World Spirit 27, 225
World War I xii, xxvi, 11, 13, 17, 20, 37,
    46–47, 63, 66, 67–70, 71–74,
    87, 110, 151, 154, 161, 168, 194
    aftermath 80–87
    peace resolution of July 19, 1917 71
World War II 8, 12, 204, 226
Worpswede, Germany 60
"Written Word as the Spiritual
    Space of the Nation, The"
    (Hofmannsthal) 105
WTB Plan 199
Wulle, Reinhold 101
Wundt, Max 113
Wyneken, Gustav 63, 86

Y

Yahweh 111
Young Conservatives.
    See Jungkonservativen
Young German League.
    See Jungdeutscher Bund
Young German Orde. *See* Jungdeutscher
    Orden
Young Germany League.
    See Jungdeutschland-Bund
Young Nationalists. *See* Jungnationalen
Young National League.

See Jungnationaler Bund
Young Plan 205
Young Right. *See* Jeune Droite
Youth Action. *See* Aktion der Jugend
Youth League Movement. *See* Bündische
Youth Movement. *See* Jugendbewegung

Z

Zarathustra 55
Zehrer, Hans xix, 10, 145–149, 217
Zeitgeist 57
Zentrumspartei. *See* Deutsche
    Zentrumspartei
Ziegler, Heinz O. 151
Ziegler, Leopold xx, xxvi, 137, 151
Zimmermann, Ferdinand Friedrich
    146, 148, 205, 212
Zionism 59
Zivilisation 74, 77–78, 92
  theories of 93
Zschaetzsch, Karl Georg 123
Zurich, Switzerland 9

Visit

WASHSUMMIT.COM

CPSIA information can be obtained
at www.ICGtesting.com
Printed in the USA
LVHW081403200720
661135LV00019B/1919

9 781593 680596